Themes in the
Social Sciences

The domestication
of the savage mind

Editors: Jack Goody & Geoffrey Hawthorn

The aim of this series is to publish books which will focus on topics of general and interdisciplinary interest in the social sciences. They will be concerned with non-European cultures and with developing countries, as well as with industrial societies. The emphasis will be on comparative sociology and, initially, on sociological, anthropological and demographic topics. These books are intended for undergraduate teaching, but not as basic introductions to the subjects they cover. Authors have been asked to write on central aspects of current interest which have a wide appeal to teachers and research students, as well as to undergraduates.

First books in the series

Edmund Leach: *Culture and Communication: the logic by which symbols are connected*
    An introduction to the use of structuralist analysis in social anthropology

Anthony Heath: *Rational Choice and Social Exchange*
    A critique of exchange theory

Philip Abrams and Andrew McCulloch: *Communes, Sociology and Society*

BY THE SAME AUTHOR

The Social Organisation of the LoWiili, 1956, reprinted Oxford University Press, 1966

Death, Property and the Ancestors, Stanford University Press, 1962

Comparative Studies in Kinship, Routledge and Kegan Paul, 1969

Technology, Tradition and the State in Africa, Oxford University Press, 1971

The Myth of the Bagre, Clarendon Press, 1972

Production and Reproduction, Cambridge University Press, 1977

EDITED:

The Developmental Cycle in Domestic Groups, Cambridge University Press, 1958

Succession to High Office, Cambridge University Press, 1966

Salaga: the Struggle for Power (with J. A. Braimah), Longmans, 1967

Literacy in Traditional Societies, Cambridge University Press, 1968

Bridewealth and Dowry (with S. J. Tambiah), Cambridge University Press, 1973

The Character of Kinship, Cambridge University Press, 1974

Changing Social Structure in Ghana, International African Institute, 1975

Family and Inheritance: Rural Society in Western Europe, 1200–1800 (with J. Thirsk and E. P. Thompson), Cambridge University Press, 1976

The domestication
of the savage mind

by Jack Goody

Cambridge University Press

Cambridge
London   New York   Melbourne

Published by the Syndics of the Cambridge University Press
The Pitt Building, Trumpington Street, Cambridge CB2 1RP
Bentley House, 200 Euston Road, London NW1 2DB
32 East 57th Street, New York, NY 10022, USA
296 Beaconsfield Parade, Middle Park, Melbourne 3206, Australia

First published 1977

Reproduced and printed by photolithography and bound in
Great Britain at The Pitman Press, Bath

Library of Congress Cataloguing in Publication Data
Goody, John Rankine.
The domestication of the savage mind.
(Themes in the social sciences)
Includes bibliographical references.
1. Philosophy, Primitive.   2. Illiteracy.
3. Ethnopsychology.   I. Title.   II. Series.
GN451.G66   301.2'1   77–6835
ISBN 0 521 21726 1 hard covers
ISBN 0 521 29242 5 paperback

Contents

Tables

Figures

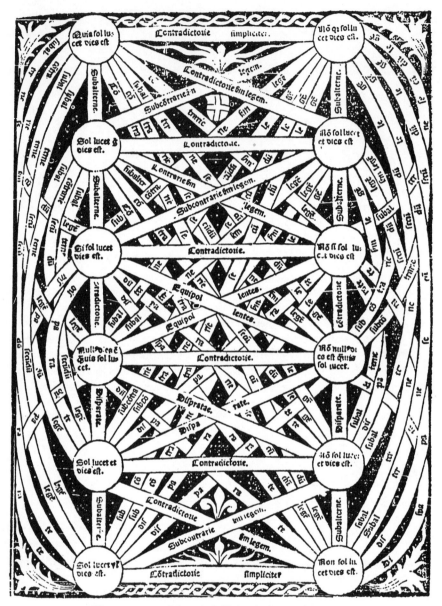

The geometry of the mind (Celaya). (From Ong 1974)

Preface

The theme of this book has an obvious continuity with the essay written by Ian Watt and myself some years ago, and with the volume I subsequently edited on *Literacy in Traditional Societies* (Cambridge, 1968). In trying to account for the Greek achievement, as well as some of the differences between other human societies, we placed much store on alphabetic literacy. My present theme is in some ways a modification and in others an extension of this thesis, since it was soon apparent that we failed to give full recognition to the achievements of other literate societies because of a preoccupation with the 'uniqueness of the West' (see Hirst 1975; Anderson 1974). Stimulated by experience of changing cultures in West Africa and by reading about what one might call the 'rise of the Middle East' (as distinct from the later 'rise of the West'), I have wanted for some time to pursue the contrast between literate and non-literate societies in order to try and push a stage further the analysis of the effects of writing on 'modes of thought' (or cognitive processes) on the one hand, and on the major institutions of society on the other.

This book tries to tackle the first of those tasks. I am only too aware that it is an undertaking of huge proportions, of which I have only touched the fringe. I am aware, too, that I have sometimes used commonplace examples to cover up my ignorance of the more exotic. I know too that I have trespassed on the well-cultivated gardens of other scholars, classicists, orientalists, psychologists, linguists, and others, without having the comprehensive understanding of their subjects which they would expect of one another. It would be futile to protest that others have plundered the rougher pastures of social anthropology for just the same ends. I would rather rest my justification on the need to cross these disciplinary boundaries if anything is to be made of the comparative study of human behaviour.

Needless to say, I could not have broached the subject without advice, conversation and discussion. In particular, my thanks are due to Ian Watt for his initial stimulation, to Robin Horton and Claude

ix

Preface

Lévi-Strauss for providing such intelligent points of departure, to Derek Gjertsen and Everett Mendelsohn for philosophical and historical remarks, to Shlemo Morag, Abraham Malamat, James Kinnier Wilson and Aaron Demsky for advice on the Ancient Near East and Geoffrey Lloyd on Greece, to John Beattie for notes on the Nyoro, to Gilbert Lewis for medical and collegial comments, to Walter Ong for illustrations, to Françoise Héritier and Claude Meillassoux for help with the domestic domain, to Michael Cole for a visit to the Vai and for psychological assistance, to Stephen Hugh-Jones for enlightenment on the oral 'literature' of the Barasana, to Patricia Williams and Michael Black for suggestions on argument and organisation, to Bobbi Buchheit and Colin Duly for editorial work, to Esther Goody for her critical attention.

Parts of this work have appeared in print or have been presented as lectures. The first chapter came out as 'Evolution and communication: the domestication of the savage mind' in the *British Journal of Sociology*, 24 (1973):1–12, having been previously given as a paper at the World Sociological Conference in Varna in 1970. Chapter 3 has appeared in *Culture and its Creators* (eds. J. Ben-David and T. Clark), Chicago University Press, 1976, and was given as a lecture to the Van Leer Foundation, Jerusalem, in 1973. Chapter 4 was a contribution to the conference of the Association of Social Anthropologists in Oxford in 1973 and has appeared in French in *Actes de la Recherche en Sciences Sociales*, 1976:87–101 under the title, 'Civilisation de l'écriture et classification, ou l'art de jouer sur les tableaux'; it will appear in English in the proceedings of that section of the conference in a volume edited by R. Jain, *Text and Context: The Social Anthropology of Tradition*, ISHI Publications, Philadelphia, 1977. The rest appears in print for the first time, though chapters five and six were given as the Monro Lectures in Edinburgh in May, 1976.

Cambridge   JACK GOODY
December, 1976

1. *Evolution and communication*

Emotion is completely Negro as reason is Greek.

Leopold Senghor

In attempting to refute the evaluation to which black reality had been subjected, Negritude adopted the Manichean tradition of European thought and inflicted it on a culture which is most radically un-Manichean. It not only accepted the dialectical structure of European ideological confrontation but borrowed from the very components of its racist syllogism.

Wole Soyinka, *Myth, Literature and the African World*

The way in which modes of thought have changed over time and space is a subject on which most of us have speculated at some time or other. It may have been to arrive at some idea of why Indians behave as they do (or we think they do), why African art differs from that of Western Europe, or (when we look at the picture in historical perspective) what lay behind developments in the Ancient Middle East, in Greece or in Renaissance Europe, where new ways of thinking appear to have replaced the old. And the same kinds of question have given rise to much discussion by anthropologists, sociologists, psychologists, historians and philosophers about the shift from magic to science, the growth of rationality, and a host of similar topics. But the problem has been complicated both by the categories and by the framework that have been used.

The trouble with the categories is that they are rooted in a we/they division which is both binary and ethnocentric, each of these features being limiting in their own way. Sometimes we are still employing the simplistic categories of our folk taxonomy; where these have been abandoned, we substitute some polysyllabic synonym. We speak in terms of primitive and advanced, almost as if human minds themselves differed in their structure like machines of an earlier and later design. The emergence of science, whether seen as occurring at the time of the

1

Renaissance in Europe, in Ancient Greece, or earlier still in Babylonia, is held to follow a pre-scientific period, where magical thought predominated. Philosophers describe this process as the emergence of rationality from irrationality (Wilson 1970), or of logico-empirical from mythopoeic thinking (Cassirer 1944) or of logical from pre-logical procedures (Lévy-Bruhl 1910). More recently, others have attempted to get over the difficulties raised by a purely negative definition of the situation (e.g. rational–irrational) by means of more positively phrased dichotomies, the wild and domesticated (or cold and hot) thinking of Lévi-Strauss (1962), and the closed and open situations of Robin Horton (1967), applying Popper.

The trouble with the framework has been that it is either largely non-developmental or else simplistically so. It has been non-developmental because the anthropologists and sociologists interested in these questions have tended to set aside evolutionary or even historical perspectives, preferring to adopt a kind of cultural relativism that looks upon discussions of development as necessarily entailing a value judgement on the one hand and as over-emphasising or misunderstanding the differences on the other. Such objections are founded not only on the appealing premiss that all men are equal. They also stem from the undoubted difficulty that speculations upon developmental sequences often create for the analysis of a particular set of data. Such problems arise whether the data is derived from a field study or from a historical society, from the present or from the past. If I assume that all societies have once had mythological forms of the kind found in South America, then I may well be led to see the Greek corpus of 'sacred tales' as the faded fragments of some former glory (Kirk 1970). If I assume that matrilineal societies have always preceded patrilineal ones, then I may be led to interpret the prominent part played by the mother's brother in a patrilineal society as a survival from an earlier period rather than examining his role in relation to the existing social system.

In accepting the functionalist and structuralist critiques, in acknowledging the necessity of proving rather than assuming difference, it is only too easy to set aside the developmental questions, as pseudo-historical, as 'evolutionary', as speculative. Yet having done so, we nevertheless fall back upon a mode of discourse, a set of categories, such as primitive and advanced, simple and complex, developing and developed, traditional and modern, pre-capitalist, etc. which implies change of a more or less unidirectional kind. Any resort to comparative work necessarily raises the evolutionary issue.[1] Even specific field studies of contemporary social life in the Third World cannot dismiss the question of short-term and long-term change. These problems are intrinsic to an understanding of our individual experience and of the world at large, both in space and in time.

Indeed, though contemporary social scientists have been wary of a developmental framework, much of the best sociology has employed just this starting point. One only has to mention the work of Comte, Marx, Spencer, Weber and Durkheim (not to mention the more obvious anthropological candidates, Maine, Morgan, Tylor, Robertson Smith and Frazer) which has displayed both comparative and evolutionary interests. The work of Spencer and Durkheim shows an extensive knowledge of writings about non-European societies; Weber has a similar command of Asia. However, even those who have displayed these interests have often derived them from a somewhat ethnocentric (but none the less important) concern associated with the rise of modern industrial society; this centred upon a question which Parsons has recently reiterated. 'Why, then, did the breakthrough to modernization not occur in *any* of the "Oriental" advanced intermediate civilizations?' (1966:4). Once again this question implies a binary opposition between 'our' type of society and 'theirs'; and its answer requires that we search the world for positive and negative cases to confirm our ideas about the relevant factors. There is nothing wrong with the search as such, but we need to recognise the ethnocentric nature of its starting point and the fact that the dichotomising of 'we' and 'they' in this manner narrows the field both of the topic and of its explanation. It pushes us once again into the use of binary categories and while it introduces developmental perspective, it attempts to look for a single breaking point, a Great Divide, though whether this jump occurred in Western Europe in the sixteenth century, or Greece in the fifth century B.C., or in Mesopotamia in the fourth millennium, is never very clear.

Of no topic is this truer than studies of the general development of the human mind or thought. Here we face squarely the dilemma of the participant observer. We look at the question not as an investigator examines geological layers, but from the inside outwards. We start with the conviction that there are important differences between ourselves (variously defined) and the rest. Otherwise how come that they are under-developed (or developing) and we are developed (or over-developed)? Or to revert to the earlier classification, why are they primitive and we advanced? We try to state the nature of these differences in very general terms – the move from myth to history, from magic to science, from status to contract, cold to hot, concrete to abstract, collective to individual, ritual to rationality. Such movement inevitably tends to be phrased not only in terms of process but of progress too; in other words it acquires a value element, a procedure that tends to distort the way we perceive the kind of development that has occurred, especially when this is seen in such very general terms as, for example, in Lévy-Bruhl's division into pre-logical and logical mentalities. The fact that the questions concerning human thought are posed in such terms means that satisfactory evidence is difficult to obtain; or, to look at the enquiry from another angle, most evidence can be made to fit the gross categories. As for the framework, writers wobble uneasily between developmental and non-developmental standpoints. But again the differences are usually seen as being dualistic in character, leading to the assumption of a global 'philosophie indigène', a single 'témoignage ethnographique', in opposition to our own.

One recent contribution in this field is Lévi-Strauss' influential study of *La Pensée Sauvage*, translated into English as *The Savage Mind*, which follows the interesting trail blazed by Durkheim's work in 'primitive classification' (1903) and which illustrates all of the dilemmas mentioned above. One needs to say straight away that in Lévi-Strauss' analysis of the human mind in different cultures he stresses both differentiation and similarity. The second line of thinking is present in *La Pensée Sauvage* as well as in the three volumes entitled *Mythologiques* and is epitomised in his essay on 'The Concept of Primitiveness' where he writes: 'I see no reason why mankind should have waited until recent times to produce minds of the calibre of a Plato or an Einstein. Already over two or three hundred thousand years ago, there were probably men of a similar capacity, who were of course not applying their intelligence to the solution of the same problem as these more recent thinkers; instead they were probably more interested in kinship!' (1968:351). The sentiment is unexceptional (it is difficult to believe that anyone could think otherwise, at least if we lessen the two or three hundred thousand to fifty thousand, the emergence of *Homo sapiens*): and we do avoid the radical dichotomy. But we do so apparently by rejecting all consideration of the specific factors, including intellectual tradition, institutional setting and mode of communication, that lay behind the emergence of a Plato or an Einstein. We move from the crude dichotomy to an ahistorical unity.

The starting point of *The Savage Mind*, on the other hand, is a dichotomy of 'mind' or 'thought' into savage (or 'prior') and domesticated. This opposition has many of the characteristics of the earlier 'we–they' division into primitive and advanced, even though the author tries to set aside some of its implications. He attempts to give the new dichotomy a more specific historical base, seeing 'savage'

4

knowledge as characteristic of the neolithic age and the domesticated variety as dominating the modern period.

At the beginning of this work, the author calls attention, as have many other writers, to the complexity of the classifications, the taxonomies, the word-sets, that appear in the languages of 'simple' societies, and he rightly criticises the view, which he attributes to Malinowski, that these systems are merely means of satisfying 'needs'. Malinowski, he says, claimed that 'primitive peoples' interest in totemic plants and animals was inspired by nothing but the rumbling of their stomachs' (1966:3). He argues instead that 'the universe is an object of thought at least as much as it is a means of satisfying needs' (1966:3).

A few pages later, the supplement becomes an alternative. Writing of the 'science of the concrete' Lévi-Strauss denies that therapeutic classification has a 'practical effect'. 'It meets intellectual requirements rather than or instead of satisfying needs.' He goes on: 'The real question is not whether the touch of a woodpecker's beak does in fact cure toothache. It is rather whether there is a point of view from which a woodpecker's beak and a man's tooth can be seen as "going together" (the use of this congruity for therapeutic purposes being only one of its possible uses), and whether some initial order can be introduced into the universe by means of these groupings. Classifying, as opposed to not classifying, has a value of its own, whatever form the classification may take' (p. 9).

The argument of this passage, while in some ways highly appealing (when the intellect is brought into the picture, man is not simply the creature of material needs), is also rather deceptive. In the first place, it depends on a special understanding of the key words. 'Needs' here are clearly to be interpreted as largely physical, otherwise why would they not include intellectual and emotional requirements, as is the case in common speech? I cannot see any justification for treating these aspects as alternatives; the curing of the toothache is very often an intellectual task in simple societies, one that involves a readjustment of man's relationship not simply with his physical environment but with the moral and supernatural universe; indeed the universe is rarely if ever divided into a pragmatic and a non-pragmatic side. Such a division is another imposition of Western observers upon the non-European world, frequently out of tune with the concepts of both worlds, but especially of the latter.

If this is so, 'the real question' (but 'real' to whom?) cannot be phrased in an either/or fashion. As we have seen above and as we see from the parenthetical statement that '(the use of this congruity for therapeutic purposes being only one of its possible uses)', Lévi-Strauss is himself in two minds about placing 'needs' and 'classifications' as alternatives. Clearly they are not. They supplement one another. Nevertheless, Lévi-Strauss insists upon seeing the search for order as dominant over the search for security.

It is difficult to see how one would begin to weigh the two in the balance. From the actor's own statements, it is usually the search for security that dominates, and there would seem great dangers in a neglect of the pragmatic orientations of the individual (interpreted in the widest sense). This is not of course to deny the intellectual 'search for order'. But if this means classification, such a system is surely inherent in the use of language itself and whatever potentialities existed in the primate world, it was this new instrument of communication that vastly extended the process of conceptualisation. There can therefore be no question of 'not classifying', only of differently classifying.[2] The implied opposition has no substance.

There is another, associated, dichotomy that creates difficulties. Lévi-Strauss rightly stresses the 'scientific' element in primitive society – a point Malinowski and others had established (though it is surprising now to think that this was ever necessary). And he rightly sees classification (or order) as being characteristic of all thought (p. 10) – though this perhaps means only that the development of both derives from the use of language. But in discussing the difference between the thought of man in primitive and advanced societies (which is after all the subject of his enquiry) he comes up against what he sees as a major paradox, and one which touches upon the distinction between magic and science, and their association with primitive and advanced respectively. 'Scientific knowledge', 'modern science', he notes, dates back only a few centuries; it was however preceded by Neolithic achievement. 'Neolithic, or early historical, man was therefore the heir of a long scientific tradition.' But from Lévi-Strauss' standpoint, the inspiration behind this achievement was different from that of post-Renaissance man. His reason for this assumption is phrased as follows: 'Had he, as well as all his predecessors, been inspired by exactly the same spirit as that of our own time, it would be impossible to understand how he could have come to a halt and how several thousand years of stagnation have intervened between the Neolithic revolution and modern science like a level plain between ascents' (p. 15). This paradox he sees as having but one solution: there must be 'two distinct modes of scientific thought'. Having set up a historical problem ('Neolithic' as against 'modern' science), he then goes on to reject the 'evolutionary' implications of his position. 'These are certainly not a function of different stages of development of the human mind but rather of two strategic

6

levels at which nature is accessible to scientific enquiry: one roughly adapted to that of perception and the imagination: the other at a remove from it' (p. 15).

But although he tries to set aside earlier views, the way he describes these two forms of knowledge displays a very definite link with early dichotomies into primitive and advanced, a dichotomy which becomes 'wild' (savage, *sauvage*) and domesticated (*domestiquée*) in his own terminology and which refers quite specifically, as in the title of the book, to the *pensée* (thought, mind) of the actors involved.

At various times the dichotomy takes the following forms, explicit or implicit:

Domesticated	Wild	References (*1962*)
'hot'	'cold'	309
modern	neolithic	24
science of the abstract	science of the concrete	3
scientific thought	mythical thought	33, 44
scientific knowledge	magical thought	33
engineer(ing)	bricoleur(-age)	30
abstract thought	intuition/imagination/perception	24
using concepts	using signs	28
history	atemporality;	348, 47,
	myths and rites	321

To this dualistic view of the world Lévi-Strauss returns at the very end of his book, showing how intrinsic it is to his general argument.

'Certainly the properties to which the savage mind has access are not the same as those which have commanded the attention of scientists. The physical world is approached from opposite ends in the two cases: one is supremely concrete, the other supremely abstract; one proceeds from the angle of sensible qualities and the other from that of formal properties.' Instead of meeting, these two courses led to 'two distinct though equally positive sciences: one which flowered in the neolithic period, whose theory of the sensible order provided the basis of the arts of civilisation (agriculture, animal husbandry, pottery, weaving, conservation and preparation of food, etc.) and which continues to provide for our basic needs by these means; and the other, which places itself from the start at the level of intelligibility, and of which contemporary science is the fruit' (p. 269).

This dichotomy follows traditional thinking and attempts to account for supposed differences between 'we' and 'they' in a blanket fashion. On one hand, it takes up a relativistic stance and tries to get round the 'evolutionary' implications by insisting that (a) the courses are 'alternatives', and that (b) they are 'crossing' in mid-twentieth century. At the same time it refers to supposed historical changes, that is, to the fundamental discontinuity in human knowledge as pursued up to the end of the Neolithic and as pursued in modern times. This discontinuity is both temporal (there is a plateau in between) and causal (the inspiration is different).

But while the rhythm of human inventiveness has often been uneven, it does not appear to display the bimodal pattern that Lévi-Strauss assumes. Just as there were many important inventions well before the Neolithic (speech, tools, cooking, weapons) so too there were many between the Neolithic and the modern periods (metallurgy, writing, the wheel). In recent writings on prehistory, the idea of a sudden revolution produced by the domestication of plants and animals has been replaced by a more gradual progression of events which take one back to the last inter-glacial. Development has been more gradual than was earlier thought but in any case Lévi-Strauss' account appears to overlook the very great achievements of the 'Urban Revolution' of the Bronze Age, the developments of the classical period in Greece and Rome, and the advances of twelfth-century Europe and of early China. I say 'appears to overlook' because the author is clearly aware of these developments in human culture and in a later volume he specifically refers to the shift from myth to philosophy in Greece as a precursor to science (1973:473). It is rather that, like the rest of us, he is a victim of the ethnocentric binarism enshrined in our own categories, of the crude division of world societies into primitive and advanced, European and non-European, simple and complex. As general signposts these terms may be permissible. But to build on so slender a base the idea of two distinct approaches to the physical universe seems scarcely justified.

I certainly do not wish to deny that there are differences in the 'thought' or 'mind' of 'we' and 'they', nor that the problems which may have concerned many observers, among them Durkheim, Lévy-Bruhl and Lévi-Strauss, are of no significance. But the way they have been tackled seems open to a whole range of queries. Perhaps I may put the central difficulty I find in terms of personal experience. In the course of several years living among people of 'other cultures', I have never experienced the kinds of hiatus in communication that would be the case if I and they were approaching the physical world from opposite ends. That this experience is not unique seems apparent from the contemporary changes occurring in developing countries where the shift from the Neolithic to modern science is encapsulated into the space of a man's lifetime. The boy brought up as a bricoleur becomes an engineer. He has his difficulties, but they do not lie at the level of

8

an overall opposition between wild and domesticated minds, thoughts or approaches, but on a much more particularistic level.

In looking at the changes that have taken place in human thought, then, we must abandon the ethnocentric dichotomies that have characterised social thought in the period of European expansion. Instead we should look for more specific criteria for the differences. Nor should we neglect the material concomitants of the process of mental 'domestication', for these are not only the manifestations of thought, invention, creativity, they also shape its future forms. They are not only the products of communication but also part of its determining features.

So even if the message cannot reasonably be reduced to the medium, any changes in the system of human communication must have great implications for the content. Indeed, our starting point must be that the acquisition of language, which is an attribute of mankind alone, is basic to all social institutions, to all normative behaviour.[3]

Many writers have seen the development of languages as a prerequisite of thought itself; the Russian psychologist, Vygotsky, characterised thought as 'inner speech'. We do not need to go into this argument, which is partly a definitional problem; it is not a question of establishing a boundary, but of determining the extension of cognitive activity that language permits and encourages. It is worth noting that the archaeological evidence of extensive human culture, as depicted in the wall paintings of the Upper Palaeolithic and in the burial practices of the Neanderthals, coincides with the appearance of a man with the larger brain that would seem to be necessary for the type of communicative and storage systems associated with speech.

Of course, the existence of language does tend to dichotomise. You either have it or you don't. Human languages appear to display few differences in their potentiality for adaption to development. Whatever differences there may be in the language of 'primitive', 'intermediate' and 'advanced' peoples, apart from vocabulary, these factors seem to have little effect in inhibiting or encouraging social change. In making this point, I am deliberately setting aside certain implications of Benjamin Lee Whorf's seminal comparison of what he called Standard Average European with the Hopi of North America, where Whorf sees aspects of the world view and cognitive processes of these societies as being intimately linked to grammatical structures. I am also discounting the multitude of anthropological analyses that tend to treat man as imprisoned by the concepts he has produced and hence fail to account for the generative aspects of his culture.

The dichotomy between those with language and those without has little to do with the kind of differences that concern us here. However, it does suggest that an examination of the means of communication, a study of the technology of the intellect, can throw further light on developments in the sphere of human thinking. For those studying social interaction, developments in the technology of the intellect must always be crucial. After language the next most important advance in this field lay in the reduction of speech to graphic forms, in the development of writing. Here we can see not one single leap but a series of changes, many of them spread through a process of diffusion that can be reconstructed in its broad terms and which culminated in the relatively simple form of alphabetic writing in widespread use today, and whose proposed adoption in China Lenin once described as the revolution of the East. Of course changes in the means of communication are not the only significant factor; the system or mode of communication also includes the control of this technology, whether it is in the hands of a religious or political hierarchy, whether indeed it is a scribal or 'demotic' system. Nevertheless differences in the means of communication are of sufficient importance to warrant an exploration of their implications for developments in human thought; and, in particular, to see whether they can give us a better account of observed differences than the dichotomies we have earlier rejected. The challenge then is not merely to criticise the existing framework (that is never very difficult) but to offer an alternative account that explains more.

If we think of changes in communication as being critical, and if we see them as multiple rather than single in character, then the old dichotomy between primitive (or 'prior') and advanced disappears, not only for 'thought' but for social organisation as well. For the introduction of writing has had a great influence on politics, religion and economics; kinship institutions seem influenced only in a secondary way, for reasons that will be mentioned shortly. In saying this I am not attempting to put forward a simple, technologically determined, sequence of cause and effect; there are too many eddies and currents in the affairs of men to justify a monocausal explanation of a unilineal kind. On the other hand, there is a halfway house between the choice of a single cause and the complete rejection of causal implications, between the diffuseness of structural causality and of functional fit and the selection of a single material factor as the dominant or even determinant cause; there is the whole area of causal arcs, of feedback mechanisms, of the attempt to weight a plurality of causes. Regarding the nature of these causal factors, a major line of thinking in sociology and anthropology, especially in that which follows the Durkheimian tradition, has tended to neglect the technological changes that other

10

disciplines, such as prehistory, have found so significant. There were two reasons for this trend. One was the attempt to establish sociology as a distinct subject dealing with a special category of facts deemed 'social'; in social anthropology there was a parallel attempt (deriving from the same Durkheimian source) to steer clear of the study of 'material culture' and concentrate exclusively upon the 'social'. The second reason lay in Weber rather than in Durkheim; his qualifications to Marx's thesis involved a partial shift in emphasis from production to ideology, from 'infrastructure' to 'superstructure', a trend that has become increasingly dominant in some later social theory.

The significance of technological factors has to be judged independently of such ideological considerations. In the cognitive sphere they are important for two special reasons. We are dealing with developments in the technology of communicative acts, a study of which enables us to make a bridge between various branches of knowledge interested in the science of society, in its cultural products and in the instruments of cultural production that it has at its command. Secondly a stress upon the implications of changes in the technology of communications can be seen as an attempt to discuss in more manageable terms a topic that has become increasingly obscure and scholastic.

In an earlier paper (1963) Watt and I tried to lay out some of the features we saw as being closely linked to the advent of writing and in particular to the invention of the alphabetic system that made widespread literacy possible. We suggested that logic, 'our logic', in the restricted sense of an instrument of analytic procedures (and we did not give the same overwhelming value to this discovery as Lévy-Bruhl and other philosophers) seemed to be a function of writing, since it was the setting down of speech that enabled man clearly to separate words, to manipulate their order and to develop syllogistic forms of reasoning; these latter were seen as specifically literate rather than oral, even making use of another purely graphic isolate, the letter, as a means of indicating the relationship between the constituent elements. It is a suggestion consistent with Luria's research in Central Asia where he found schooling associated with an acceptance of the highly artificial assumptions on which logical syllogisms were based (Scribner and Cole 1973:554). A similar argument applies to the law of contradiction, which Lévy-Bruhl deemed absent in primitive societies. From one standpoint his claim was nonsense. Yet it is certainly easier to perceive contradictions in writing than it is in speech, partly because one can formalise the statements in a syllogistic manner and partly because writing arrests the flow of oral converse so that one can compare side by side utterances that have been made at different times and at

11

different places. Hence there is some element of justification behind Lévy-Bruhl's distinction between logical and pre-logical mentality, as well as behind his discussion of the law of contradiction. But the analysis is totally wrong. Because he fails to consider the mechanics of communication, he is led to make wrong deductions concerning mental differences and cognitive styles.

The same kinds of consideration apply to numbers as apply to other words. The development of Babylonian mathematics also depended upon the prior development of a graphic system, though not an alphabetic one. The relationship between writing and mathematics holds true even at an elementary level. In 1970 I spent a short time revisiting the LoDagaa of Northern Ghana, whose main contact with literacy began with the opening of a primary school in Birifu in 1949. In investigating their mathematical operations I found that while non-school boys were expert in counting a large number of cowries (shell money), a task they often performed more quickly and more accurately than I, they had little skill at multiplication. The idea of multiplication was not entirely lacking; they did think of four piles of five cowries as equalling twenty. But they had no ready-made table in their minds by which they could calculate more complex sums. The reason was simple, for the 'table' is essentially a written aid to 'oral' arithmetic. The contrast was even more true of subtraction and division; the former can be worked by oral means (though literates would certainly take to pencil and paper for the more complex sums), the latter is basically a literate technique. The difference is not so much one of thought or mind as of the mechanics of communicative acts, not only those between human beings but those in which an individual is involved when he is 'talking to himself', computing with numbers, thinking with words.

There are two other general points I want to make about the mental processes involved. I remarked that most LoDagaa were quicker in counting large sums of cowries. Indeed my method caused some amusement since I was seen as moving the shells in an uneconomic manner, one by one, I later observed that only schoolboys, accustomed to the more individualising ways of 'abstract' counting, used the same technique. When a normal bridewealth payment adds up to 20,000 cowries, counting can be a time-taking procedure. The LoDagaa themselves recognised a special mode of 'cowrie counting' (*libie pla soro*), where they moved first a group of three, then two, to form a pile of five. Apart from being a fraction of twenty, which was the base for higher calculations, five represented a number which a person could check by a glance as he moved his hand forward again to collect the next group of cowries.[4] The possibility of such a double check clearly

12

increased the accuracy of the computation. Four piles of five were then aggregated into a pile of twenty; five twenties into a hundred, and so on till the bridewealth was counted. But the point I want to make has nothing to do with the speed or accuracy of counting, but with the relative concreteness of the procedure. When I first asked someone to count for me, the answer was 'count what?'. For different procedures are used for counting different objects. Counting cows is different from counting cowries. We have here an instance of the greater concreteness of procedures in non-literate societies. It is not the absence of abstract thought, as Lévy-Bruhl believed; nor is it yet the opposition between the 'science of the concrete' and the 'science of the abstract', of which Lévi-Strauss speaks. The LoDagaa have an 'abstract' numerical system that applies as well to cowries as to cows. But the ways in which they use these concepts are embedded in daily living. Literacy and the accompanying process of classroom education brings a shift towards greater 'abstractedness', towards the decontextualisation of knowledge (Bruner *et al.* 1966:62), but to crystallise such a developmental process into an absolute dichotomy does not do justice to the facts either of 'traditional' society, or of the changing world in which the LoDagaa now find themselves.

The other general point is this. There are some specialist groups of traders, such as the overseas Yoruba, whose ability to calculate relatively complex sums is linked to their role as distributors of European goods, breaking down bulk items into small packages. Such transactions require a careful consideration of the profit and the loss, and this attention the Yoruba certainly give. How far their ability in this direction is a feed-back of literate achievement is difficult to know; the 'table' is essentially a graphic device, yet it is used as an instrument of oral calculation. Among the Yoruba this ability to calculate is normally transmitted in 'family' lines; it is subject to the limitations of oral transmission, which tends rapidly to incorporate or reject outright a new element in the body of knowledge. I have already mentioned that the absence of writing means that it is difficult to isolate a segment of human discourse (e.g. mathematical discourse) and subject it to the same highly individual, highly intense, highly abstract, highly critical analysis that we can give to a written statement. But there is also a further point, for which I provide a simple illustration to show the difference made by writing. If an individual Yoruba were to develop a new mode of calculation, the chance that this creative achievement would survive him depends primarily upon its 'utility'. I do not give this term the narrow meaning assigned by Lévi-Strauss in his dismissal of Malinowski (1966:3) but simply intend to infer that it is a now or never matter; there is no chance that his discovery will be acclaimed at a later date; there is no store for subsequent recall.

This is no trivial consideration; what happens here is part and parcel of the tendency of oral cultures towards cultural homeostasis; those innumerable mutations of culture that emerge in the ordinary course of verbal interaction are either adopted by the interacting group or they get eliminated in the process of transmission from one generation to the next. If a mutation is adopted, the individual signature (it is difficult to avoid the literate image) tends to get rubbed out, whereas in written cultures the very knowledge that a work will endure in time, in spite of commercial or political pressures, often helps to stimulate the creative process and encourage the recognition of individuality.

The growth of individualism is another of the vague generalities applied to the cognitive development of mankind. Once again, there is something to be explained. Durkheim tried to do so by means of another dichotomy, the shift from mechanical to organic solidarity; the growth of the division of labour meant the increasing differentiation of roles; advanced society was characterised by heterogeneity as against homogeneity and this state of affairs was reflected in the *conscience collective* of uncomplicated societies, and in the kinds of solidary bond that existed between persons and groups.

Again there is something to the Durkheimian argument. But the process he describes is more likely to produce a series of partially differentiated sub-groups rather than the kind of activity usually associated with the growth of individualism in the West. There was certainly more than one factor involved in this vaguely defined process; but the changes in human communication that followed the extension of alphabetic literacy in Greece and the introduction of the printed word in Renaissance Europe were surely important factors. Yet they are given no consideration at all in his argument.

Another common theme in differentiating between societies, one that is discussed by Lévi-Strauss as well as by Cassirer before him, has to do with the contrast between myth and history (Goody and Watt 1963:321–6). There is, of course, a simple-minded sense in which history is tied to the use of documentary material and hence is inseparable from literate cultures; before that, all is prehistory, the prehistory of societies dominated by myth. Without going into the many ambiguities involved in the definition of myth, there is a sense in which this concept often involves a backward look at that which is either untrue or unverifiable. And in the most literal sense the distinction between *mythos* and *historia* comes into being at the time when alphabetic writing encouraged mankind to set one account of the universe or the pantheon

14

beside another and hence perceive the contradictions that lie between them. There are thus two senses in which the characterisation of the 'savage mind' as 'pre-historical' or atemporal relates to the distinction between literate and pre-literate societies.

While the focus of this book is specifically upon cognitive factors, it is worth indicating two other sociological discussions that would gain from a consideration of the consequences of the changes that have taken place in systems of communicative acts, even though these relate to social institutions. The written word does not replace speech, any more than speech replaces gesture. But it adds an important dimension to much social action. This is especially true of the politico-legal domain, for the growth of bureaucracy clearly depends to a consider-able degree upon the ability to control 'secondary group' relationships by means of written communications. Indeed it is interesting to note that the terms in which Cooley originally defined the primary group are very close to those used for pre-literate societies. 'By primary group, I mean those characterised by intimate face-to-face association and co-operation. The result of intimate association, psychologically, is a certain fusion of individualities in a common whole, so that one's very self, for many purposes at least, is the common life and purpose of the group' (1909:23). A face-to-face group has no great need of writing. Take the example of the domestic group, the prototypical primary group, which brings us back to the reasons why writing has had little direct influence on kinship, since intercourse between kin is largely oral and often non-verbal.

Other social institutions are affected more directly. I mentioned above the problem of communication in large states. This is not the occasion to enter upon an extended discussion of the links between the means of communication and the political system. Max Weber pointed out that one of the characteristics of bureaucratic organisations was the conduct of official business on the basis of written documents (Weber 1947:330–2; Bendix 1960:419). But it needs stressing that some of the other characteristics of bureaucracy he mentions are also closely related to this fact. The depersonalisation of the method of recruitment to office often involves the use of 'objective' tests, that is, written examinations, which are ways of assessing the applicants' skill in handling the basic material of administrative communication, letters, memos, files and reports. As Bendix notes in his valuable commentary on Weber, in earlier systems of administration 'official business is transacted in personal encounter and by oral communication, not on the basis of impersonal documents' (1960:420). In other words, writing affects not only the method of recruitment and the occupational skills

15

but also the nature of the bureaucratic role itself. The relation with both ruler and ruled becomes more impersonal, involving greater appeal to abstract 'rules' listed in a written code and leading to a clear-cut separation between official duties and personal concerns. I do not wish to suggest that such separation is totally absent from non-literate societies; nor would I endorse the observation that unwritten tradition 'endorses the unprincipled arbitrariness of the ruler' (Bendix 1960:419). But it is clear that the adoption of written modes of communication was intrinsic to the development of more wide-ranging, more depersonalised and more abstract systems of government; at the same time, the shift from oral intercourse meant assigning less importance to face-to-face situations, whether in the form of the interview or audience, of personal service or national festivals in which the renewal of ties of obedience was often as significant as the religious rites.

I have tried to take certain of the characteristics that Lévi-Strauss and others have regarded as marking the distinction between primitive and advanced, between wild and domesticated thinking, and to suggest that many of the valid aspects of these somewhat vague dichotomies can be related to changes in the mode of communication, especially the introduction of various forms of writing. The advantage of this approach lies in the fact that it does not simply describe the differences but relates them to a third set of facts, and thus provides some kind of explanation, some kind of mechanism, for the changes that are assumed to occur.

A recognition of this factor also modifies our view of the nature of those differences. The traditional characterisation is essentially a static one in that it gives no reason for change, no idea of how or why domestication occurred; it assumes the primitive mind has this particular character, the advanced has that, and it is due to the genius of the Greeks or the Western Europeans that modern man emerged. But modern man is emerging every day in contemporary Africa, without, I suggest, the total transformation of processes of 'thought' or attributes of 'mind' that existing theories imply. The content of communication is clearly of prime significance. But it is also essential, for social theory and historical analysis, for present policy and future planning, to recall the limitations and opportunities offered by different technologies of the intellect.

In the chapters that follow, I try to analyse in a more particular way the relation between means of communication and modes of 'thought'. In this endeavour I want to maintain a balance between the refusal to admit of differences in cognitive processes or cultural developments

16

on the one hand and extreme dualism or distinction on the other. The thought ways of human societies resemble each other in many respects; individual intellectual activity is a feature of the social life of the LoDagaa of Northern Ghana as it is of Western cultures. Indeed the next chapter is directed to making this very point, the point that some versions of the dualistic view tend to overlook. On the other hand, the extreme form of relativism implicit in much contemporary writing neglects the fact that the cognitive activities of individuals differ from society to society in many ways. Some of the general differences that marked the binary approaches can be attributed to the new potentialities for human cognition that are created by changes in the means of communication. Social scientists readily acknowledge this point for language itself, but tend to ignore the influence of subsequent events in the development of human interaction.

The general influence of writing on the growth of knowledge is discussed in the third chapter, where I try to look at some of the features thought to be characteristic of 'simple' and 'complex' societies from this point of view, paying particular attention to the treatment of the important comparison and contrast between Western science and African traditional thought that has been made by Horton.

The next four chapters switch from the general to the particular, attempting to specify more exactly certain ways in which the use of writing seems to have influenced cognitive structures. Here I am more interested in the non-speech uses of language in writing than the obvious speech-like ones, as exemplified in the use of tables, lists, formulae and recipes for the organisation and development of human knowledge. It is these 'figures of the written word' rather than 'figures of speech' on which the account focuses. In trying to assess the importance of these instruments of cognitive manipulation, of intellectual processes, I examine (with very much of an amateur's eye) some of the first products of writing systems, drawing upon the earliest writing systems of all, those of the Middle East, that were so central in facilitating great advances in human knowledge. And at the same time I look at the more recent introduction of writing into hitherto oral societies, a process that can be observed in West Africa at the present day. In that region an attempt can be made to assess not only the external impact of both Arabic and European writing upon non-literate societies, a subject which I have discussed in earlier essays (Goody 1968a; 1972b), but also the actual process by which individuals and societies acquire writing and become literate.

While the impact of foreign systems can tell us much, this situation is necessarily influenced by the content of the tradition of which the system of writing is a part, Islam in one case, Christianity (or modern Western culture) in the other. During the first half of the nineteenth century, some members of one West African society did invent their own script, stimulated by a knowledge of the advantages that writing gave to the European and to the Arab (and possibly to the Cherokee). This well-documented discovery was made by the Vai of the Liberia-Sierra Leone border, who provide a limited opportunity to see the ways in which the advent of writing can influence a society in the absence of formal educational organisation and without the importation of a ready-made literate culture. This particular situation is currently being investigated intensively by Michael Cole, Sylvia Scribner, and a number of their collaborators. I had the good fortune to be invited to participate briefly in the project and so had the opportunity of 'testing' my suggestions concerning the implications of literacy (and in particular the role of lists) by looking at the content of a body of Vai documents. The results of this brief encounter have been published in *Africa* (1977), in collaboration with Cole and Scribner, under the title 'Writing and formal operations: a case study among the Vai'. It is an essential supplement to the present account and can be taken to indicate, in terms of the distinction used by Scribner and Cole (1973), that while cognitive capacities remain the same, access to different skills can produce remarkable results. Indeed I myself would go further and see the acquisition of these means of communication as effectively transforming the nature of cognitive processes, in a manner that leads to a partial dissolution of the boundaries erected by psychologists and linguists between abilities and performance.

Domestication as an individual experience

2. *Intellectuals in pre-literate societies?*

> When they reached the Dragon Gate, the guild head pointed to it, and said, 'This is the gate for scholars'. They went into a corridor with examination cells on both sides, and the guild head told them, 'This is Number One. You can go in and have a look'. Chou Chin went in, and when he saw the desk set there so neatly, tears started to his eyes. He gave a long sigh, knocked his head against the desk, and slipped to the ground unconscious.
>
> But to know whether Chou Chin recovered or not, you must read the next chapter.
>
> Wu Ching-Tzu, *The Scholars*, p. 25[1]

The drift of the argument, then, is not to build an iron curtain nor even a paper screen, between the cognitive processes of societies that one would clearly distinguish on any technological index, but to disentangle the particular features of 'modes of thought' that appear to be affected by changes in the means of communication. But a word of warning is necessary. In suggesting that some of the arguments concerning myth and history, the development of mathematical operations, the growth of individualism and the rise of bureaucracy were closely connected with the long and changing process of introducing graphic symbols for speech, of the shift from utterance to text, I do not mean to imply that pre-literate societies are without history, mathematics, individuals or administrative organisations. Rather I am interested in the further developments in these various facets of social life that seem to be associated with changes in the means and modes of communication.

I would like to develop this point by considering not whether intellectual activity is found in pre-literate societies, for this seems to me self-evident, but what kind of intellectual activity and whether we can speak of intellectuals in any sense, since the presence of such individuals is sometimes said to characterise 'advanced' societies, 'hot' societies, as distinct from static, traditional ones.

19

The domestication of the savage mind

If one defines intellectuals as members of a profession in any narrow sense, their identification in pre-literate societies would be difficult, though not perhaps impossible. Certainly there were no scholars of Chou Chin's kind. If we define the term in a larger sense, of individuals engaged in the creative exploration of culture (see Shils 1968), then I would argue that this type of activity is more clearly present, even in the 'simpler' societies. As a result of certain tendencies in the social sciences, the presence of this kind of activity, this kind of individual, has been obscured. The contribution of the intellect in simple societies has been played down to such an extent that one is sometimes moved to ask 'Do natives think?'. Or do they just have constraining structures, special systems of classification, undomesticated thoughts?

Let me begin towards the beginning. It was Sir James Frazer in that massive, influential and still fascinating volume, *The Golden Bough* (1890), who claimed that the first form of specialisation lay in the realm of magic, that the magician gave way to the priest, and the priest to the priest-king and subsequently to the divine king. I do not want to discuss the proposition that political roles developed from religious ones, except to point out that Sir Henry Maine used a parallel argument in tracing the development of law from Themistes, and Fustel de Coulanges applied similar notions to his reconstruction of Ancient Greece; indeed the thesis is simply the general hypothesis behind much writing on social development, namely that progressive differentiation is combined with increasing secularisation.

I mention this discussion for two reasons. The first is to suggest that one area we should examine for evidence of creative intellectual activity is the religious sphere. The second is to suggest that we need to be thoroughly aware of the implications of that line of thought which has criticised and rejected the so-called 'intellectualist' approach to the religion of non-literate societies attributed to the English scholars, Tylor and Frazer. The critique began with the French school that has exercised such a dominating influence in comparative sociology, and it forms the polemical starting point for one of the most influential books on the sociology of religion, Émile Durkheim's *Elementary Forms of the Religious Life* (1912 [1915]).

One cannot say that Durkheim was an 'anti-intellectualist' as far as simple societies were concerned. He wrote at the beginning of his book:

> For a long time it has been known that the first systems of representations with which men have pictured to themselves the world and themselves were of religious origin. There is no religion that is not a cosmology at the same time that it is a

speculation upon divine things. If philosophy and the sciences were born of religion, it is because religion began by taking the place of the sciences and philosophy. But it has been less frequently noticed that religion has not confined itself to enriching the human intellect, formed beforehand, with a certain number of ideas, it has contributed to forming the intellect itself. . .

At the roots of all our judgments there are a certain number of essential ideas which dominate all our intellectual life; they are what philosophers since Aristotle have called the categories of understanding: ideas of time, space, class, number, cause, substance, personality, etc. They correspond to the most universal properties of things. They are like the solid frame which encloses all thought. . .They are like the framework of the intelligence (1915:9).

Durkheim, then, was certainly not anti-intellectualist to the extent that he avoided the consideration of things intellectual in the world of elementary forms. But it is essentially the social aspects of these categories and speculations in which Durkheim is interested. The nature of his concern is explicit in his emphasis upon 'social facts', upon the 'conscience collective' and its 'collective representations' and above all in his brilliant and seminal work on 'primitive classification' where he attempts to relate concepts of time and space to the 'social morphology' of particular communities. One of the consequences of such an approach is to deflate the contributions of specific individuals. In the same opening chapter he writes of:

a special intellectual activity. . .which is infinitely richer and complexer than that of the individual. From that one can understand how the reason has been able to go beyond the limits of empirical knowledge. It does not owe this to any vague mysterious virtue but simply to the fact that according to the well-known formula, man is double. There are two beings in him; an individual being which has its foundation in the organism and the circle of whose activities is therefore strictly limited, and a social being which represents the highest reality in the intellectual and moral order that we can know by observation – I mean society (1915:16).

Thus for Durkheim, the highest intellectual activity was essentially social. One sees his point – people build on what is there; knowledge is cumulative, culture continuous. But the nature of his argument leads him on to play down the individual intellectual activities of members of the simpler societies in a rather surprising way. At one point in his discussion Durkheim is trying to dismiss Tylor's argument about the

21

importance of dreams in the origin of religious belief. Man, he says, can certainly tolerate contradiction and may hold beliefs of a scarcely intelligible kind. As an example, he refers to the belief in many Australian societies that the child is not physiologically the offspring of his parents. He goes on:

> This intellectual laziness is necessarily at its maximum among the primitive peoples. These weak beings, who have so much trouble in maintaining life against all the forces which assail it, have no means for supporting any luxury in the way of speculation. They do not reflect except when they are driven to it. Now it is difficult to see what could have led them to make dreams the theme of their meditations (1915:58).

When Durkheim argued, he argued hard. Why is he driven to these extremes from which the slightest acquaintance with their creative activities would have forced his retreat? His attitude partly reflects the fact that he had no other way of explaining ideas that have tantalised many, namely the apparently absurd physiological concepts of the Australians (which in some ways resemble those of the Trobriand Islanders discussed by Malinowski). But he was also anxious, for theoretical reasons, to attribute as much to the social factors in the situation as he possibly could. Society is *sui generis;* religion is defined in terms of the Church and its relation to a community, its maintenance and generation of moral values. Definitions apart, he interpreted religious rites and beliefs not so much from the point of view of the problems which the actors are trying to solve (indeed he appreciated the fact which many anthropologists overlook, that contradictions need not necessarily be resolved, mediated, or otherwise disposed of), but as expressions of, as 'symbols' of, some other reality, namely 'society'. Religion was social, and religious rites and beliefs stood for something other than what they appeared to stand for. So we are led on to that preposterous statement that God is *société divinisée.*

Preposterous not because of any question of theism or atheism but because it is meaningless. Its import, in so far as it had one, was once again to direct attention to the social aspects of religion and hence away from the individual ones. The influence and advantage of this approach were manifest, especially in the field of the sociology of knowledge (Merton 1945); in the early paper on primitive classification, Durkheim tried to show how variation in the categories of thought were related to group structure and relations. The insight was clearly a fruitful one; it led to Marcel Granet's attempt to relate typical Chinese conceptions of time and space (time is round, space is square) to the 'feudal' organisation and to the rhythmic alternation of the concentrated and dispersed phases of the life of the group.[2] The same insight was applied by many other French scholars, outside as well as inside the group centred around the journal he edited, *Année Socio-logique*.[3] In the study of pre-literate societies, the theme is most explicitly developed in Evans-Pritchard's account of the concepts of space and time among the Nuer (1940), a volume which has served as a secondary source of diffusion of these ideas.[4] But one consequence of this valuable approach was an inflation of social thinking and a devaluation of individual thinking. Indeed one could argue that the very nature of Durkheim's dichotomy between individual and society virtually precluded a consideration of the individual contributor (except as a provider of what already, in some sense, existed, as a bringer of coals to a cultural Newcastle), despite the fact that, at the very least, the individual was required to mediate any changes in the categories of thought brought about by changes in the 'social morphology'.

This emphasis of Durkheim had a pervasive influence upon the work of French social scientists and even more of British anthropologists (in America there was some escape, largely through neglect of these developments). The cultural character of categories of the understanding, the nature of primitive classification, the stress on the social aspects of religious rites and beliefs, all this was taken up in a variety of forms by a wide range of scholars. One of the most obvious examples was the work of the French philosopher, Lévy-Bruhl. In England his ideas influenced Evans-Pritchard's pioneering study *Witchcraft, Oracles and Magic among the Azande* (1937). Though characteristically (because so few of the monographs of the British anthropologists explicitly declared their intellectual progenitors), the name of the Frenchman is barely mentioned, Evans-Pritchard's work was based upon extensive reading of the French school and some considerable sympathy for certain aspects of Lévy-Bruhl's thesis, the clearest evidence of which came out in three articles on the sociology of religion written when he was Professor of Sociology at Cairo. In the *Bulletin of the Faculty of Arts* of that University, he wrote on Tylor and Frazer, on Pareto and on Lévy-Bruhl. The comments on Tylor and Frazer follow closely those of Durkheim, being critical of their 'intellectualist' stance or what he later describes as the 'if I were a horse' position.

There was an equally heavy influence on French studies of non-literate societies, especially clear in the work of Lévi-Strauss. While he has been credited by Geertz and Kirk among others, with restoring the speculative component in anthropological studies, the speculation is essentially that of the observer rather than of the actor; the latter remains a shadowy figure, caught in a structural maze, a prisoner of his classificatory schemata. It is essentially a social rather than an individual intellectualisation. Or, to put it another way (since a discussion in terms of alternatives can be misleading), his emphasis is on the social aspects of the intellectual activities rather than on the individual ones. For example, while he does not interpret myth in the same way as Malinowski, who saw it as a charter of social institutions, he still sees it as a social product in some general but undefined way. The emphasis is on the myth as a social fact, a cultural statement, the key to a code, a window on structure, as well as a product of the human mind *tout court*, but not on the process of creation itself. His approach thus tends to treat myth as a static factor in a society, closely linked to the cultural framework, and to that extent removed from the manipulation of particular individuals, individuals who might have some particular gift for the verbal arts. Myth partakes of the exteriority of Durkheim's social facts, hence problems of change (of which creative activity is a significant part) are relegated to the background. Inevitably it also tends to concentrate upon the observer's rather than the actor's framework, the etic rather than the emic. For example, in the first volume of his *Introduction to a Science of Mythology*, Lévi-Strauss explicitly excludes from consideration the intellectual, cognitive aspects of myth; as a means of communication between men, myth has: 'no practical function. We need to reduce it to systems of inter-relations of which it is doubtful, to say the least, whether the natives of central Brazil... have any understanding'. (1970[1964]:12). He is looking for the syntax rather than the semantics of South American mythology.

This approach implies a sharp distinction between the way one examines the verbal acts and cognitive processes of 'simpler' and 'advanced' societies, of 'other cultures' as opposed to our own, of, say, 'myth' as opposed to 'poetry' or other literary forms. Significantly, much recent discussion of myth is set within the dichotomy between *la pensée sauvage* and *la pensée domestiquée*. Savage thought is essentially social thought, apparently quite dependent upon given categories of the understanding, upon forms of *primitive* classification. Even though Lévi-Strauss displays more understanding of the world of the so-called bricoleur, the cultural handy-man, the opposition is unacceptable both as a statement of fact and because of the consequences for analysis. Like a good deal of structural or functional analysis, it tends to interpret primitive thought 'symbolically' rather than 'cognitively'. I would not reject the interpretation of, for example, a story about a hyena and a rabbit as a statement about matrilineal relationships (Beidelman 1961); this element may well be present, although the

24

theme is found where matrilineal systems are not (Finnegan 1970). But one can go too far in trying to explain away thinking in pre-literate societies by interpreting it in this way, as Malinowski's approach tended to do on the social rather than the cultural level. One runs into similar problems (sometimes insurmountable ones) by interpreting such thought in terms of a series of categories which clearly fall outside the actor's frame of reference, as is often the case with Lévi-Strauss's 'structural' approach (1970:12), and in a different way, with the approach of those Freudian writers who also engage in the crypto-phoric interpretations of myth and ritual (Goody 1962:38). In other words, meaning to the actors, surface meaning, becomes less important than the 'underlying' themes detected by the observer, the 'deeper meaning', an elucidation of which explains the apparent meaningless-ness, non-rationality, even absurdity, of the utterance, the ritual, the interaction under review.

In such a scheme there is little place for intellectuals, nor yet for creative activity of a more than superficial kind. Indeed, it leans in the same direction as that considerable body of literature written about European ballads and folk song, interpreting them as works of commu-nal consciousness and group authorship rather than, as in more 'civi-lised' communities, of an individual bard or artist. As Ruth Finnegan observes, this view looked upon such compositions as 'handed down word for word from the dim before time' or 'far back ages', for 'no individual creativity or imagination could be expected of primitive peoples' (1970:36). Such a view of oral society was connected with a world view that developed with the rise of nationalist and socialist movements in Europe in the second half of the nineteenth century. For not only did many writers hark back to tribal and vernacular roots (Germanic, Slavic or Celtic) in opposition to the Graeco-Roman con-tribution which had been stressed before the dawning of the Romantic era, but they also emphasised the communality of village life, re-affirmed the countryside against town, especially the old countryside as against the modern town. The co-operative quality of peasant exis-tence was diagnosed in the extended families of the *zadruga*, in the redistributive workings of the *mir*, as well as in the social elements of belief and story epitomised in the rural folktale, the national epic or the mysterious ballad, where even the process of composition was visualised not as an individual one but as emerging from the mass, a cultural given, a product of the *gemeinschaft* that was and will be, rather than the *gesellschaft* that is now but will disappear.

One feature of all these approaches, both the earlier and the later (and they have their merits as well as demerits), is that they fail to give

sufficient consideration to the individual creative process; some tend
to dismiss such activity altogether. Ruth Finnegan sees the limitations
of the earlier theories as arising from 'the same basic evolutionist
approach' (now largely rejected, she claims, 'by the majority of professional anthropologists') which treats oral literature as essentially
different from written literature (1970:37). Hence her desire to employ
both the term 'literature' and the forms of literary analysis for written
and oral products alike.

While we need to reject the radical dichotomy that has dominated
so many approaches to this problem, it would be a great error to substitute a diffuse relativism that fails to recognise the differences implicit
in the means. of communication implied in the terms 'oral' and
'written', and which fails to take account of other changes in the modes
and content of verbal interaction. Medieval ballads are different from
nineteenth-century ballads, not just because they were composed in
different epochs of time but because they were subject to different
processes of transmission, which in turn affect the process of composition. The medieval ballad is not simply an individual creation, but
an individual creation in an oral medium; the process of transmission
means that it is subject to continuous composition, to continuous
creation, and hence betrays some of the characteristics that earlier
writers attributed to the mysterious process of collective invention.
The objection to those earlier formulations is to the lack of interest in
the mechanics, to the elimination of the individual element and to the
over-formalisation of the difference, in other words the failure to try
and account for the particularities of difference in a concrete way.
For the differences cannot be neglected; to make the point in an
extreme way, one cannot imagine a novel or a symphony in a society
without writing, even though one finds narrative and orchestra; the
former are intrinsically literate modes of expression. However, the
differences here, as elsewhere, do not relate primarily to differences of
'thought' or 'mind' (though there are consequences for these) but to
differences in the nature of communicative acts.

The point is well made by Parry and Lord in their important work
on Homeric and Balkan narrative; they rightly emphasise that 'the oral
poet learns his songs *orally*, composes them *orally*, and transmits them
orally to others' (Lord 1960:5). It is not simply the performance that
distinguishes the oral narrative from the literary epic but the mode of
composition; the narrative is composed during the performance.

Lord continues: 'If the reader interprets oral learning as listening to
something repeated in exactly the same form many times, if he equates
it with oral memorization by rote, then he will fail to grasp the peculiar

process involved in learning oral epic. . .with oral poetry we are dealing with a particular and distinctive process in which oral learning, oral composition and oral transmission almost merge. . .' (1960:5). But we must be careful about drawing too sharp a distinction. While individual oral creativity is more continuous, often being intrinsic to performance, part of the process of composition and creation may still be private even though its final expression is always public. My own experience would suggest that shorter songs are often composed, not in full-scale performances, but rather in practice sessions where a man has more opportunity to work out an idea – I am thinking specifically of the composition of songs for the xylophone among the LoDagaa of Northern Ghana.

What are the implications of this argument about the role of the individual in creative, artistic activity? Much of the discussion and much of our thinking about other cultures has been based on the misinterpretation of the nature of oral 'tradition'. One of the features of oral communication in pre-literate societies lies in its capacity to swallow up the individual achievement and to incorporate it in a body of transmitted custom that can be considered as the approximate equivalent to what Tylor called 'culture' and Durkheim 'society' (or rather the 'social factor'), which both writers regarded as *sui generis.* In considering the nature of this tradition and the process by which it is created, it is important to recognise the difference between oral and literate cultures (though overlooked in many of the general arguments), because it bears upon the question of the individual's role in the creative process and hence the whole problem of the intellectual. In oral societies a man's achievement, be it ballad or shrine, tends to get incorporated (or rejected) in an anonymous fashion. It is not that the creative element is absent, though its character is different. And it is not that a mysterious collective authorship, closely in touch with the collective consciousness, does what individuals do in literature cultures. It is rather that the individual signature is always getting rubbed out in the process of generative transmission. And this process affects, though in a different degree, not merely what in its written form we would call 'literature', but more generally the categories of the understanding and systems of classification themselves, for a dialectical relationship always exists between the individual as a creator and the culture as a given.

In the remaining part of this chapter I want to refer to particular societies in Northern Ghana, in order to point to some characteristic areas where creativity emerges in non-industrial communities. I comment briefly on two societies in which I have worked, not simply as a matter of self-congratulation, but because a study of the similarities and differences between them assists in the development of my argument.

The first of these, the LoDagaa, were a 'tribal' society, without central government, who, until the recent introduction of schools, had a completely oral culture. Where did the kind of creativeness associated with intellectual activity tend to arise?

Firstly, it must be remarked that there was little institutionalisation of narrative, of telling stories or histories in any form, the one exception being a long recitation associated with the Bagre society. This recitation provides an interesting illustration of the role of the intellectual in a non-literate society. It dramatises man's relationship with God and the beings of the wild. But it is also concerned with man's problems in an experiential sense. I mean by this that it has to do with disease and death, with breeding and growing. And more widely still, it considers the problem of evil (Goody 1972a:197–8). One major theme that runs through the work could be paraphrased in the following way: 'God, who can accomplish all, has withdrawn from the world because if he were involved in it, he would be called upon to set all to rights, and because mankind has been led astray by the beings of the wild.' And after building up the Bagre ritual, which is the way of the beings rather than of God, as a means of overcoming disease and even death, the final message of the myth is highly sceptical about the implications of the rites which have just been performed.

> '...we still perform,
> so that one day
> we may help each other.
> These things we do,
> though they can't banish death?'
> 'But this our matter [ritual],
> I had thought that
> it was able
> to overcome
> death?'
> 'It can't do that' (1972a:290).

There is a delicate balance here between belief and disbelief, between caring and not caring, between commitment and scepticism. It is as if to say: 'God has created the world but the world is not as we would wish it to be. The creator has distanced himself from us and we have to deal with intermediate beings, not necessarily intermediaries. These beings are the ones who have led us astray from God's way, but we have been led away so long that their way has become our way'.

But although the story recounts the quest of the two first men for truth about the world, the quest is never ended. Indeed, it is open-ended, as is much African religion, leaving available the possibility of further development, of alternative solutions.

Before I expand this point, let me refer to the role of creativity in the poetry itself. The poem is a standardised one, in that it is passed on in a particular context, by selected people and in a special style; people are encouraged to listen to and then recite the myth and a premium or reward is given to those who can do this well. But while the LoDagaa sometimes talk as if there were one correct version of the myth, this is not in fact the case. In the poem itself, people are actually encouraged to incorporate elements which they have learned at other recitals. During the recital itself, new elements are being introduced all the time, as is now clear from the successive versions we have recorded. Which of those elements are repeated on the next occasion is a matter of speculation, but certainly something new gets incorporated all the time, just as something old gets dropped. We have here a process of composition that resembles certain forms of ballad poetry and gives rise to a great number, indeed, an infinite number of variants.[5] This continuous creation means that it is impossible to analyse myths of this (or any) sort, as if one were dealing with a finite number of manuscripts of an author's work; each reciter is an author, though some are more creative than others. Nor can it be assumed that all the versions of the myth, collected and uncollected, have a similar 'structure', unless by that word one is conveying very little. A brief examination of the new versions of the Bagre recorded in 1970 shows the omission of elements which seemed essential to the published version, written down in 1951.

Let me turn now to the element of creative activity in the area of the religious life. Many nineteenth-century writers, including Frazer and Marx, saw religion (and even more, magic) as the most static aspect of the social system. Fixed cosmologies, established rites, deep-seated beliefs, supported the status quo and helped insulate it from change. Consequently, it was hardly a likely sphere for intellectual activity. This view requires some modification.

If we regard a certain amount of magico-religious activity as orientated towards relatively pragmatic goals, such as the health of one's children or the fertility of one's wife, then appeals to a particular shrine or agency must necessarily fail from time to time. Certainly this is true of cures for witchcraft. A person appeals to a shrine and perhaps obtains relief from suffering, but then witchcraft is seen to return because children still die and people still fall ill. Monotheistic religions have certain ways of dealing with this problem, although many fall back on a pluralistic universe where one may switch one's attention from one aspect (or intermediary) of a deity to another. This latter solution is adopted in many simple societies and accounts for the turnover phenomena, the circulation of certain types of shrine. The fact that there is a turnover means that some individuals in that society are rethinking aspects of the conceptual universe. Not necessarily in its totality, but the whole is made up of parts and it is as parts of man's relationships with gods, or with various medicinal plants or prohibited foods that they are reconsidering when they adopt a new shrine ('fetish', 'god') with its associated prohibitions and injunctions on the behaviour of mankind. To consider these innovations as simply repetitions of what has always been does less than justice to the situation. The agents who introduce or invent these new shrines are often responding to the pressure from below, the demand for new ways. These men are among the intellectuals of non-literate societies.

Closely related to this category of person, and often involving the same individuals, is the diviner. This practitioner is faced with a somewhat different problem. His clients may want to know which of the plurality of agencies has been responsible for the misfortunes through which they are going. In directing people to this agency rather than that, he is inevitably concerned with the organisation of the universe, with man's relationship to his gods. Moreover he is operating a specialised technique which often involves numerical manipulation as well as a certain degree of mystification. When writing appears, then it is often the most popular divinatory technique precisely because of the access to 'secrets' which it makes possible. Hence diviners are led to play with complex ideas, and to relate different aspects of the universe to one another, as in the manner of the Pythagoreans and in the way with which we are familiar from Cabalistic literature. They are similarly led to adopt new methods, since failure to give an effective diagnosis may eventually rebound not only on the practitioner but on the technique.

Finally, there is one area in which intellectual activity is clearly seen to pay off, and that is in the area of praising leaders and manipulating chiefs. The incidence of this kind of activity is obviously related in a very direct way to the political system. Hence it is common among the centralised states such as the Hausa of Northern Nigeria (Smith 1957), but less common, indeed almost non-existent, among the acephalous LoDagaa. In the former case, the continual recourse to praise-songs leads to the emergence of part-time specialists of various kinds of music; in the latter one very occasionally finds a visiting minstrel playing to a group of senior men.

30

Intellectuals in pre-literate societies?

The kingdom of Gonja lies to the south of the LoDagaa, bordering upon the important forest state of Asante. It was the home of a number of market towns which served as entrepôts for the exchange of goods between forest and savannah lands, some of which made their way across the Sahara to the Barbary coast. Islam, and hence Islamic writing, followed a similar route, giving rise to a tradition of what I have called 'restricted literacy' (1968a). This tradition, restricted as it was, produced not merely the kind of intellectual we have traced among the LoDagaa, but scholars of a kind recognisable in all parts of the world where literacy has penetrated. Indeed, as among the Nupe of Northern Nigeria, they might also be said to have a group of literati, of men of letters (Nadel 1942). These scholars were specific, named individuals concerned with the manipulation of the written word. Driving north from Kumasi to Tamale in Northern Ghana, the traveller passes through the small administrative centre of Salaga with its mud houses, a few tin roofs and nowadays, one or two concrete shops. At the end of the nineteenth century this unimpressive town provided the setting for a school of learning under the leadership of al-Ḥajj 'Umar, who had travelled down from the Hausa town of Kano with his father in about 1874. He was originally a trader and subsequently settled down as a scholar in Salaga, first producing a volume on epistolary styles in 1877 which was subsequently published in Cairo. His later works in both Arabic and Hausa cover a wide range of topics and exhibit a literary quality which mark him off as one of the major intellectual figures in West Africa. In 'Umar's library inherited from his father, were the odes of the pre-Islamic poet, 'Imru' al-Qays, in an edited copy said to have been made in Katsina in the latter part of the eighteenth century. The British administrator-anthropologist Rattray, met 'Umar and wrote how he had spent many years of his life wandering through Arabia, during which time he had made a special study of the work of this Arabian poet and had finally translated his thirty-four odes into Hausa. These works had also been rendered into English by writers such as Arnold, Lyall and Lady Anne Blunt (and subsequently by Arberry); Rattray considers 'Umar's the best and most scholarly of all these attempts. There was good reason why this should be so, for among his library was to be found a manuscript copy of a work on Arabic prosody written about A.H. 200. Using this, writes Rattray, ''Umar had fully worked out the forms and names of the different metres for each of the thirty-four odes in the original'.

One of this writer's most widely read poems, found in manuscript in Northern Nigeria as well as in Ghana, was on the Christian conquest.

It displays a capacity for a critical commentary on the world and its contemporary problems:

> I've set out this poem in rhyme. . .
> For the profit of intelligent folk. . .
> Anyone with brains will heed it.
> From our words,
> He'll grasp our intention.
> The sun of disaster has risen in the West,
> Glaring down on people and populated places.
> Poetically speaking, I mean the catastrophe of the Christian.
> The Christian calamity has come upon us
> Like a dust-cloud.
> At the start of the affair, they came
> Peacefully,
> With soft sweet talk.
> 'We've come to trade,' they said,
> 'To reform the beliefs of the people'
> 'To halt oppression here below, and theft,'
> 'To clean up and overthrow corruption.'
> Not all of us grasped their motives,
> So now we've become their inferiors.
> They deluded us with little gifts
> And fed us tasty foods. . .
> But recently they've changed their tune. . .
> (Translated by B. G. Martin in Braimah and Goody 1967:192)

Thus at the time of the advent of the Europeans there was already, in parts of Northern Ghana, an intellectual culture of the literary sort, a community of scholars whose members commented critically upon contemporary affairs and composed accounts of recent events. The same was true of other parts of West Africa influenced by Islam, especially Northern Nigeria. Indeed, some of the foremost literary figures of Hausaland were the politico-military leaders of the Fulani conquest, Dan Fodio and his brother, Abdullah, the latter being the 'propagandist' of the new regime and the one most concerned in his writings to bring the practice of government into line with Islamic precept. The widespread circulation of books and manuscripts made such a venture possible: the use of writing enabled the literati to see how far short a regime fell from Muslim ideals and so was perhaps an element in leading such intellectuals to rebel. The exegesis of a Koranic text, the critical perusal of a commentary, could well be a precursor of more overt political actions destined to bring the world to a state closer to that envisaged by the Prophet. Already then, at the time of the Colonial conquest, many societies in Africa and Eurasia were influenced by the advent of literacy which even in a restricted form produced its own scholarly tradition. Even in non-literate societies there is no evidence that individuals were prisoners of pre-ordained schemes, of primitive classifications, of the structures of myth. Constrained, yes; imprisoned, no. Certain, at least, among them could and did use language in a generative way, elaborating metaphor, inventing songs and 'myths', creating gods, looking for new solutions to recurring puzzles and problems, changing the conceptual universe.

One is reminded here of the dispute between Popper and Kuhn over the role of paradigms in 'normal' science. Popper argues against Kuhn's thesis, what he calls the 'myth of the framework'. 'I do admit that at any moment we are prisoners caught in the framework of our theories; our expectations; our past experiences; our language. But we are prisoners in a Pickwickian sense: if we try, we can break out of our framework at any time. Admittedly, we shall find ourselves again in a framework, but it will be a better and a roomier one; and we can at any moment break out of it again.

'The central point is that a critical discussion and a comparison of the various frameworks is always possible. It is just a dogma – a dangerous dogma – that the different frameworks are like mutually untranslatable languages. The fact is that even totally different languages. . .are not untranslatable. . .' (1970:56).

It is clear that certain tools and certain situations make it easier to break out of frameworks and in this respect the role of an intellectual is more prominent in a literate than in a non-literate society; he is transformed into a scholar, a specialist in communication rather than in, say, production.

In more recent times, the advent of European literacy, with its simple alphabet, its printed books, its formalised systems of instruction, has led to further great changes, especially in the content and organisation of intellectual activity. In West Africa, such activity fell increasingly into the hands of those who had been educated in the new schools, and later the universities, whether in the metropolitan country or (later) in their own land. Much of what is produced falls within the established tradition of scholarship or literature; in some fields, such as African history, ethnography and literature, substantial achievements have now been registered. But it is also the case that in this new situation many of the first products (at least in the sense of published works), often fell between European and other traditions, as if the writers were exploring ways of trying to make sense of their new

33

intellectual universe. I refer here especially to work on the history and culture of Ghana, especially that of Karl Reindorf, the Ga author, and in a later generation to the Akan studies of J. B. Danquah, and more recently the writing of J. A. Braimah, the first author (under the new dispensation) of Northern Ghana. Much of Danquah's writing is specifically aimed at considering Akan culture within the same framework as has appeared relevant to the study of European society. Hence concepts of the deity and philosophical ideas from the two settings are compared in a quite deliberate manner. The discovery of similarity leads to an assumption of historical continuity between West Africa and the Mediterranean, so that the conceptual parallels are ultimately seen as deriving from a common source. Like other writers in this position, he places great emphasis upon supposed verbal resemblances (e.g. the Akan *kra* and the Egyptian *ka*, both associated with beliefs about the soul), upon similarities in place-names and upon likenesses in custom. By such means, the local society and its members are genetically linked to the civilisations of Europe and Asia.

The same impetus is found not only among Ghanaian writers but also among some European authors of the same period and of a similar position, who were concerned to discover in West Africa the signs of Mediterranean influence. These writers include scholar-administrators like Bowdich, priests like Father J. Williams and the Rev. Balmer, teachers like E. Meyerowitz, all of whom tried to 'place' the particular societies with which they had come to empathise, in a wider temporal and spatial context. It is not difficult to criticise this work on historical and ethnographical grounds (see Goody 1959 and 1968b). But it is also important to see it as the achievement of individual intellectuals trying to make sense of their new universe (which included both Africa and Europe), and to produce a synthesis of the two traditions that was personally meaningful to them. In so doing they are pursuing the role of the intellectual in society, whether that society is simple or complex, literate or non-literate, colonial or traditional. But they were doing so with the aid of the instruments of intellectual activity provided by the radical developments that had taken place in the means of communication, developments that produced not only writing but the culture of the printed book to which these later authors belonged.

The long-term change in intellectual activity has been largely in the direction of the religious to the secular and the technical. Such a process can be seen as part of the overall process of secularisation and growth of science which has resulted in an intellectual activity incomparably more complex in its organisation, and one that depends upon a much more widespread use of literacy than heretofore, a literacy that is intrinsic to the organisation of government and the economy, as well as to the organisation of intellectual life. That such sweeping changes have taken, and are taking, place is obvious; we have already looked at some of the general implications in the opening chapter and will look at certain implications for the growth of knowledge in the chapter that follows. But it would be a fundamental error (though in keeping with some trends in sociological and anthropological thinking) to imagine any human society without its quota of what one may legitimately call creative intellectual activity, and even intellectuals.

3. Literacy, criticism and the growth of knowledge

The Word was made flesh, and dwelt among us.

John, i. 14

As I suggested in the opening chapter, the division of societies or modes of thought into advanced and primitive, domesticated or savage, open or closed, is essentially to make use of a folk-taxonomy by which we bring order and understanding into a complex universe. But the order is illusory, the meaning superficial. As in the case of other binary systems, the categorisation is often value-laden and ethnocentric.

I certainly do not find that any such simple design provides an adequate framework for the examination of human interaction and development. Yet neither is it possible to accept the opposing tendency, adopted by many social scientists heavily committed to cultural relativism, which leads them to treat all societies as if their intellectual processes were essentially the same. Similar, yes; the same, no. And once one allows this, the specification of difference is not in itself enough; one needs also to point to mechanisms, to causal factors.

Towards this end I want to pursue further an argument that has been outlined elsewhere,[1] and points to the role of changes in the mode of communication in the development of cognitive structures and processes and to illustrate the thesis by reference to developments in the growth of human knowledge and in the growth of man's capacity to store and to augment that knowledge. For some, at least, of the differences in intellectual processes that are indicated in a very general way by means of terms like 'open' and 'closed' can be related not so much to differences in 'mind' but to differences in systems of communication.

In using the words 'thought' and 'mind', I am referring to what might more technically be described as the content and processes of cognition. I take it as axiomatic that these two aspects are very closely intertwined, so that a change in one is likely to effect a change in the other. In other words, we are dealing with what Cole and Scribner, following Luria, describe as 'functional cognitive systems' (1974:194). I am interested here in certain general dimensions of such systems that are related to what historians of culture perceive as 'the growth of knowledge'. While this has to do with 'content', it also presupposes certain processes which are related, I argue, to the modes of communication by which man interacts with man and, more especially, transmits his culture, his learned behaviour, from generation to generation.

Culture, after all, is a series of communicative acts, and differences in the mode of communication are often as important as differences in the mode of production, for they involve developments in the storing, analysis, and creation of human knowledge, as well as the relationships between the individuals involved. The specific proposition is that writing, and more especially alphabetic literacy, made it possible to scrutinise discourse in a different kind of way by giving oral communication a semi-permanent form; this scrutiny favoured the increase in scope of critical activity, and hence of rationality, scepticism, and logic to resurrect memories of those questionable dichotomies. It increased the potentialities of criticism because writing laid out discourse before one's eyes in a different kind of way; at the same time increased the potentiality for cumulative knowledge, especially knowledge of an abstract kind, because it changed the nature of communication beyond that of face-to-face contact as well as the system for the storage of information; in this way a wider range of 'thought' was made available to the reading public. No longer did the problem of memory storage dominate man's intellectual life; the human mind was freed to study static 'text' (rather than be limited by participation in the dynamic 'utterance'), a process that enabled man to stand back from his creation and examine it in a more abstract, generalised, and 'rational' way.[2] By making it possible to scan the communications of mankind over a much wider time span, literacy encouraged, at the very same time, criticism and commentary on the one hand and the orthodoxy of the book on the other.

To argue this way is not to subscribe to a 'great divide' theory; it is an attempt to get away from the non-developmental perspective of much thinking about human thought and, at the same time, to link the discussion to the history of scientific endeavour in its broadest context – an undertaking that involves modifying certain categories of most historical and philosophical approaches to the subject.

It might be argued that there is all the difference in the world between the scientific attitude towards the control of nature that is adopted by the modern world and the mystical attitude seen as characteristic of pre-literate societies. But is this difference as radical as it

37

appears? Robin Horton, who has given us the most intelligent of the available accounts of African traditional thought and its relationship to Western science, denies that this is so. He attempts to treat African traditional religious beliefs as 'theoretical models akin to those of the sciences' and argues that, if we recognise the aim of theory to be the demonstration of a limited number of *kinds* of entity or process underlying the diversity of experience (1967:51), then recent analyses of African cosmologies make it clear that 'the gods of a given culture do form a scheme which interprets the vast diversity of everyday experience in terms of the action of a relatively few *kinds* of force' (1967:52). The gods are not capricious; spiritual agencies are at work behind observed events, and there is a basic modicum of regularity in their behaviour. Like 'atoms, molecules, and waves, then, the gods serve to introduce unity into diversity, simplicity into complexity, order into disorder, regularity into anomaly' (1967:52).

While I would argue towards the same conclusions, I would do so along different lines. For in stressing resemblances, the author has laid himself open to the criticism directed at earlier comparisons or contrasts of this kind (e.g. by Evans-Pritchard 1934, and Beattie 1970:260), namely, that he has compared the religious thought of simple societies with the scientific thought of complex ones instead of comparing the latter with the technical thinking of traditional societies. It was on this technical aspect, what one might call proto-scientific rather than pre-scientific thought, that Malinowski, and after him Lévi-Strauss, laid much stress. Note also that by 'science' Horton usually refers to modes of thought rather than to an activity, an organisation, or a body of knowledge. The semantic leeway that surrounds the concept 'science' allows considerable latitude in many discussions about its growth.

I would suggest that we may compare entities of the modern scientific kind not only with specifically religious concepts but also with a more generalised kind of element (air, fire, water, etc.) based upon perceived objects or processes but also used more generally to break down the surface structure of the physical world. The generalisation of these elements, which is a way of analysing the nature of the world in its spiritual as well as its physical aspects, takes elaborate forms in early literate civilisations. The reasons will be discussed in the following chapters but such elaborations are clearly based upon simpler forerunners. Take, for example, the account of creation (or procreation) found in the Bagre myth of the LoDagaa of West Africa to which I have already referred. In the second part of the Black Bagre, the first man goes to the sky to visit God.

When he arrives there,
God says that our ancestor
should come forward.
When he came,
[God] took some earth,
and pressed it together.
When this was done,
he spoke again
and called a young girl,
a slender girl,
to come there too.
She came over,
and when she had done so,
he told her
to take a pot.
She took it,
and stood up with it.
Then he told her
to look for okra
to bring to him.
He chose a piece,
put it in his mouth,
chewed it to bits,
spat them out
into the pot.

(Goody 1972a:230–231)

Here we have a 'symbolic' representation of procreation, the sap of the okra being sticky and white like semen and the pot being a receptacle resembling the vagina. As a result of this bringing together of the elements that go to make up human-kind, a child is born, and the man and woman who observed the act of creation quarrel over the ownership of the child. But this is not the only part of the narrative which gives an account of procreation. Later on the girl goes into the woods and sees snakes at play. She then goes back to tell her husband how pleasurable intercourse can be. In a sense a difference is being pointed out between the (first) spiritual act of creation and the (continuing) animal act of procreation, the first having to do with the supernatural, the latter with the natural. However, I am not primarily concerned with the interpretation of these processes but with the fact that the human body is seen as compounded of elements, of earth and water (or semen) and (elsewhere) of blood. So, in this society (and in its verbal constructs) we find the world analysed not only in terms of supernatural entities but also, at least in an embryonic way, in terms of natural elements, including fire and air, blood and water. It did not need the elaborations of Taoist, Mohist, or Greek to introduce us to these basic notions. In all probability, such elementary ideas, like the kernel of the wave theories, which Joseph Needham links with developments in Chinese science, and the essence of those atomistic ideas developed in the West, are universally present.[3] The bases for such general notions of science exist much more widely in human societies than many of our current dichotomies allow, whether these dichotomies are viewed in a developmental way (*from* magic *to* science) or not.

Indeed, what lies behind Joseph Needham's idea of these developments in human thought turns out to be a more sophisticated version of the simple dichotomy between primitive and advanced that we have been trying to qualify. He sees two kinds of thinking emerging from 'primitive thought',[4] namely, the causal account of natural phenomena associated with the Greeks and the 'co-ordinative or associative thinking' typical of the Chinese, which attempts 'to systematise the universe of things and events into a pattern of structure, by which all the mutual influences of its parts were conditioned' (1956:285). In the scientific or proto-scientific ideas of the Chinese, this conceptualisation depended upon two fundamental principles or forces in the universe, first, the Yin and the Yang, the negative and positive projections of man's own sexual experience, and, second, the five 'elements' of which all process and all substance were composed (1956:279). For, he concludes, 'once a system of categorisations such as the five-element system is established, then anything can by no means be the cause of anything else' (1956:284).

In writing of the concept of Yin and Yang, Needham himself suggests that we could be dealing with ideas of such simplicity that 'they might easily have arisen independently in several civilisations' (1956:277). Such 'independent invention' must surely have occurred, both with the dualistic divisions and with the concept of elements; indeed, in their most general form such ideas seem intrinsic to human thought, to the use of language itself. I have already suggested that the notion of elements is present in embryonic form in LoDagaa mythology and in similar verbal forms. Other writers have found, indeed pursued, dualisms in many parts of the globe among a variety of peoples, where they have invariably succeeded in discovering at least some 'opposition' between right and left, male and female; while, even for purely oral societies, some authors have erected much more elaborate schemes, which appear to display all the features of the 'co-ordinative or associative thinking' said to be characteristic of the Chinese.

I would therefore extend Horton's analysis further than he does himself; for the comparison between science and religion overlooks the comparison between science and proto-science (or simple technology), and this starting point tends in turn to distort the differences between simple and complex societies. The result is seen in the second part of Horton's discussion, where he deals with the differences rather than the similarities. Here he adopts Popper's distinction between what he calls the 'closed' and 'open' predicaments, which are defined in the following words: 'in traditional cultures there is no developed awareness of alternatives and anxiety about threats to the system; openness, with scientifically oriented cultures, such an awareness is highly developed' (1967:155); it is 'the awareness of alternatives which is crucial for the take-off into science'. Closure is associated with lack of awareness of alternatives and anxiety about threats to the system; openness, with the opposite.

Horton attempts to link these general characteristics with the more specific features of traditional thought. While I would accept most of these statements as pointing to certain differences between two broad groups of societies, the West and the rest, the dichotomies need to be treated as variables, both as regards the societies and as regards their characteristics. A dichotomisation of this kind is often a useful pre-liminary for descriptive purposes;[5] once we accept it as such, we can go further and attempt to elucidate the possible mechanisms that bring about the differences, a step that usually involves modifying or even rejecting the original dichotomy. Without in any way insisting upon a single-factor theory, I want to try to show how these differences can be partly explained (rather than simply described) by looking at the possible effects of changes in the mode of communication.

Horton isolates two major features of the difference between closed and open systems, the first of which has four aspects, the second three. These characteristics can be summarised as follows:

1. The absence of alternatives, which is indicated by:

(a) a magical versus non-magical attitude to words. In traditional thought, words, ideas, and reality are intrinsically bound up; in science, words and reality vary independently.

(b) ideas-bound-to-occasions against ideas-bound-to-ideas. In the scientific situation, the thinker can 'get outside' his own system, because it is not bound to occasions, but to reality.

(c) unreflective versus reflective thinking. In traditional thought there is no reflection upon the rules of thinking, hence there can be no Logic (rules) or Epistemology (grounds for knowing) in the limited sense.

(d) mixed versus segregated motives. While traditional thought deals with explanation and prediction, it is also influenced by other factors, e.g. emotional needs, especially for personal relations of a surrogate kind. This personalisation of theory gets eliminated only with the application of the rules of the game.

2. Anxiety about threats to the system, which is indicated by:

(a) protective versus destructive attitudes towards established theory. In traditional thought, failures are excused by processes of 'secondary elaboration' which protect beliefs; the questioning of basic beliefs, on divination, for example, is a blocked path 'because the thinkers are victims of the closed predicament' (1967:168). Contrast the scientific attitude. It is above all his *essential scepticism towards established beliefs* that distinguishes the scientist from the traditional thinker (1967:168 [my italics]). Having said this, Horton introduces a caveat by referring not only to Kuhn's discussion of normal science but also to the 'magical' attitude of the modern layman towards theories invented by scientists.

(b) protective versus destructive attitudes to the category system. Following Douglas' analysis, he sees 'taboo' as related to events and actions which seriously defy the established lines of classification in the particular culture. Taboo is the equivalent of secondary elaboration, a defensive measure.

(c) the passage of time: bad or good? Horton relates the 'widespread attempt to annul the passage of time' (1967:178) to the closed predicament; for scientists, the future is in their bones, but traditional societies lack any idea of Progress.

Let us examine these features from a different angle and ask what it is that lies behind the closed situation. Is the absence of awareness of alternatives due simply to the fact that traditional societies were not presented with other choices until Europe intervened? Or are we dealing with closure of a more inherent sort, a feature of the traditional mind? I doubt whether Horton would ask us to accept the latter proposition, which is essentially circular. What about the first? Here we seem to be offered a view of African societies which ignores historical complexity. The Kalabari, of whom he writes, have, after all, been in contact with Europeans for a number of centuries, and many other African societies have been influenced by Islam for a much longer period. Quite apart from these northern imports, there was certainly much traffic in ritual, much exchange of religious ideas and theories, among the 'indigenous' societies themselves. Some might claim that central beliefs in the efficacy of witchcraft and the powers of diviners remained unquestioned by such contact, being common to all these societies; but even this very general statement is open to query; certainly the forms of divination and the intensity of witchcraft changed under both internal and external pressures.[6] The religious systems of simple societies are indeed open and very far from closed. The well-established mobility of cult is incompatible with the complete closure of thought, closure and openness being in any case variables rather than binary oppositions. Horton has himself pointed to the true situation in non-literate societies: if traditional cultures see ideas as bound to occasions – if, for example, general statements arise in the context of healing rather than as abstract programmes about what we believe – then, when the contexts change (because of famine, invasion, or disease) or when individual attitudes change (because of the recognition that the remedy has not worked), the ideas and practices will themselves change. They seem more likely to do so here than in societies where ideas, religious or scientific, are written down in scholarly treatises or in Holy Writ.

This observation raises the question of the relationship between modes of thought and modes for the production and reproduction of thought that lies at the heart of the unexplained but not inexplicable differences that so many writers have noted. As I have said, Horton argues that traditional and scientific thought differ in the 'essential scepticism' of the latter towards established beliefs. However, we saw in the previous chapter that many observers have described Africans as being sceptical, especially about witchcraft, divination, and similar matters. What seems to be the *essential* difference, however, is not so much the sceptical attitude in itself but the accumulation (or reproduction) of scepticism. Members of oral (i.e. 'traditional') societies find it difficult to develop a line of sceptical thinking about, say, the nature of matter or man's relationship to God simply because a continuing critical tradition can hardly exist when sceptical thoughts are *not* written down, *not* communicated across time and space, *not* made available for men to contemplate in privacy as well as to hear in performance.

In many cases it is 'oral' and 'literate' that need to be opposed rather than 'traditional' and 'modern'. Awareness of alternatives is clearly more likely to characterise literate societies, where books and libraries give an individual access to knowledge from different cultures and from different ages, either in the form of descriptive accounts or of utopian schemes. But it is not simply the awareness of being exposed to a wider range of influences. Such openness would be largely mechanical and would be available to the inhabitants of a city like Kano, with its variety of trans-Saharan travellers, as much as to the inhabitants of eighteenth-century Boston or Birmingham. It is rather that the *form* in which the alternatives are presented makes one aware of the differences, forces one to consider contradiction, makes one conscious of the 'rules' of argument, forces one to develop such 'logic'. And the form is determined by the literary or written mode. Why? Because when an utterance is put in writing it can be inspected in much greater detail, in its parts as well as in its whole, backwards as well as forwards, out of context as well as in its setting; in other words, it can be subjected to a quite different type of scrutiny and critique than is possible with purely verbal communication. Speech is no longer tied to an 'occasion'; it becomes timeless. Nor is it attached to a person; on paper, it becomes more abstract, more depersonalised.

In giving this summary account of some of the implications of writing or, at any rate, of extensive literacy, I have deliberately used words with which others have spelled out the traditional–modern dichotomy. Horton speaks of the differences between personal and impersonal theories; and while he is referring to a rather different aspect of the problem (personal gods as against impersonal forces), the points are related. Again he speaks of thought being tied to occasions (hence in a sense less abstract or less abstracted), an idea which can also be discussed more concretely in terms of systems for communicating signs and symbols. Writing makes speech 'objective' by turning it into an object of visual as well as aural inspection; it is the shift of the receptor from ear to eye, of the producer from voice to hand.

Here, I suggest, lies the answer, in part at least, to the emergence of Logic and Philosophy. In the opening chapter it was noted that Logic, in its formal sense, is closely tied to writing: the formalisation of propositions, abstracted from the flow of speech and given letters (or numbers), leads to the syllogism. Symbolic logic and algebra, let alone the calculus, are inconceivable without the prior existence of writing. More generally, a concern with the rules of argument or the grounds for knowledge seems to arise, though less directly, out of the formalisation of communication (and hence of 'statement' and 'belief') which is intrinsic to writing. Philosophic discourse is a formalisation of just the kind one would expect with literacy. 'Traditional' societies are marked not so much by the absence of reflective thinking as by the absence of the proper tools for constructive rumination.

Let me now turn to the second category of contrasting aspects, those related to anxiety about threats to the system. As Horton appreciates, traditional thinkers are not the only people who find change threatening; so too, Kuhn claims, does 'normal science' (1962:81). It is certainly true that growth, progress, change is more characteristic of 'modern' societies, but it is not absent from other cultures. Nor, as we have seen, is scepticism. With regard to concepts of time, we find a difference of emphasis which can reasonably be related to differences in technology, in procedures for the measurement of time (Goody 1968c). Indeed, too much weight is often placed upon differences between cyclical and linear approaches. For example, the concept of chronology is linear rather than circular; it needs numbered series starting with a fixed base, which means that some form of graphic record is a prerequisite.

Note that in talking of anxiety about change, Horton is not referring to observed reactions to threats but rather what are hypothesised as possible defences against such threats. My own experience has not revealed major difficulties of this kind on the individual level; people accommodate the aeroplane flying overhead into some classificatory scheme, as Worsley (1955) pointed out in the context of Groote Eyland totemism, without finding themselves threatened because it cuts across their distinction between birds that fly in the air and machines that move on the ground. I make this point because Horton sees one of the main distinguishing features of African thought as the 'closure' of the systems of classification and follows Mary Douglas' discussion of taboo as a reaction to events that seriously defy the established lines of classification.

In support of this theory, incest is seen as flagrantly defying the established category system because it treats the mother, for example, as a wife and is therefore subject to taboo. Equally, twins are dangerous because multiple births confuse the animal and the human world; the human corpse is polluting because it falls between the living and the dead, just as faeces and menstrual blood occupy the no-man's-land between animate and inanimate. But what does this mean?

Let us take incest. The argument is difficult to follow, for several reasons. Societies in West Africa often classify potential wives as 'sisters' (this is indeed a feature of permitted cousin marriage and a Hawaiian terminology); nevertheless, men find no difficulty in sleeping with some and not others. Equally, some 'mothers' are accessible as sexual partners, just as, in our society, some 'mothers' are 'superior' to childbirth. If we look at systems of classification from the actor's stand-point, there is little problem in coping with overlapping categories; as we shall see, the Venn diagram is as relevant a model as the Table. Moreover, the whole discussion seems to rest upon a simplistic view of the relationship between linguistic acts and other social behaviour. What is at issue here is the question of 'taboo' as a category requiring explanation, either in the terms of Douglas or Horton. Neither classificatory closure nor taboo seems very satisfactory as defining characteristics of traditional thought.

Another aspect on which Horton comments is the contrast between the magical and non-magical use of the word.[7] The author himself points out – for he is very sensitive to questions of similarity and difference – that the outlook behind magic (at least in the sense of the dominance of the word, its entailment with ideas and action) is an intellectual possibility even in scientifically oriented cultures (e.g. in the dominance of mind over matter). I would go further and say that even the problem of classification (a mode of bringing data under control which is intrinsic to the whole range of sciences) is not far removed from the magical use of words in spells. Today the magic of the printed word has in a sense replaced the magic of the spoken one. Nevertheless, there certainly is some truth in Horton's contention concerning the shift away from word magic. What truth there is, I suggest, turns once again on the effect of separation, of objectification, which writing has on words; for words assume a different relationship to action and to object when they are on paper than when they are spoken. They are no longer bound up directly with 'reality'; the written word becomes a separate 'thing', abstracted to some extent from the flow of speech, shedding its close entailment with action, with power over matter.

Many of the differences that Horton characterises as distinctive of open and closed systems of thought can be related to differences in the systems of communication and, specifically, to the presence or absence of writing. But this does not mean that we are dealing with a simple dichotomy, for systems of communication differ in many particular respects (for example, ideographic from phonetic scripts). There is no single 'opposition' but rather a succession of changes over time, each influencing the system of thought in specific ways. I do not maintain that this process is unidirectional let alone monocausal; thought feeds back on communication; creed and class influence the kind and extent of literacy that prevails; only to a limited extent can the means of communication, to use Marx's terminology from a different context, be separated from the relations of communication, which together form the mode of communication. In drawing attention to the significance of this factor, I attempt to avoid the conceptual slush into which one flounders when such differences are attributed either to 'culture' (who denies it, but what does it mean?) or to vague, descriptive divisions such as open and closed, which themselves need explaining rather than serve to explain.

The above discussion has attempted to show that it is not so much scepticism itself that distinguishes post-scientific thought as the accumulated scepticism that writing makes possible; it is a question of establishing a cumulative tradition of critical discussion. It is now possible to see why science, in the sense we usually think of this activity, occurs only when writing made its appearance and why it made its most striking advances when literacy became widespread. In one of his essays (1963, chap. 5, esp. pp. 148–52), Karl Popper traces the origin of 'the tradition of critical discussion [which] represents the only practical way of expanding our knowledge' to the Greek philosophers between Thales and Plato, the men who, as he sees it, encouraged critical discussion both between schools and within individual schools. Kuhn, on the other hand, sees these forms of activity as having no resemblance to science.

> Rather it is the tradition of claims, counterclaims, and debates over fundamentals which, except perhaps during the Middle Ages, have characterised philosophy and much of social science ever since. Already by the Hellenistic period mathematics, astronomy, statics and the geometric parts of optics had abandoned this mode of discourse in favour of puzzle solving. Other sciences, in increasing numbers, have undergone the same transition since. In a sense...it is precisely the abandonment of critical discourse that marks the transition to a science. Once a field has made that transition, critical discourse recurs only at moments of crisis when the bases of the field are again in jeopardy (1970:6–7).

Let us leave aside the discussion about the distinction between critical discourse and puzzle-solving, between innovative and normal science, with Kuhn's implication of incompatibility (an implication Popper would strenuously deny). Thales' thought is not science as we know it, rather an essential preliminary to the kind of problem-solving involved in science, and it is significant that this kind of critical discourse is seen as emerging in one of the first widely literate societies.

This point relates to another of the concepts that have been much discussed by philosophers and anthropologists as a critical feature in cultural development, namely, rationality (see, e.g. Wilson 1970). As with scepticism, rationality is often seen as one of the differentiating features of the 'modern mind', of the scientific view. This is not a debate I find very promising. For, as with logicality, the argument is conducted in terms of an opposition between rationality and irrationality (with the occasional introduction of the non-rational as a third term), and rationality is seen as characterising certain operations rather than others. The usual way of avoiding the radical dichotomy is

47

by resort to diffuse relativism (all societies are rational). However, if we look more closely, a third possibility emerges. Take as a starting point Wartofsky's definition of rationality. Science is 'concept-ordered', but the use of concepts is intelligent, not yet rational: 'rational practice entails. . .the self-conscious or reflective use of concepts; i.e. the critical attitude towards scientific practice and thought, which constitutes not simply scientific knowledge alone (which is its necessary condition), but the *self-knowledge* of science, the critical examination of its own conceptual foundations' (1967:151). Rationality in this sense implies metaphysics, which is 'the practice of rationality in its most theoretical form' (1967:153); 'a rational theoretical science is continuous with the tradition of metaphysical theory-construction' (1967:154); metaphysics is a 'heuristic for science'. Whether or not we agree with Wartofsky, it seems clear that the kind of reflective use of concepts required by his definition of rationality is greatly facilitated by the process of giving speech some permanent embodiment and thus creating the conditions for an extension of reflective examination.

Since my theme has been the relationship between processes of communication, the development of a critical tradition, and the growth of knowledge (including the emergence of science), I want to conclude by offering an illustration of the way in which literate techniques operate as an analytic tool, promoting criticism leading to the growth of knowledge. My example is taken from a book on this subject, edited by Lakatos and Musgrave (1970), which discusses Thomas Kuhn's *The Structure of Scientific Revolutions* (1962). For Kuhn, a scientific revolution consists of a change in paradigm, a gestalt-switch, from one set of assumptions and models to another. Otherwise, science (normal science) proceeds to work within one paradigm by solving the puzzles offered by it. The very boundaries of a paradigm are a condition of growth of a subject, a development from a pre-paradigmatic stage, since, by limiting the scope of enquiry, they create specialist areas of concentration, based on positive results. Contrast this approach to that of Popper, who sees criticism as lying at the heart of the scientific enterprise, which is a state of 'revolution in permanence'. The difference between the two views is essentially between science as a closed community and as an open society.

For any discussion of Kuhn's contribution to the history of science, some agreement on the word 'paradigm' is essential. Yet in his book, as Margaret Masterman points out in a favourable essay, he has used the word in some twenty-one different ways, which she attempts to reduce to three major clusters of meaning (1970:65):

    (1) *metaphysical paradigms*, associated with a set of beliefs;

48

(2) *sociological paradigms,* a universally recognised scientific achievement;

and (3) *artefact or construct paradigms,* which turn problems into puzzles.

In his reply to criticisms, Kuhn acknowledges the ambiguity of his usage and suggests a substitution of disciplinary matrix for cluster (2) above (1970:271), and *exemplars or problem-solution paradigms* for (3), though he sees (3) as contained in (2) (1970:272). In other words, the author explicitly qualifies his earlier use of the term paradigm and hence can no longer talk of a pre- or post-paradigm period when describing the maturation of a scientific speciality. His footnote on p. 272 explains this somewhat radical modification, which waters down the whole concept in the process of clarifying it.

Let us suppose (I will complicate the assumption later) that Kuhn's reformulation, which makes a 'revolutionary' statement seem to fall well within the bounds of 'normal' science, was due to Masterman's criticism. How, from the standpoint of technique, was that criticism developed? Her first footnote explains the circumstances of the composition of her chapter.

> This paper is a later version of an earlier paper which I had been asked to read when there was to have been a panel discussion of T. S. Kuhn's work in this Colloquium; and which I was prevented from writing by getting severe infective hepatitis. This new version is therefore dedicated to the doctors, nurses and staff of Block 8, Norwich Hospital, who allowed a Kuhn subject index to be made on a hospital bed (1970:59).

In other words, the detection of ambiguity or inconsistency leading to a reformulation of the argument was effected by reference to a box of filing cards which kept track of different usages of one key word in the author's argument. It was effected by a purely graphic technique, which permitted a more systematic exploration of a written text than was possible by the more casual techniques of visual inspection usually undertaken by critics of a written text and which form the basis of the kind of criticism offered by Watkins or Feyerabend in the same volume.

My point here is that, by putting speech down on to paper, one creates the possibility of what is almost a different kind of critical examination. Imagine (though it is a fanciful task) Kuhn's book as an oral discourse. No listener, I suggest, could ever spot the twenty-one different usages of the word 'paradigm'. The argument would flow from one usage to another without anyone being able to perceive any discrepancy. Inconsistency, even contradiction, tends to get swallowed up in the flow of speech (*parole*), the spate of words, the

49

flood of argument, from which it is virtually impossible for even the most acute mind to make his mental card-index of different usages and then compare them one with another.

I am not suggesting that the differences (or shades) of usage were deliberately manipulated to confuse the reader and to carry the argument. Kuhn's acceptance of the criticism shows that he recognises what he did not earlier perceive, that his new concept (new in this context) was largely unanalysed. It was a kind of self-deception. My point is that the oral mode makes this kind of self-deception easier to carry out and less easy to detect. The process of (constructive) criticism, whether by the speaker or by another, is inhibited, made more difficult.

Equally, the more deliberate deception of the orator is perhaps less easy to overcome than the unintentional ambiguities of the writer, whose inconsistencies stand out by themselves. By means of rhetoric, through the gift of the gab, the 'tricks' of the demagogue are able to sway an audience in a more direct way than the written word. What is at issue here is in part the *immediacy* of the face-to-face contact, the visual gesture and tones of voice, that marks oral communication. It is the play seen, the symphony heard, rather than the drama read, the score studied. But, more than this, the oral form is intrinsically more persuasive because it is less open to criticism (though not, of course, immune from it).

The balance of my argument continues to be a delicate one. In the first place, I have attempted to set aside radical dichotomies; in the second, I reject diffuse relativism. The third course involves a more difficult task, that of specifying particular mechanisms. In the chapter I have tried to analyse some aspects of the processes of communication in order to try to elucidate what others have tried to explain by means of those dichotomies. This is not a great-divide theory. It sees some changes as more important than others, but it attempts to relate specific differences to specific changes.

The effort to compare and contrast the thought ways of 'traditional' and 'modern', literate and pre-literate, societies may seem of marginal interest to the more recent history of human knowledge. So it is from many standpoints. But from the most general of these, it serves to define the problem we are dealing with. For example, the development of science in Western Europe in the seventeenth century is sometimes seen as resting upon views about (1) the lawfulness of nature, which permits comprehension, and (2) man and nature as antagonists, and the outcome of the ideology of the control of nature as 'growth'. If we are to understand the particular contributions of Western (or any other) science to the development of human thought, then we must be a good deal more precise about the matrix from which it was emerging, about the pre-existing conditions and the nature of 'pre-scientific thought'. Thus the attempt to gain precision leads us inevitably into an examination of the ways of thinking of earlier times and of other cultures, as well as of the manner in which these ways of thinking were related to particular modes of communication between man and man, man and God, man and nature. All of these were influenced by major changes in the means, such as the development of scripts, the shift to alphabetic literacy, and the invention of the printing press. I repeat that I am not proposing a single-factor theory; the social structure behind the communicative acts is often of prime importance. Nevertheless, it is not accidental that major steps in the development of what we now call 'science' followed the introduction of major changes in the channels of communication in Babylonia (writing), in Ancient Greece (the alphabet), and in Western Europe (printing).

4. *Literacy and classification: on turning the tables*

*A vigorous letter from a salesman of
the Lord:
Ethan Amos Boyd to his wife Maura*

JULY 5, 1910   BOSTON, MASSACHUSETTS

Blessed One,

I think of you hundreds of miles away, and of our dear green innocent Vermont and reconcile myself with difficulty to these torrid streets. If it were not for Faith, for my earnest Belief that Spirit is All and the ALL THINGS REAL proceed from it, I think I should find Business unbearable. My love, I am alone among the Sadducees!

It is to preserve my ideals in this Egypt that I've taken to playing Moses and have drawn up a set of Tablets which, my dearest wife, I am eager to share with you that you may be better instructed in my simple ways.

Eschew	*Engage In*
Late Hours	Early Bed
	(Never After 9.00 p.m.)
Stuffy Rooms	Daily Exercise
White Bread	Brown Bread
Animal Food (Flesh and Fowl)	Raw Vegetables
Alcohol	An Occasional Pipe (for me)
Gossip	Philosophy
Novels	Mercy
Expense	Baths

I am pleased to say I have been successful in keeping to this regime, and feel the better for having eaten nothing but vegetable food this past week.

(Anne Stevenson, *Correspondences*, 1973)

We have seen how the understanding of cognitive processes and structures of knowledge in non-literate societies has suffered from the

Literacy and classification: on turning the tables

binary, ethnocentric categories that have been employed. Equally the explanation of such differences that appear to exist is affected by the failure to consider changes in the means by which they are communicated from one individual and from one generation to the next. But it is also the case that the nature of these processes and structures have been partially misrepresented because of an incomplete understanding of the transformations involved in organising verbal concepts in the ways required (or at least favoured) by graphic reductionism.

In this chapter I look at how observers, particularly those who have been influenced by the important work of the French sociological tradition, have organised the knowledge of members of oral societies in tabular form. In so doing, they have tended to arrange, categorise, formalise those concepts in ways that seem more consistent with literate rather than with non-literate forms of communication and tradition. In the following chapters I break down the table used by these writers into its constituent parts, for it is a matrix of vertical columns and horizontal rows. By taking two critical examples, the list as an example of the column, the formula of the row, I move from considering how the use of literate procedures inhibits the study of pre-literate modes of thought, to examining the ways in which these procedures have influenced the cognitive structures and processes that have developed subsequent to the advent of writing.

But first to the table, in which form the communicative acts of other cultures, non-literate and literate, are increasingly presented. It is of course true that all enquiry in the field of the social sciences involves the abstraction, generalisation and formalisation that are associated with many forms of tabular presentation. Here I want specifically to comment upon the table as a way of organising knowledge about classificatory schemes, symbolic systems, human thought, and I am especially concerned with tables that involve the representation of the actor's concepts at the manifest level, i.e. the semantics of linguistic manifestation rather than what Greimas calls 'une sémantique fondamentale'. Any deeper structures that exist, any more abstract models that may be postulated, must in any case be referred back to this level, where the problem of evidence is already of considerable complexity (Mounin 1970:213).

What, then, is a table?

The *Shorter Oxford Dictionary* gives three main meanings. There is the meaning we first encounter, as learners of the language, the table at which we eat and write.

Second, there is 'a flat slab or board', sometimes 'a tablet bearing. . . an inscription. . .; as the stone tablets on which the ten commandments

were inscribed'. Not only the ten commandments but also the Twelve
Tables (B.C.E. 451–450) of early Rome, as well as similar legal documents of Ancient Greece and those golden ones sent down many
centuries later to Joseph Smith, who copied them down to give us the
Mormon Bible. Such boards may be used not only for writing but also
for games which require a squared background, such as backgammon,
from which is derived the phrase 'to turn the tables'.

The third meaning runs as follows: 'An arrangement of numbers,
words or items of any kind, in a definite and compact form, so as to
exhibit some set of facts, or relations in a distinct and comprehensive
way, for convenience of study, reference, or calculation. Now chiefly
applied to an arrangement in columns and lines occupying a single page
or sheet, as the multiplication tables, tables of weights and measures,
insurance tables, time-tables etc. Formerly sometimes merely: An
orderly arrangement of particulars, a list. Late M.E.'.

The kind of table I want to consider here is of this third kind.
In commenting critically on some examples, I am certainly not attempting to throw out all use of tables, numerical and classificatory, much
less to reject all formal analysis. I do contend, however, that since the
table is essentially a graphic (and frequently a literate device), its fixed
two-dimensional character may well simplify the reality of oral communication beyond reasonable recognition, and hence decrease rather
than increase understanding.

I examine three examples, which in the end derive their inspiration
from the first, that is from the work of Durkheim and Mauss on
'primitive classification' (1903[1963]). Indeed, one of the tabulators I
consider, Rodney Needham, produced an English edition of the work
by Émile Durkheim and his nephew, Marcel Mauss, while the other
example is a table of correspondences from the work of Griaule and
his associates, which also represents the French tradition of ethnographic analysis deriving from Mauss.

When we discuss systems of classification, we need first to define
the range of linguistic material under consideration, and to specify
whether this comes from the specialist or the non-specialist, whether
it is derived from narrative forms, from ritual speech, or from all
published utterances (the total semantic universe). The problem is
illustrated in the three examples of tables I am discussing. Durkheim
and Mauss are specifically dealing with the contents of a body of
narratives, the Zuñi origin myths. Griaule also claims to be examining
Dogon 'myth', but we must understand this word in quite a different
sense, because he is dealing with 'sacred' talk of all kinds, and specifically that elicited from a particular specialist, the blind Ogotemmêli.

54

Needham takes a more eclectic view and draws his material from all published works on the Nyoro. Different bodies of empirical material could well lead to different classificatory systems, even within the same society. Since all these are in some sense partial abstractions from the totality of linguistic acts, all raise questions concerning their status, especially when this selective material is seen as revealing 'primitive thought', or indeed thought of any kind.

Table 1   Zuñi clans

Region	Clans
north	crane, or pelican
	grouse, or sagecock
	yellow wood, or evergreen oak (clan almost extinct)
west	bear
	coyote
	spring-herb
south	tobacco
	maize
	badger
east	deer
	antelope
	turkey
zenith	sun (extinct)
	eagle
	sky
nadir	frog, or toad
	rattlesnake
	water
centre	macaw, the clan of the perfect centre

Let me begin with Durkheim's view of 'primitive classifications'. In fact, he concluded, these are not exceptional, being continuous with the first scientific ones. Like the latter, they are 'systems of hierarchised notions', not isolated groups, but interrelated having a 'purely speculative purpose'. They are intended to 'unify knowledge' and form 'a first philosophy of nature' (Durkheim and Mauss 1963:81). But at the same time, they are social; men classified things because they were divided into clans, and the forms of classification are based on the divisions in society. Just as the classes and their relations are social in origin, so the total system is modelled on society. Durkheim discusses four examples of classificatory schemes, the Australian, the Zuñi, the Sioux, and the Chinese. Of these he produces a table for the Zuñi as well as a diagram for the Sioux. The Zuñi table is fairly simple (Table 1) but the text implies a more complex set of correspondences, which I list in

Table 2 Zuñi correspondences

Region	Clans	Colour	Regions of:	Prey animal	Seasons	Elements
north	crane, or pelican grouse or sagecock yellow wood, or evergreen oak (clan almost extinct)	yellow	force and destruction war	mountain lion	winter	wind, breeze or air
west	bear coyote spring-herb	blue	peace ('war cure') hunting	bear	spring and its damp breezes	water
south	tobacco maize badger	red	heat, agriculture, medicine	badger	summer	fire
east	deer antelope turkey	white	sun, magic and religion	white wolf	end of the year	earth, seeds, frosts which bring the seeds to maturity
zenith	sun (extinct) eagle sky	'streaked with colours like the play of light among the clouds'	} diverse combinations of these functions	eagle		
nadir	frog or toad rattlesnake water	black		prey mole		
centre	macaw, the clan of the perfect centre	'all colours simultaneously'				

Table 2. While the authors do not arrange these correspondences in tabular form, the tendency to seek fixed, linear sets of associations seems likewise to be connected with the written mode of communication. However this may be, the authors claim that all the correspondences which they present were derived from an examination of the Zuñi origin myths, so it is necessary to look at the way this was done before we can assess the validity of the tables.

In an article on the Zuñi origin myths, Ruth Bunzel points out that three English versions had already appeared, by Cushing, Mrs Stevenson and by E. C. Parsons. The third version is 'the basic account of the early history of the people which is generally current in folklore'; it was collected through an interpreter. Mrs Stevenson's version is 'an attempt to give a comprehensive and coherent account of Zuñi mythology in relation to ritual'. The use of the term 'coherent' is significant and will be encountered again. Now turn to the third and earliest version, which is the one used by Durkheim and Mauss.

> The Cushing version contains endless poetic and metaphysical glossing of the basic elements, most of which explanatory matter probably originated in Cushing's own mind. Cushing, however, hints at the true character of Zuñi mythology. There is no single origin myth but a long series of separate myths... There is not, however, any collected version which is 'the talk' because no mind in Zuñi encompasses all knowledge, the 'midmost' group to which Cushing refers, being a figment of his own imagination. These separate myths are preserved in fixed, ritualistic form and are sometimes recited during ceremonies, and are transferred like any other esoteric knowledge.

Bunzel quotes the example of the 'talk' of Käklo, parts of which found their way into Mrs Stevenson's version. 'Into the general outline have been introduced whatever bits of special information she had acquired.' While the main outlines of the origin myths are known to all, the esoteric texts, such as she herself gives, 'belongs to the priests'. The latter are relatively standardised but the 'history myth is not fixed in form or expression and varies in comprehensiveness according to the special knowledge of the narrator' (Bunzel 1932:548). In other words, the material is both specialised and variable (at least in part).

There is another aspect of the analysis of myth that is raised in Bunzel's discussion of Cushing's work. She notes that her predecessor recorded 'the myth of the sky cohabiting with the earth to produce life, indicating that the notion was current in that day.' She comments: 'It has completely vanished at the present time. I have recorded Zuñi creation myths...and all commence the same way, nor do the Zuñi recognize in these myths the implications of profounder cosmological concepts' (1932:488). This situation is open to two possible explanations. The first assumes that a change in the mythological structure has taken place over time; the second assumes that Cushing was guilty of overinterpretation. If the first is true, then we may see the change as connected with changes that have taken place in other aspects of the social system; or, obviously, we may see them as lacking any specific connection, the changes in mythology being part of the relatively free play of man's creative imagination. The second possibility, that of overinterpretation, is also on the cards, as Bunzel's whole analysis implies. However, it should also be said that some of Cushing's data are certainly supported by her own observations, for example, the division of the world and of animal species into corresponding categories:

north – mountain lion	east – wolf
west – bear	above – knive-wing
south – badger	below – gopher

In other words, certain of the correspondences hold, at least in some contexts.

If the material supplied by Cushing is in many respects already far removed from the observational data he collected (and this is the only possible conclusion from Bunzel's studies), then the yet more abstract and elaborate scheme drawn up by Durkheim and Mauss is clearly of limited value for interpreting Zuñi linguistic acts or thought processes. The integrated form of the myth on which the table of correspondences is based is illusory, since the myth constitutes no defined and comprehensive body of data that one can subject to so precise an analysis. Both myth and table are deliberate, literary elaborations of the actor's world-view, functions of the ethnographer's *exigence d'ordre*, not of any requirement of the actors.[1]

The second example I take is from the elaborate analysis of religious beliefs among the Dogon of Mali presented by Marcel Griaule and his colleagues. Their approach is firmly established within the French tradition stemming from Durkheim and culminating (at least in a temporal sense) in the work of Lévi-Strauss and more formal structuralists such as the Marandas (1971).

At the end of Griaule's *Dieu d'eaux* (1948[1965]), an elaborate table is presented to the reader (pp. 222–223) which is related to the 'genealogy of the Dogon people' given on page 167. It is not entirely clear how the table derives from the text, but the relationships to the categories considered by members of the Durkheimian group, e.g. left/right, below/above, male/female, etc. are obvious. Some of the categories are immediately recognisable to persons acquainted with other languages in the area. Others (such as the colour categories) are typical neither of the area nor of Africa as a whole; indeed, they run somewhat counter to the general theory of colour classification (e.g. Berlin and Kay 1969). In other words, the categories listed in the table are sometimes those of the actor, sometimes those of the observer.

One way of discovering which they are is by examining the context of elicitation, as Malinowski fruitfully insisted and as most linguists would concur. Let us first suppose that such systems have been correctly elicited. I refer here to the procedures used, as well as to the concept of reproducibility, which is an essential part of any systematic development of knowledge; to be able to reproduce is to be able to check; it serves the same (often tiresome) purpose as the academic footnote and the repeated experiment. When the procedure has been ascertained, it then remains to be seen whether the categorisation offered represents the key to the understanding of the culture, as is implicitly suggested.

Let me turn to a concrete case in order to establish what I mean. In her article 'Classification des végétaux chez les Dogon', G. Dieterlen writes of a list of about 300 vegetables which was collected among the Dogon of the Bandiagara cliffs in 1950 and 1952.

> The preliminary enquiries. . .have revealed a systematic classi-
> fication into 'families' of the plants that the Dogon know and
> use. Like all the categories of beings and things of the universe
> conceived by the Dogon (e.g. stars, textiles, animals, institu-
> tions, etc. . . . .) vegetables are classed in twenty-two principal
> families to which may be added two complementary families,
> which brings the total to twenty-four.[2]

Each category of being and of object is in correspondence with all the others theoretically rank by rank (for example the fourth of one corresponds to the fourth of all the other categories). Moreover, each of the twenty-two principal families of each category is linked to one of the twenty-two parts of the human body, itself considered as a whole.

The totality offers a coherent system of cosmobiological correspondences which is a synthesis of knowledge for the Dogon: so, for the Dogon, the whole universe fixes itself, in each of its parts, in the human being, a special expression of the microcosm (Dieterlen 1952:115).

Systems of botanical and zoological classification have been attested for many societies. But such all-encompassing tables of correspondence do raise problems, for example concerning the complex numerical patterns, the $22 + 2 = 24$ as compared with the $8 \times 10 \times 8$ of *Dieu d'eaux*.

59

This apparent difference raises the problem of whose knowledge (individual, social group, society) we are dealing with and for whom the schema is coherent.

The implicit claim is that this system is consciously held by the actors, though only by learned men. As with Zuñi myths, it is specialised knowledge. The authors are attempting to construct a system of sacred knowledge, *le mythe*, which though restricted can be assumed to be shared and hence to provide a key to culture. Unlike the Zuñi case, this one involves no shared text (i.e. written myth), so that the status of the claim is more difficult to judge. But it could be maintained that knowledge of this sort might hold a peripheral rather than a central place in the culture concerned. As an example of what I mean, and as a counterpart to the quotation on Dogon knowledge, take the first entry from a book that has remained in print in this country, though first published in 1649, and that was often consulted by our grandparents. The book is *Culpeper's Complete Herbal: with nearly four hundred medicines, made from English herbs, physically applied to the cure of all disorders incident to man: with rules for compounding them: also, directions for making syrups, ointments, etc. etc. etc.*

This entry is for a herb called Amara Dulcis; 'some call it mortal, others bitter-sweet; some woody night-shade, and others felon-wort'. There follows a detailed description of the plant, where it is found, and the time of its appearance, all of which account falls within the domain of 'science', though whether primitive or not, the product of wild or domesticated thought, I would find impossible to judge; indeed, the question has little meaning here, except in terms of the history of science, or more broadly of human knowledge.

The final section is headed 'Government and Virtues'. It runs as follows:

> It is under the planet Mercury, and a notable herb of his also, if it be rightly gathered under his influence. It is excellent good to remove witchcraft both in men and beast, as also all sudden diseases whatsoever. Being tied around about the neck, is one of the admirablest remedies for the vertigo or dizziness in the head that is; and that is the reason (as Tragus saith) the people in Germany commonly hang it about their cattle's necks, when they fear such evil hath betided them: country people commonly use to take the berries of it, and having bruised them, they applied them to felons, and thereby soon rid their fingers of such troublesome guests.
>
> We have now shewed you the external use of the herb, we shall speak a word or two of the internal, and so conclude.

Take notice, it is a Mercurial herb, and therefore of very subtle parts, as indeed all Mercurial plants are; therefore take a pound of the wood and leaves together, bruise the wood, which you may easily do, for it is not so hard as oak, then put it into a pot, and put to it three pints of white wine, put on the pot-lid and shut it close; let it infuse hot over a gentle fire twelve hours, then strain it out, so have you a most excellent drink to open obstructions of the liver and spleen, to help difficulty of breath, bruises and falls, and congealed blood in any part of the body; it helps the yellow-jaundice, the dropsy and the black jaundice, and to cleanse women newly brought to bed. You may drink a quarter of a pint of the infusion every morning. It purgeth the body very gently, and not churlishly, as some hold; and when you find good by this, remember me.

They that think the use of these medicines is too brief, it is only for the cheapness of the book; let them read those books of mine, of the last edition, viz. – Riverius, Veslingus, Riolanus, Johnson, Sennertus, and Physic for the Poor.

It is easy to set this statement aside as a survival from earlier times and to dismiss its significance. Clearly, the correspondences it presents had more significance in the seventeenth century when it was first published. But even then, such schemata as Culpeper put forward, while resting on many fragments of common belief, were often:

(i)   specialist syntheses,
(ii) elaborations of secret knowledge contained in 'books', spae books, Latin texts, expensive volumes of various kinds,
(iii) variable in content, though certain features like the seven planets clearly provided some fixed points of reference.

As a consequence, such productions could hardly be regarded as keys to British culture; though they might make a neat acrostic, provide a temporary understanding of the phenomenal world, they constitute a specialist's elaboration rather than a fundamental cultural code. In fact, this particular schema had a close connection with the advent of the printing press, as the last sentence of the quotation indicates.[3] The first edition of the Herbal was an English translation of the College of Physicians' Pharmacopoeia; characteristically, Culpeper was a Puritan who used the vernacular to break the monopoly of medical knowledge just as other dissenters had earlier done with Holy Writ itself. It was an act which brought him the enmity of the medical profession as well as the benefits of an enormous circulation.

Is there any evidence that the schemata offered for the Dogon and other peoples are essentially different from Culpeper's Herbal? Do they have a wider circulation, a more central significance? To the first part of this question the answer is probably in the negative, since we are admittedly dealing with specialist knowledge of a secret kind. Before returning to the second point, I turn to a third type of table which has recently had much currency.

These tables are typically laid out in the form of two columns, headed by the pair male/female or left/right. Their form again owes much to Durkheimian concerns (for example, to Hertz's essay on the left hand) as well as to the more recent interest of Lévi-Strauss in the simplest types of marriage exchange in moiety systems, that is, to that longstanding anthropological topic of dual organisations (see Lévi-Strauss 1956, 1960; Maybury–Lewis 1960). The Durkheimian thesis on primitive classification would naturally lead one to look for parallels between the organisation of groups and of categories; elementary forms of kinship would have their counterparts in elementary forms of classification, which the happy arrival of computer technology allowed to be described as 'binary oppositions'.[4] Some of the analysis of conceptual systems in binary terms has been carried out on African material where the marriage systems are hardly 'elementary' in the original sense of the term, despite recent attempts to view them (or their hypothetical originals) as such. Indeed, in these studies we have shifted to the examination of some general, and hence basic, constituents of human thought rather than of the intellectual processes of a single society. But in the case of Durkheim's discussion of primitive classification (which included China), the implications of applying such techniques to the examination of European (supposedly non-primitive, non-elementary) systems of thought were never explicitly discussed. Yet we have left the sphere of dualist systems, left that of simple societies, and moved to a pan-human arena.

Confining our attention to 'other cultures', we may examine these techniques further by looking at Needham's analysis of the 'symbolic classification of the Nyoro of East Africa', an article that has already been the subject of a critical review by Beattie (1968), author of many studies on the Banyoro.[5] Needham's aims, apart from investigating a puzzle in Nyoro ethnography, were to 'make a further contribution to the understanding of secular-mystical diarchy or complementary governance' and 'to carry out a *routine* exercise in the structural analysis of symbolism, in a continuing attempt to isolate its general principles' (Needham 1967:425). The specific problem that puzzles him is why the diviner holds cowrie shells with his left hand.

It might be claimed that the problem would hardly exist but for the assumption that left must be 'hated' in all circumstances if it is hated

Literacy and classification: on turning the tables

Table 3 Right and left in Nyoro symbolic classification

Scheme of Nyoro symbolic classification

Right	Left	Right	Left
normal, esteemed	hated	security	danger
boy	girl	life	death
brewing	cooking	good	evil
giving (social intercourse)	sexual intercourse	purity	impurity
king	queen	even	odd
man	woman	culture	nature
fertility	barrenness	classified	anomalous
heaven	earth	order	disorder
white	black		

in one, an idea that automatically follows from the allocation of a single position in a fixed matrix (Table 3). As a possible solution to the problem he raises, Needham suggests that the Nyoro 'may well conceive' of the diviner 'as an agent of the powers of darkness, and the left hand is the readiest symbol of this condition' (Needham 1967:437). In a footnote he also guesses that LoDagaa ideology might be accounted for in a similar way, pointing to my 'unexplained' footnote that *gobr* means a left-handed man, a term which is applied to diviners (Goody 1962:256n). I do not believe that any LoDagaa would conceive of diviners as agents of darkness, but in any case the problem of the left hand has a simpler explanation to which I shall return. Needham also tries to identify the diviner with females by showing that:

1 The left hand is inauspicious.
2 Reversal occasionally occurs, for which parallels are adduced from Indonesia, showing that 'a logic of symbolism which has a more essential significance than have mere differences of tradition' (1967:431) e.g. left hand, right hand, is part of 'a general contrast of symbolic values. . .which has indeed a world-wide distribution' (1967:429).
3 A similar reversal occurs in the case of a princess, who is physically female but socially masculine (1967:432) while the diviner is 'physically male, but through his left hand he is symbolically associated with the feminine' (1967:432).
4 The suggestion is supported by the fact that the diviner is associated with things black, a colour which 'connotes night, death, evil and danger' (1967:433). He is also associated with the odd numbers, especially with three, which is also feminine (1967:435).

There are several questions we need to ask about Needham's table.

The domestication of the savage mind

1 Does it have actor or observer status?
2 Why should vastly different cultures provide such similar 'symbolic' statements?
3 What is the status of the analogies and the oppositions (to use Lloyd's terms), i.e. the columns and the rows?
4 Are these associations fixed or variable, rigid or manipulable?

The first question is one we have asked of other tables and we have found the answer equivocal. Clearly, concepts such as left and right, male and female, occur in the Nyoro language. But is this true of all those listed? Is it true for example of 'nature' and 'culture'? This opposition has penetrated so deeply into cultural analyses that we regard it as 'natural', inevitable. However, the division between nature and culture is in some ways rather artificial. For example, many foods fall into an intermediate category, being uncooked yet cultivated, or only collected by human hand. In his paper on the Three Bears, E. A. Hammel (1972) places honey in the realm of nature and porridge in that of culture. On the breakfast table and on the farm, the opposition is scarcely so obvious. Indeed, the dichotomy raw/cooked might be more appropriately applied.

If the dichotomy is not all that obvious in our own society (nature being to some extent a residual category rather than standing in defined opposition, a matter of presence and absence rather than of contrasts, i.e. A/ – A rather than A/B), in many other cultures we find no corresponding pair of concepts. If the Nyoro have any explicit classification of this kind, Needham provides no supporting evidence. I would claim that there is no such pair in either of the two African languages known personally to me (LoDagaa and Gonja). Though there is certain 'opposition' of 'bush' and 'house', 'cultivated' and 'uncultivated', there is nothing that would correspond to the highly abstract and rather eighteenth-century dichotomy that is current in Western intellectual circles – though less evident in popular usage.[6]

Of course, the fact that there is no specific conceptualisation of the nature-culture opposition does not prevent us from employing some such dichotomy for analytical purposes. But such a usage can only be described as 'Nyoro symbolic classification' in a very different way from categories related to left- and right-handedness or to colour terminology. The whole evidential base is changed and, indeed, the inclusion of both actor and observer classifications in one table represents something of a sleight of hand.

The second question has to do with the widespread similarities between this and other tables from other cultures, similarities, which clearly can no longer be related to differing social conditions. Two of

64

these widespread identifications are left–sinister–female and black–night–evil. In these cases it is clear that we are dealing with associations, which, as Needham and others before him have pointed out, are transcultural. But does that mean they reflect certain basic features of the human mind, of human nature? Or is there some other explanation? I suggest that some of the associations of right and left are less reflections of the structure of human thought than of the structure of the human body (mediated, of course, by the mind). It is hard to see how any linguistic system could avoid such an elementary opposition. Nor, given the structure of the brain, is it difficult to understand how left gets negatively valued and right positively. A similar argument applies to the second set of associations. It could as well be the structure of the situation as the structure of the mind that gives rise to such identifications.[7]

What does Needham think his table represents? What is he looking for? 'Rather than look for some banal social function,' he writes, 'we should take seriously the principle of order which Nyoro collective representations not only exemplify but state, i.e. the relation of complementary opposition' (1967:446). Nyoro values are 'reflected in the myth by an ultimate contrast with their opposites', the myth being 'a chronological expression of an ideological and symbolic scheme which is defined in its entirety by opposition and made unitary by analogy (see Table). The narrative describes a transition from nature to culture; it states the perennial and complementary opposition between order and disorder' (1967:446).

The banal social function has to do with the interpretation of the myth as a way of justifying the advent of a new dynasty, an interpretation which a number of authors have made of similar stories of regal origin. Polemics apart, there is no reason to suppose these varying interpretations are incompatible one with another; and in any case the concept of banality appears as applicable to empty reductionism of the kind exemplified in the final sentence as it does to the plausible allocation of social function. As Beattie points out, Nyoro myth could be interpreted in completely the opposite way.

With regard to the last of these points, clearly Needham recognises that the associations are reversible, even manipulable. But for him they are all manipulable in terms of a single specific schema. Ambivalence, even vagueness, is suspect, as is clear from his discussion of Beattie's comment on the number three; indeed, many anthropologists appear to view ambivalence and ambiguity as unacceptable to the 'savage mind', as having to be eliminated by classification or smothered by taboo. Could such an approach, so inimical to the analysis of much poetic speech, be a result of *our* tables rather than *their* thoughts?[8]

65

The domestication of the savage mind

More complex issues are raised by the discussion of black. Radcliffe-Brown pointed to the virtually universal association of day=white=good, night=black=bad (1922:331–3), an association on which I commented for the LoDogaa (1962:109, 395; 1969; 137) and on which many others have made similar remarks. But the symbolic association is not a simple one which works only in a straightforward positive or negative direction. For not only is black=evil, but also, for Africans, black=evil =us. It is inconceivable that the symbolic network could be so simplistic as to insist upon a fixed set of equivalents of the order: black=evil= us. Whatever element of self-denigration may exist in the relationships of blacks with whites, especially under colonial conditions, such a view of self must necessarily contain more positive constituents; hence the opposition black/white can never be in any permanent relationship with evil/good. Black is beautiful as well as evil. Whitewashing is covering up as well as cleansing. And this ambiguity cannot just be treated as a matter of reversal, of change of dominant direction. For both implications are often present in the black/white contrast; the relationship is therefore ambivalent or polysemic. The kind of ambivalence I am thinking of is recorded by Turner for the Ndembu: 'black=excreta or bodily dissolution=transition from one social stratus to another viewed as mystical death; black=rain clouds or fertile earth =unity of widest recognised group sharing same life values' (1967:89). The relevant reference is sorted out on a *contextual* basis; no tables of equivalences or oppositions can be universally applicable (see Beattie 1968:438).

My own enquiries among the speakers of a number of Northern Ghanaian languages lead to similar conclusions. As in many pairs of the world, the notion of blackness (L.D. *sebla*) is linked with darkness (night) and with its various dangers, especially the black arts. Whiteness on the other hand is light, clean, and harmless; when my belly is white (*n puo pelena*), I cannot practise witchcraft or harbour envy. It would however be a gross error to suppose that in all contexts these colours had the same significance; to talk about 'we black people' (*ti nisaal sebla*) is not to place ourselves below whites, who are in some ways more tricky, more 'shady' in their dealings. Indeed, sometimes whiteness is positively rejected, as in the case of the unfortunate albino, who is the unhappiest of sights in a jostling African crowd.

Such compartmentalisation of the 'classificatory' schema is the common knowledge of literary critics and others used to studying our own semantic processes. Because black has sinister associations, it would be ridiculous to suppose that one could not use the word in a positive sense, as in 'the black earth'; clearly, one needs to examine a wider

66

semantic field than a limited number of connotations of a single morpheme.

Looked at from this standpoint there is no problem of the diviner as
a left-handed man among the LoDagaa; for it is in his left hand that
he holds the divining stick, leaving the right free for other purposes
such as holding a rattle, as my friend K. G. pointed out when I wrote
to him asking for his explanation; indeed, he thus confirmed the interpretation I offered in my footnote to the Bagre (1972a:206). The
xylophone player is another left-handed man; the ability to play an
independent rhythm with the left hand is one of the first things one
has to acquire as a musician – it is a task difficult to master and one
that is certainly not devalued by the LoDagaa. Indeed one would only
assume left-handedness was devalued in all contexts of utterance if one
was concerned to establish a fixed pattern of associations in the form of
a single table of 'symbolic classifications'.

The same point is even more clearly made when we take the element
'girl', which also appears on the left side of the Nyoro table. According
to Needham, the symbolic classification equates 'barrenness' with
women and 'fertility' with men. One could point out a number of
contexts in which such an identification must make nonsense of Nyoro
thought and action. Not that the association is necessarily wrong, but
it is strictly contextual and cannot be reasonably subjected to this kind
of simplistic treatment. The trouble arises from applying a crude
written technique (the table) to a complex oral process, then claiming
one has the key to a culture, to a symbolic system.

The complexity of these tables lessens as the range of material
widens. This lessening of complexity is accompanied by the attribution of increasing generality to the results. Durkheim and Mauss
link forms of classification to particular societies; they see certain
features of the former as typical of a specific type of society, the tracing
of such connections deriving from their view of the origin of these
schemas. Griaule looks upon his results as suggesting a common religion in the area with which he is concerned (1965:217–18).[9] Needham's
schema seems very much like other tables derived from a wide variety
of cultures, a similarity that is consistent with his (or Lévi-Strauss')
later view that these systems of symbolic classification are related to
the structure of the human mind. Hence we should look for internal
rather than external relationships, a view which seems to run counter
to the earlier attempt to link binary oppositions with prescriptive
marriage, though it offers the possibility of identifying homologous
relationships at a much more abstract level.

But the basic trouble lies in the attempt to apply a simple graphic device (the table) to the study of 'symbols' in an oral culture. It is doubtful if words and their meanings can ever be subjected to such reductionism with any degree of profit, though some sets may be more amenable than others to this manner of treatment. For this simplification produces a superficial order that reflects the structure of a matrix more obviously than the structure of the (or a) human mind, and thus produces gross general similarities in all this type of construct. Indeed it is not irrelevant that the first form of writing known to man, the 'cuneiform' writing of Sumer, was probably organised in just such columns and rows, read first from top to bottom. Later the tables were turned through ninety degrees and read from left to right.

If we turn from tables created by an observer to those created by the actor, we find that the type of 'thinking' these schemata reflect is more characteristic of the early phases of literate societies than it is of oral cultures. Look, for example, at Joseph Needham's description of Chinese thought. This he sees as differing both from 'primitive thinking' on the one hand and from European causal and 'legal' or nomothetic thinking on the other. This associative or co-ordinative thinking gave 'a picture of an extremely and precisely ordered universe, in which things "fitted" so exactly that you could not insert a hair between them' (1956:286). Thinking of this sort has a natural affinity for number-mysticism of the kind practised by the Pythagoreans (1956:287).

If we discount the evidence for different types of thinking and concentrate rather on the products of thought, it is critical to note that both the Pythagoreans, with their magical tetrahedrons, and the Chinese with their horoscopes, were dealing in literary artefacts, in the results of the graphic manipulation of concepts. One of the features of the graphic mode is the tendency to arrange terms in (linear) rows and (hierarchical) columns in such a way that each item is allocated a single position, where it stands in a definite, permanent, and unambiguous relationship to the others. Assign a position, for example, to 'black' and it then acquires a specific relationship to all the other elements in the 'scheme of symbolic classification'.

I do not mean to argue that 'associative thinking' of some kind is absent from non-literate societies. Clearly, systems of classification have a greater flexibility the fewer the constraining factors, such as the 'scientific' penetration of the external world; the fit of the periodic table of elements operates at a more restricted level than the linking of animals and clans, or seasons and humours. One of the consequences of literacy in pre-Renaissance cultures was to encourage the kind of systematised classification that appears in the signs of the zodiac

Table 4 The signs of the zodiac and their associations (from Hussey 1967: 22) *

Temperament	Humour	Element	Colour	Condition	Quality	Age	Season	Wind	Sign of Zodiac	Part of body
Sanguine	Blood	Air	Red	Liquid	Hot-moist	Childhood	Spring	South	ARIES TAURUS GEMINI	Head Neck Shoulder
Choleric	Yellow bile	Fire	Yellow	Gaseous	Hot-dry	Youth	Summer	East	CANCER LEO VIRGO	Upper body
Melancholic	Black bile	Earth	Black	Dense	Cold-dry	Maturity	Autumn	North	LIBRA SCORPIO SAGITTARIUS	Lower body
Phlegmatic	Phlegm	Water	White	Solid	Cold-moist	Old age	Winter	West	CAPRICORNUS AQUARIUS PISCES	Thigh Knee Foot

* I am grateful to Diana Burfield for pointing out that there are alternative versions of the above table, especially as regards the grouping of the signs.

(Table 4) or in the interpretative tables of Middle Eastern magic (Goody 1968a:18). The reduction of cultures to writing, whether by actors or by observers, by Cabalists or by anthropologists, tends to order perception in similar ways, providing simplified frameworks for the more subtle systems of oral reference, whose less organised form is probably better indicated by tables that do not attempt to emulate the tightly woven correspondence of Durkheimian tradition.

It is a legitimate conclusion from the post-Durkheimian approach that Tables of Opposites represent indigenous forms of classification in the simpler societies. In fact, they present all types of differentiation and similarity in a single form, which misrepresents the thought processes of those societies, and can easily lead to the problem of what Mounin calls *fausse synonymie* (1970:203). Gay and Cole have emphasised that the Kpelle of Liberia have 'a graded series of terms comparing things and sets of things. These terms can be translated as "equal to", "the same as", "similar to", and "appears to be like". They range from strict equality to vague similarity' (1967:46). Dissimilarity too can be expressed in a number of ways.

The construction of a Table of Opposites reduces oral complexity to graphic simplicity, aggregating different forms of relationship between 'pairs' into an all-embracing unity. The contradictions in this situation are realised and exploited by Aristotle, as Lloyd points out in his excellent analysis of Greek forms of argument. Aristotle discussed the problem of the isolation of elements by the Platonic method of Division and brought out the complexities of the relationship of 'similarity' and 'opposition' ('same', 'like', 'other', 'different', 'contrary', and 'contradictory'), thus clarifying logical procedures. In other words, while these tables neglected to differentiate between the various kinds of opposites that existed in oral discourse, they led Aristotle to formulate these distinctions which in turn laid the basis of the Square of Opposition and hence of the Law of Contradiction and the Law of Excluded Middle (Lloyd 1966:161). In historical terms, the tables can be seen as a useful catalyst to a more productive approach. The reason for the Greek concern with opposites lies not so much in their debt to an earlier oral culture as in their relationship to a contemporary literate one. Indeed, Lloyd rightly notes that 'the extent to which present-day primitive peoples themselves consciously formulate the system that underlies their dualist beliefs is often difficult to determine from the reports of the anthropologists. Neat Tables of Opposites...generally represent the fieldworker's own analysis of a complex series of beliefs and practices, rather than a verbatim report of the notions entertained by a particular member of the society investigated' (1966:63). Certainly, as manifest models of communicative acts these tables leave much to be desired, more particularly when they take a purely binary form. I would go further and ask whether such systems do not 'overlay' rather than 'underlie', noting that in a number of cases the 'field-workers' are in fact commenting on published material about a language, a semantic system, that is unknown to them (as indeed to me).

The suggestion that such schematic treatments of categories of the understanding, and hence of knowledge itself, are encouraged by written communication receives some striking confirmation in the further developments that took place with the invention of movable type in the fifteenth century. During the course of the following century, educational reformers were engaged in suggesting changes in the curriculum of rhetoric, especially the elimination of 'artificial memory' (Yates 1966:228). Foremost among these reformers was Peter Ramus (Pierre de la Ramée, 1515–1572, massacred as a Huguenot), who attempted to replace the earlier techniques of memory with new ones based upon 'dialectical order', a 'method', a 'logic' resting on the analytical study of texts, which as Ong has pointed out owes a great deal to the diffusion of printed texts and the reproduction of charts by means of the newly invented typography (Ong 1971:167). This order was set out in schematic form in which the 'general' or inclusive aspects of the subject came first, descending thence through a series of dichotomised classifications to the 'specials' or individual aspects. Once a subject was set out in its dialectical order it was memorised in this order from the schematic presentation – the famous Ramist epitome (Yates 1969:229). In other words the mechanisation of script by printing, with the ability to produce multiple copies of diagrams quickly and cheaply, led to a further step toward more formalistic schemes, which anthropologists are only too ready to see as features of 'primitive classification' (Table 5).

In his essay on Goldilocks and the Three Bears, Hammel points out that 'Analysis is always the examination of variation, not of uniformity. Thus if binary logic is indeed universal, then there is not much point in examining it, and if it is not, but is only fundamental to the philosophy and analytical techniques of the observer, it cannot be demonstrated to exist in another culture' (1972:7). 'If anything is universal, it is not binary logic so much as the tendency of philosophers (and the rest of us) to engage in this kind of standardisation' (1972:8). What I have suggested here is that this standardisation, especially as epitomised in the Table consisting of k columns and r rows, is essentially the result of applying graphic techniques to oral material. The result is often to freeze a contextual statement into a system of permanent

71

Table 5   What logic is 'really' like (Ramus, ed. Freige) (From Ong 1974)

P. RAMI DIALECTICA.
TABVLA GENERALIS.

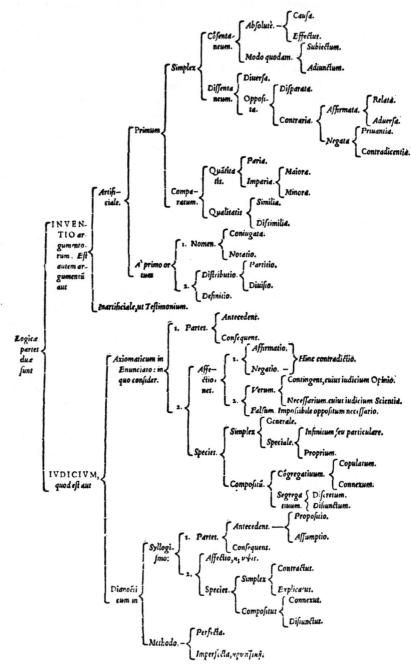

oppositions, an outcome that may simplify reality for the observer but often at the expense of a real understanding of the actor's frame of reference. And to shift frames of reference and regard such tables as models of the camshaft behind the jigsaw is to mistake metaphor for mechanism.

5. *What's in a list?*

s. d.

Item, for De Regimine Principum, which containeth
45 leaves, after 1 penny a leaf, which it is right well worth   3   9
Item, for Rubrishing of all the Book   3   4

63   5

<table>
<thead>
<tr><th></th><th>£</th><th>s.</th><th>d.</th></tr>
</thead>
<tbody>
<tr><td>Sum received .   .   .   .   .   .</td><td></td><td>22</td><td>4</td></tr>
<tr><td>Sum unpaid   .   .   .   .   .   .</td><td></td><td>41</td><td>1</td></tr>
<tr><td>Sum Total .   .   .   .</td><td>3</td><td>3</td><td>5</td></tr>
</tbody>
</table>

[From his bookseller to Sir John Paston, 1469?]

The Inventory of English Books, of John Paston, made the 5th
day of November, in the . . . year of the reign of Edward IV
3. Item, a black Book, with the Legend of Ladies; [La Belle
   Dame] sans Mercy; The Parliament of Birds; The Temple
   of Glass; Palatyse and Scitacus; the Meditations of . .;
   [Sir Gawain and the] Green Knight . . . worth
4. Item, a Book in print of the play of [the Chess].
5. Item, a Book lent Midelton . . .
   Item, a copy of Blazonings of Arms, and the names to be
   found by Letter . . .
   Memorandum; my Book of Knighthood; and the manner of
   making of Knights; of Jousts, of Tournaments; fighting in
   Lists; paces holden by soldiers; Challenges; Statutes of
   War; and de Regimine Principum. . .worth
   Item a Book of new Statutes from Edward the iiii.   1479?
   [From *Selections from the Paston Letters*, Harrap 1949]

The table that anthropologists and others employ to study the 'primitive classifications', the symbolic systems, the modes of thought of oral

74

cultures is, then, a graphic method of analysing concepts and categories, the use of which raises major theoretical issues. It consists
essentially of a matrix of columns and rows, or of what can be regarded
from another angle as one or more vertical lists. In this chapter I want
to move from discussing how social scientists have employed this procedure in quite questionable ways, to an attempt to show how recurrent a feature of early writing systems this kind of behaviour was.
And while I do not see the making of tables, lists and formulae as
originating entirely with the coming of writing, I would maintain that
the shift from utterance to text led to significant developments of a sort
that might be loosely referred to as a change in consciousness and
which in part arose from the great extension of formal operations of a
graphic kind. The very features that hamper the study of oral communication are critical to the understanding of the literate variety,
especially in its early phases.

In an earlier paper, Watt and I examined some of the consequences
of literacy, the implications as I later preferred to call them. Here I
want to go back a further stage in the development of graphic systems,
and discuss the influence of writing itself on cognitive operations,
especially in the forms in which this seems to have occurred at the
earliest period in Mesopotamia and Egypt.

One of the problems in the earlier discussion was that, like Havelock
(1963; 1973), we attached particular importance to the introduction of
the alphabet because of its role in Greece. In doing so, we tended to
underemphasise the achievements of societies that employed earlier
forms of writing and the part these played in social life and in cognitive
processes. While these systems did not equal the alphabet in its ease
of operation, they could nevertheless be used to achieve some of the
same ends. The lack of fluency mattered much less when they were
mainly used for transcribing words rather than speech; indeed, it was
perhaps an advantage in providing a very definite spatial framework
for verbal concepts and thus enabling them to be subjected to the kind
of formal manipulation available even to those graphic systems that
symbolise objects (i.e. pictograms) rather than words (i.e. logograms).
Let us treat this argument in two parts. Firstly, there is no need to
abandon the claim that the alphabet made reading and writing much
easier, and made it available for more people and more purposes (including writing down one's 'thoughts'). But, in their turn, earlier
syllabic and 'consonantal alphabets' were simplifications of Sumerian
logograms, and had similar, though not so far-reaching effects. It is
clear that the greater abstraction and simplification of progressive
changes in the writing system increased the number of literates,

75

potentially and sometimes in practice. Of the consonantal alphabet of the Ugarit texts of the fourteenth and thirteenth centuries B.C.E., Nougayrol writes that they greatly extended the number of 'lettrés' (1962:29). For Ugaritic scribes that had to learn Akkadian, a long apprenticeship was necessary since it meant acquiring a second language as well as the complex cuneiform script; for Akkadian was never written alphabetically, and the vernacular, Ugarit, was never written in syllabic cuneiform.

While alphabetic systems extended the field of literates,[1] it is also the case that earlier writing systems, and indeed yet earlier graphic devices scratched on the walls of caves, on pieces of birch bark or more temporarily in the sand itself, had an influence both on the organisation of social life and on the organisation of cognitive systems.[2] It is the particular influence of these earlier, pre-alphabetic writing systems that I want to explore in this chapter.

Part of the failure to give sufficient attention to these earlier developments arose from the way the problem was formulated. Writing was seen as providing speech with an 'objective correlative', a material counterpart to oral discourse. Indeed it is a general assumption, when considering the difference that writing makes to the use of language, and perhaps directly on cognitive processes (though I see the new technique as providing tools rather than as dictating results), that writing gives a permanent form to speech. Words become enduring objects rather than evanescent aural signals. This transformation means that communications over time and space are altered in significant ways. At the same time, the materialisation of the speech act in writing enables it to be inspected, manipulated and re-ordered in a variety of ways (Goody and Watt 1963).

I don't wish to retract this line of argument, which requires both supplementing and developing. But the general assumption that writing duplicates speech needs modifying in one major respect, for in certain very significant ways it changes the nature of language use. The failure to accord this fact adequate recognition is partly due to a universal acceptance of the linguists' dichotomy between *langue* and *parole*, the latter being located in the oral mode. But what about the written mode? Is this just a recording device? Is the semiotic of writing simply a material reduplication of the semiotic of speaking? Is there not a linguistic triangle rather than a dichotomy, a triangle which is not simply a formal arrangement, but an indication of vectorial forces? It it not likely that as speech is the major determinant of writing, so writing to a lesser degree will influence speech and the associated cognitive processes?

76

What's in a list?

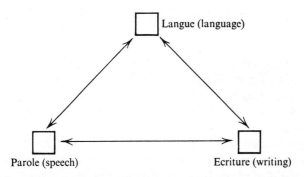

The idea of the distinctiveness of the spoken and written languages has been resisted by many linguists. De Saussure accepts the view that writing simply represents language;[3] the same opinion is asserted by Sapir, Hockett, and yet more vigorously by Bloomfield, who insisted that 'writing is not language, but merely a way of recording language by means of visible marks' (1933:21). Against this general trend, we have the self-styled 'functionalist' approach of some scholars associated with the Prague Linguistic Circle, especially Vachek (1939, 1959, 1973) who writes of 'the co-existence, in one and the same language, of two norms, the spoken and the written' (1973:15; see also Pulgram 1951, 1965).

> The SPOKEN NORM of language is a system of phonically manifestable language elements whose function is to react to a given stimulus (which, as a rule, is an urgent one) in a dynamic way... duly expressing not only the purely communicative but also the emotional aspect of the approach of the reacting language user.
>
> The WRITTEN NORM of language is a system of graphically manifestable language elements whose function is to react to a given stimulus (which, as a rule, is not an urgent one) in a static way...concentrating particularly upon the purely communicative aspect...

Thus written language is seen as 'the marked member of an opposition', intensified by printing with its 'depersonalized character', for writing is used for specialist purposes often serving higher cultural purposes.

A recognition of this distinction has been somewhat impeded by the concentration upon linguistic universals rather than upon developmental or evolutionary factors (see Kay 1971), which leads to a neglect of the process of the gradual increase in the functional capacity of language (Vachek 1973:34). In any case, the research and discussions that have taken place are related mainly to problems of the correspondence of phoneme and grapheme (hence, to interests in 'English as a foreign language', in alphabetic reform, or in shorthand) rather than to an examination of the implications of writing for semantics or for cognition.

We have seen that there are two main functions of writing. One is the storage function, that permits communication over time and space, and provides man with a marking, mnemonic and recording device. Clearly this function could also be carried out by other means of storage such as the tape-recording of messages. However, the use of aural reproduction would not permit the second function of writing, which shifts language from the aural to the visual domain, and makes possible a different kind of inspection, the re-ordering and refining not only of sentences, but of individual words. Morphemes can be removed from the body of the sentence, the flow of oral discourse, and set aside as isolated units capable not simply of being ordered within a sentence, but of being ordered outside this frame, where they appear in a very different and highly 'abstract' context. I would refer to it as a process of decontextualisation, even though the word involves some conceptual difficulties.

I do not wish to imply that these processes cannot take place in oral discourse. For example, we may suddenly stop the flow of speech and repeat something we have just said: 'Thistle', commenting, 'that's a curious word.' So too one may correct a part of speech or rephrase a sentence even after it has been composed or spoken in order to avoid splitting an infinitive or ending with a preposition. But the very statement of these possibilities makes it obvious how writing can facilitate the process of reorganisation, as well as affecting more permanently the sphere of verbal communication. For there are two oral situations: that which prevails in the absence of writing and that which prevails in its presence. These two situations are certainly different, for writing is not simply added to speech as another dimension: it alters the nature of verbal communication. In an extreme case, the written language may exist in the absence of the spoken, preserving it over time when it would otherwise have died as an instrument of current communication, as with learned Latin, 'a language spoken by millions but only those who could write it' (Ong 1971:17). Or in classical Chinese, which Rosemont (1974) and others have argued was far removed from the speech of ordinary men. Indeed it may never have been a 'natural language' at all.

The potential effects of writing can be assessed from an ethnographic analysis of contemporary writing or from a historical study of earlier written materials. It is the second of these approaches I want to undertake here because the problem emerges with particular clarity from the very earliest texts produced by man, on the cuneiform tablets of the Fertile Crescent.

The 'pictographic' kind of writing that first developed in Mesopotamia towards the end of the fourth millennium was mainly used for 'the simplest administrative notations' (Kramer 1956:xix). Later the system lost its pictographic character and became 'a highly conventionalized and purely phonetic system of writing'. Kramer claims that by the second half of the third millennium, it became 'sufficiently plastic and flexible to express without difficulty the most complicated historical and literary compositions'. We may doubt whether any non-cursive system, especially a non-alphabetic one, could become quite so flexible. Nor is it likely that these modifications alone meant that 'only a few literary documents' from the earlier period 'have as yet been excavated, although this same period has yielded tens of thousands of economic and administrative tablets and hundreds of votive inscriptions' (p. xix). For literary documents in any quantity did not appear till the first half of the second millennium, that is, at a time when Sumerian was no longer a spoken language but only a written (or 'dead') one, when it had become purely a graphic system rather than a combination of phonological and graphic codes.

The same point was made for the later Assyrian period by D. J. Wiseman. He begins a review of 'the content of Assyriological studies' with a discussion of a class of literature known as 'the stream of tradition'. The first category of materials he treats are the fifty or so epics or 'mythological' texts, of which several have known Sumerian prototypes dealing with the creation of the earth, of mankind, and of the arts, and recounting the exploits, rivalry and suffering of numerous deities, texts which are fastened upon not only because of their affinities with Sumerian, Hebrew and Homeric literature, but also because of the light they shed on the 'intellectual adventures' of these early civilisations.

But what is the topic of the bulk of the written material? Even in Assyrian times, it is not the main 'stream of tradition', either in the form of literary creations or the recording of myth and folktale, but rather the administrative and economic documents found in temples and palaces throughout Babylonia and covering a wider geographical and chronological extent than the more academic records; three quarters of all the extant cuneiform inscriptions, numbering some 150,000 in all, fall in this class, an enormous quantity compared with the epic material (Wiseman 1962:22). Among them are letters and legal documents, including 'deeds of sale and purchase, rental, loan, adoption, marriage bonds, and wills together with the ledgers, lists, and memoranda of shopkeepers, secretaries, and bankers as well as the census

79

and tax returns which comprise the necessary output of a highly developed bureaucratic system of government' (p. 22).

Particularly in the early phases of written cultures in the first fifteen hundred years of man's documented history, such materials are often presented in a form which is very different from that of ordinary speech, indeed of almost any speech. And the most characteristic form is something that rarely occurs in oral discourse at all (though it sometimes appears in ritual), namely, the list.

THE LIST

'List' is one of those polysemic words in which English abounds. The O.E.D. gives (lists) seven substantive usages, relating to listening and lusting, etc. The third has to do with 'the border, edging, strip, selvage of a cloth'. Closely associated with this meaning is that of a boundary, for example, 'a place within which a combat takes place'; hence 'to enter the lists' means to go into the area marked out for combat. The notion of a boundary, or rather the increased visibility, the greater definition of a boundary, is an important attribute of the kind of list I am considering, that is, number six in the O.E.D., which is probably derived from the third sense of a 'strip' of paper, and is defined as; 'a catalogue or roll consisting of a row or series of names, figures, words, or the like. In early use, *esp.* a catalogue of the names of persons engaged in the same duties or connected with the same object'. I want to distinguish three broad kinds of lists. The most usual is a record of outside events, roles, situations, persons, a typical early use of which would be a king-list. It is a kind of inventory of persons, objects or events.

Distinct from this kind of retrospective list (which can be used to sort data stored long term as well as observed data stored short term) is the shopping list, which serves as a guide for future action, a plan. Items get struck off, mentally or physically, as they are dealt with. One example that is currently found among systems of restricted literacy in West Africa as well as in early writing systems in the Middle East, is the itinerary used, for example, to map out the route an individual has to take on the pilgrimage to Mecca.

In addition to the inventory and the shopping list, we find another series of very important texts in Mesopotamia, that is the lexical lists which have given rise to a particular branch of knowledge known as *Listenwissenschaft*. This very extensive series of Sumerian tablets provides a kind of inventory of concepts, a proto-dictionary or embryonic encyclopaedia.

What's in a list?

My concern here is to show that these written forms were not simply by-products of the interaction between writing and say, the economy, filling some hitherto hidden 'need', but that they represented a significant change not only in the nature of transactions, but also in the 'modes of thought' that accompanied them, at least if we interpret 'modes of thought' in terms of the formal, cognitive and linguistic operations which this new technology of the intellect opened up.

A characteristic of the presentation of information in the form of lists is that it must be processed in a different way not only from normal speech but from other ways of writing, ways that we may consider at once more typical and closer to speech. I do not wish to assert that lists cannot be presented in linear form; that would be clearly untrue. Nor do I wish to assert that listing does not occur in oral cultures (by which I mean deliberately to exclude the very important category of lists that are purposely placed in memory store from written originals and then recited); a certain amount of nominal listing does occur, especially in some ritual situations, as with names in a genealogy, words for food crops or animals, but it occurs less frequently and more flexibly than is often thought. However, the contrast with oral societies and their modes of learning is one that I want to leave for subsequent consideration. Here I would rather stress the positive features of the written list.

The list relies on discontinuity rather than continuity; it depends on physical placement, on location; it can be read in different directions, both sideways and downwards, up and down, as well as left and right; it has a clear-cut beginning and a precise end, that is, a boundary, an edge, like a piece of cloth. Most importantly it encourages the ordering of the items, by number, by initial sound, by category, etc. And the existence of boundaries, external and internal, brings greater visibility to categories, at the same time as making them more abstract.

In all these ways lists differ from the products of oral communication, and are more related to the table discussed in the previous chapter and to the formula discussed in the next. They do not represent speech directly. Or rather they stand opposed to the continuity, the flux, the connectedness of the usual speech forms, that is, conversation, oratory etc., and substitute an arrangement in which concepts, verbal items, are separated not only from the wider context in which speech always, or almost always, takes place, but separated too from one another, as in the inventory of an estate, that runs: cows, 5; donkeys, 14; land, 5 dunams; chairs, 8; tables, 2.

From one standpoint then, lists are very different from speech forms, treating verbal items in a disconnected and abstract way. Yet it is precisely this type that occurs so frequently when speech is (as we say) reduced to writing, either in contemporary Africa, or in the ancient Near East.

It is generally assumed that the first complete system of writing was developed by the Sumerians about 3000 B.C.E. from a forerunner which has been suggested as a possible ancestor of other scripts. Evidence from Uruk shows that the simplest and earliest forms consisted of clay tags or labels with holes and traces of the string by which they were tied to objects. These tags contain nothing more than the impression of a cylinder seal, in other words the property marks of the sender of the objects. Even for these restricted purposes, the limitations were considerable, because a detached tag could not be linked with its object. So the system was elaborated by drawing signs for these objects and by replacing the impressions of the seals with written signs.

These tablets bearing details of names and objects led to the development of ledgers. For example, one tablet lists a series of nouns together with numbers, the latter being added up to give a total of 54 cows (Gelb 1963:64). At this stage, Uruk writing consists of word signs limited to the expression of numerals, objects, and personal names (p. 65). It is a system which, Gelb observes, owes its origin to the needs arising from public economy and administration. With the rise in productivity of the country, resulting from the state-controlled canalisation and irrigation systems, the accumulated agricultural surplus made its way to the depots and granaries of the cities, necessitating the keeping of accounts of goods coming to the towns, as well as of manufactured products leaving for the country (p. 62).

It is not literary works, then, but administrative lists that dominate the uses of writing in ancient Mesopotamia (Oppenheim 1964:230). These lists can take a whole variety of forms, receipts of tribute, itemisation of war booty on the income side, distribution of rations, payments to officials, among the expenditures. A recording of these transactions is specially important in a bureaucratic system of the Mesopotamian kind, whose economic activities were based upon the movement of personnel and goods (staples, materials, or finished products) 'through the channels of bureaucracy under the supervision of personally responsible officials who serve for a definite term of office'. In so-called 'redistributive' economies such as those centred upon palaces and temples, officials recorded incoming taxes, tribute, and the yield of the royal or priestly domain and workshops as well as the distribution of materials and rations to craftsmen and workers, a type of recording which was 'strictly formalized and astutely co-ordinated', and which was very much in evidence wherever writing on clay has led to the preservation of early documents. Whilst state systems approximating to this kind of elaboration did arise in Central America, without the advent of a true writing system (Gelb 1963:57–58) but using a system of recording by means of knotted ropes, the complexities of which are only just being understood, it is clear that the presence of writing both facilitated and promoted the development of such an economy as well as the polity that organised it.

Lexical lists are initially less common than administrative ones, though even as early as 3000 B.C.E. we find some word lists intended for study and practice (Kramer 1956:3). Beside the 'school texts' (such as the VAT 9130 from Fara) we find documents that illustrate the process of regrouping material that turns up again and again in early writing systems; for example, in the first column of one early text, we find the grouping together of a series of signs containing the element KU (see no. 340, Falkenstein 1936:44). By 2500 B.C.E., in ancient Shuruppak, a considerable number of 'text-books' are found. When these lists contain items that are grouped together under different classes, they constitute specialised 'text-books', or rather 'text-lists', and represented the 'first steps in the direction of an Encyclopaedia' (Gardiner 1947:i, 1) as well as of the kind of systematic enquiry into the natural world that has become institutionalised in schools and universities. The emphasis here is not on the process of enquiry, but on the degree of systematisation, of formalisation. From Tell Harmal, outside Baghdad, we have what Kramer describes as a 'botany-zoology textbook', dating from the early part of the second millennium. 'It is inscribed with hundreds of names of trees, reeds, wooden objects, and birds. The names of the birds, more than one hundred of them, are listed in the last three columns from the right' and end with the class sign *mushen*, bird (Kramer 1956:280). In other words, in the written as distinct from the spoken language, a determinative is added placing the items in a specific lexical category. The revolutionary significance of the lists for conceptual processes will be discussed later in the context of the Sumerian lexicon and the Egyptian onomastica. But here I begin by referring to a special kind of list, not of words or things but of signs (that is, sign-lists) which are basic to the communicative channel itself. With alphabetic writing, the list is a simple one of between twenty-five and thirty characters. With logographic systems, like the Chinese or Egyptian, the list is immensely long. Syllabic systems, and most forms of writing which make use of the phonetic principle in one way or another, fall somewhere in between, closer to the alphabetic pole. But the majority of writing systems required a good deal of precise and decontextualised learning before they could be worked, and the signs that needed learning to operate the system were usually set out in sign-lists. Writing of the Mesopotamian material, Oppenheim (1964:245) notes the existence of three early types. One contains syllable-signs grouped according to the vowel sequence u-a-i (e.g. bu-ba-bi); another arranged the signs according to their forms, while the third, the Ea-lists – where the signs were 'written carefully one underneath the other – were eventually provided on the left with their reading in Sumerian (expressed in simple syllabic signs) and, on the right, with their Akkadian names. Thus three column syllabaries came into being in which vertical lines neatly separated the individual columns (pronunciations: sign: sign name)' (1964:245).

Listings of this kind clearly played an important part in early proto-alphabetic systems. Indeed the very fact of listing may itself have contributed to the development of the alphabet, which occurred in the Phoenician–Palestinian area. The earliest cuneiform tablet from this region was found in Byblos dating from a time around 2000 B.C.E. (Ur III) when a prince of this town was viceroy to the king of Ur. This tablet presents a phonetically arranged vocabulary of cuneiform charac-ters 'proving that the Byblians were already trying to master the diffi-cult cuneiform script by use of methods not yet attested in Mesopo-tamia' (Albright 1968:99).

I would like to take this example as indicating the generative possi-bilities of graphic reductionism. In a writing system that represents words by signs, the resulting logograms can be arranged either by similarity of form or by similarity of sound. Arrangement by similarity of form is difficult because of the number of signs involved, and in any case has little potential for further analysis. Arrangement by sound leads to groupings which can suggest a further reduction into a syllabary. The optional number of signs needed will naturally depend upon the phonetic structure of syllables in a particular language (CV requiring fewer than CVC, for example), the simplest system producing, say, 105 signs (e.g. a matrix of 21 consonants or mouth positions and 5 vowels). Again a phonetically ordered listing of a syllabary i.e. one that arranged the signs on the basis of the sound of the initial consonant, could sug-gest the further step in the analysis of sounds that leads to the alphabet itself.

ADMINISTRATIVE LISTS

Writing therefore provides a locational sorting device. Let me take its influence upon the contributions to a LoDagaa funeral, which form an important part of the long-term reciprocities so essential to the continuation of their social life. For an individual who is responsible for a funeral, the information about these contributions, which he will later need to return in similar circumstances, comes to him sporadically during the course of a very busy and complicated burial performance lasting some three days. People arrive from here and there, in the middle of a particular rite, and make offerings that differ from individual to individual, depending upon specific factors such as the state of his granary, his chickens or his pocket, the state of his relationship with the deceased or his relatives, etc. To sort the information on contributions so that it can be retrieved for future action of a reciprocal kind is no easy matter and requires the application of intellectual skills which are only inadequately summarised under the heading of 'memory' or 'recall'.

With writing, the information can be listed in an enduring form as it comes in a chronological order, 1, 2, 3 – possibly with the names and amounts, thus making use of vertical placement in a column. But a nominal list can also be sorted into separate columns (or pages, or books) to distinguish men and women, use being made of horizontal placement and of locational shifts.

An indication of the potentialities of writing, for cultures and for individuals, is given by the kind and quantity of text that is produced when writing is first used. It is obvious that the context of written communication will be affected by the models followed, the materials used (e.g. stone or paper) and the wider social situation (e.g. a centralised state will have different uses for writing than an acephalous tribe, a mercantile economy than a pastoral one). It is also clear that any body of data we make use of represents only a small proportion of the original materials, and that what has survived may be biased in certain directions. With these warnings in mind, we may look at the tablets excavated since 1929 at the Syrian port of Ugarit (the present Ras Shamra), most of which are written in a Semitic language known by the name of the port and date from the first half of the fourteenth century B.C.E. (the Amarna Age). The texts are written in a 27 letter alphabet (beginning AB) with few vowels, an alphabet which it is claimed is typologically but not chronologically earlier than the Phoenician–Hebrew alphabet (Gordon 1965:12); the Phoenician letters may have appeared by the eighteenth century B.C.E. and the alphabetic idea had already occurred in Egypt. Words are often divided and this word divider could also be used for purposes of tabulation, to divide items (on the left) from numbers (on the right); unlike Phoenician–Hebrew, the direction of writing was left to right, though some examples from Palestine have been found with 'mirror writing'. Other devices to assist tabulation occur, such as ruled lines, wedged lines and elongated signs which maintain lateral direction (i.e. the row).

In this case the corpus consists largely of poetic texts and administrative lists; there is little connected prose. Even letters and royal grants are short and formulaic. The poetry is based not so much on metrical regularity as upon the repetition of meaning in parallel form, as much other poetry in the Middle East (Albright 1968). However by far the bulk of the material consists of administrative and other lists, often just of names, goods and numerals.

The categories of text are as follows:

1	Literary texts	33
2	Religious or ritual texts	31
3	Epistles	80
4	Tribute	5
5	Hippic tests	2
6	Administrative, statistical, business documents:	
	I Quotas (conscription, taxation, obligations, rations, supplies, pay, etc.)	127
	II Inventories, miscellaneous lists and receipts	28
	III Guild and occupational lists	52
	IV Household statistics and census records	6
	V Lists of personal and/or geographical names	59
	VI Registration and grants of land	16
	VII Purchases and statements of cost or value	5
	VIII Loans, guarantees and human pledges	7
7	Tags, labels or indications of ownership	18
8	Other	31

Out of 508 documents, some two-thirds consist of lists rather than consecutive prose or poetry. That is to say, the bulk of the materials is not composed of the written equivalent of speech, the text equivalent of the utterance. It is not the result of a literate observer recording oral performance, as when I myself have written down the Bagre myth recited by the LoDagaa of Northern Ghana, or when an individual writes down and possibly reshapes a poem, song or narrative in his own language. What is being written down here are lists of individuals, objects or words in a form that may have no oral equivalent at all.

I mean this statement to be taken in several senses. Some of the lists could be derived directly from observation, e.g. the inventory of an estate (1152), or 'households including daughters-in-law, sons, brothers, and animals' (329); language intervenes only in a silent manner, by way

86

of the inner ear. Others are derived from information (in whatever form, oral or visual) that the writer receives at various times and places. I do not know how this type of information is stored in the long-term memory and then retrieved according to some specified criteria. But the general outline of the kind of sorting that occurs through writing is clear enough, and is illustrated in the list of 'rituals and sacrifices to various gods according to the days of a certain month' (3). The fact that these events have been written down as they occur means that they can now be resorted according to different criteria, such as the name of the god, kind of ritual, or by calendrical position (which is a more abstract statement of the timing of the events themselves). But not only is information given simultaneously greater fixity and greater flexibility (for re-ordering) by being put in a written form, this system of storage also provides man with a short-circuiting device. If I write down a list of the contributions of those who attend a funeral, I do not need to make use of my long-term memory at all, except of course for holding the speech code, the reading procedure and the location of the piece of paper on which I have made the list. Apart from the latter, the skills involved are generalised ones that I maintain in shape for a multitude of purposes. What interests me is not simply where the information is stored, but how it is stored. When the brain retains the information on funeral contributions, the input is highly contextualised. People bring a pot of beer, a basket of grain, a handful of cowrie shells, as they arrive at differing stages of the funeral, when many other activities are going on. Recollecting to whom and for what one is indebted (so that one can thank and later reciprocate) is a complex process. By contrast the written record takes a highly simplified and highly abstract form, which is already categorised; it consists of name and quantity, possibly adding town of residence and often enumerating the contributors, 1, 2, 3, 4. I refer here to an actual procedure that I have seen operating among the LoDagaa of Northern Ghana and have mentioned in a previous publication (1972b).

The lists in the Ugarit tablets do not provide information on funeral contributions, for they are national rather than local records.[4] But they record tribute (2107) and other types of receipt, as well as outgoing payments (2105). Other lists indicate not past income or outgoings, but future ones e.g. quotas and rations, what people should pay and should receive; such prospective lists constitute plans or programmes, rather than simple records, though the two are not to be kept altogether distinct.[5]

In earlier Sumerian records one use of lists for recording transactions was the writing down of items offered in sacrifice, an example of which is provided by tablets from Drehem (Nesbit 1914:26). The same source provides the following list:

      4 fattened kids
     26 fattened goat-heifers
    319 pastured sheep
     64 pastured he-goats
     98 pastured ewes
     66 pastured goats
     33 weaned lambs etc. (p. 51)

Statements concerning contributions to sacrifice or inventories of personal wealth are not confined to literate societies; but their presentation in writing not only provides a record of a transaction (and hence possibly of a debt) or of an estate at a particular time, it also institutes a more formalised way of conceiving that transaction or that property.

When I wrote that these Ugarit lists are simple, abstract, and categorised, I meant that they are simple in form, largely because the information was abstracted from the social situation in which it had been embedded, as well as from the linguistic context. If we turn for a moment from people to things (e.g. an inventory of implements and animals, 172), we find that it is only very rarely in oral situations that we process words (in this case nouns for animals, etc.) separately. Normally they are embedded in sentences. But in these written lists, they are not; they stand alone, with a bare quantity attached (and sometimes an ordinal number) making enumeration, simple arithmetic in the shape of addition, a much easier, almost an inevitable process. Names of individuals are rather different, since they are more likely to appear as separable 'bits of speech' in an oral context, but even so such listings would be rare (though not impossible).

Quality tends to suffer a further reduction to quantity when items with very different material properties are equated as contributions or as taxes and then totalled up by means of a set of common units. In Egypt, writes Woolley, 'All taxes were paid in kind and stored in the royal magazines; it is illuminating to find that all the goods thus brought in, grain, cattle, wine, linen, are invoiced indiscriminately as "labour"; in other words, they are put on precisely the same basis as the *corvée* whereby Pharaoh's serfs, the people of Egypt, were called up to build a pyramid or to clean out a canal' (1963:624). In this way accounting procedures can be used to develop a generalised system of equivalences even in the absence of a generalised medium of exchange.

Another process that is greatly facilitated by lists, partly because of the advantages of eye over ear, is the sorting of information according to a number of parallel criteria. Moreover, once sorted, the items can afterwards be resorted, rearranged. Take the Ugarit text no. 2068. 'Men arranged in two lists; the first list gives the name of each man mentioning whether he has a wife and child; men without wives have their locality indicated, or, in the last entry, the man's trade; the second list enumerates the king's personnel telling whether each man has a wife and child, and in an instance where he has none his trade is stated'. Here we have an example of a complex list, virtually a table, which anticipates the kind of double-entry book-keeping that appears in some of the scores of thousands of accounting tablets found in Babylonia four thousands years ago (Albright 1968:53). Moreover, the lists appear in alternative forms. We have a register of fields according to owners (85) and we have men in relation to land (152); we have rations for personnel (1100) and we have personnel with rations (1059?).

But apart from this kind of pragmatic arrangement, there was also the reorganisation of information, along apparently non-utilitarian lines, almost for play purposes. For example, text 16 is a 'list of words beginning with y–' which Gordon suggests might have been a writing exercise. Another text (2022) gives the names of men beginning with the letter i, which he suggests might represent 'a rudimentary use of alphabetizing in personnel management'. While it would be theoretically possible to arrange a list by initial sound in an oral culture, this particular type of exercise seems an inevitable outcome of the written list.

As well as considering the characteristic aspects of lists, it would be as well to establish their generality. Other early writing systems display similar preoccupations. In Sumer we have the lists of kings (Jakobson 1939). The Egyptian 'Execration Texts' contain long lists of place and tribal names together with the names of chieftains who ruled these towns or tribes, dating from the late twentieth and nineteenth centuries B.C.E. (Albright 1968:48). Even in the Old Testament, in many places a model of consecutive prose, of narrative style, a supreme product of the consonantal alphabet, lists abound, of places, tribes, taboos, etc.

For more modern situations where writing has been introduced, the use of lists among the LoDagaa of Northern Ghana to record contributions to funerals has already been mentioned. Here I am discussing the uses of writing at a village level, since the administration had already shifted to a literate base in colonial times. With the introduction of schools, writing is used for sending letters, and in its magical role it has entered into one form of divination. But the most insistent public use that I observed in the settlement of Birifu was for the recording of funeral contributions and for keeping the records (that is, lists of members and their contributions) of the Young Men's Society. Writing is employed in both of these ways among a number of other, previously non-literate groups, such as the Tallensi and the Ashanti, especially among migrants into towns.

Other societies in Ghana have used Arabic writing for a longer period. Perhaps owing to the emphasis on collecting documents of historical and literary interest, listing plays a comparatively little part in the body of recorded materials, although some documents of this character have emerged from Alfai in Eastern Gonja (Goody and Wilks 1968:245). However, Levtzion has drawn my attention to an earlier example of 'playing' with lists from the same kingdom. The Gonja Chronicle is a year-by-year record of events of the kind I have spoken about earlier, kept during the eighteenth century. On the verso of the final page of one copy (IASAR 10) we find extracted from the annual events a list of kings of Gonja, by name, with their Arabic names attached. In other words here we have the creation of a king-list from a listing of annual events. It was the keeping of such chronicles and the re-ordering of materials by means of the visual inspection of the written word, that permitted wider developments in the growth of human knowledge, more particularly in knowledge of the past, but also in knowledge about the natural world.

EVENT LISTS

I have spoken of some of the micro-effects of the reorganisation of information by means of lists. But there are more wide-ranging effects as well, which relate very closely to the scientific and intellectual achievements of the societies of the Fertile Crescent. I begin with the role of lists in the development of history, which in the present context I take to be the achievement of fuller and more accurate understanding of the past. In an earlier paper (1963), Watt and I related the distinction between *historia* and *mythos* to the emergence of literacy in early Greece. The relatively simple writing system of Ancient Greece, combined with the absence of scribal or ecclesiastical control, was certainly instrumental in the emergence of historical scholarship as we know it, that is, in the works of Herodotus and Thucydides. But at an earlier period, the existence of writing itself, and the appearance of king-lists, annals and chronicles, were essential as preliminary steps, and ones that are widely found to accompany the invention or introduction of a script. The effect that the existence of these lists produces, and their relationship to 'myth', is well illustrated by developments in Sumer. Noting the parallels between the early Sumerian literature of the 'Heroic Age' c. 2400 B.C.E. and the introductory chapters of the

Old Testament (Gen. I–II). Wiseman comments that by the early second millennium one Semitic epic of Atrahasis ('the very devout') 'links together events from the Creation to the Deluge in a single account. To do this it makes use of summary "king-lists" or genealogies (Heb. toledot)...In Egypt one such list of the forebears of a local ruler, Ukhotep, spans some 600 years...in genuine chronological order'. Thus the piecing together of 'epic' material into a 'historical' form is seen as developing out of the ability to produce lists of this kind. 'The Sumerians adapted their writing first for the classification of observed phenomena rather than the expression of abstract thought. Lists were arranged in varying order, including chronological, and were soon used for recording daily events or facts behind a given situation. Thus "king-lists", year formulae and other data necessary to the law became the basis of historical writing.' From records of this kind, plus the descriptions of disputes, 'the step to annals and chronicles was not long delayed'. Such records formed the basis of written reports to the national god and to the nation itself. Moreover these accounts were subject to revision and reorganisation. 'Each successive edition during a long reign might require the rewriting or paraphrasing of part of the history to adapt it to the purpose required'. Individual journals were kept and Babylonian scribes took note of 'the dates of all public events, accessions, deaths, mutinies, famines and plagues, major international events, wars, battles, religious ceremonies, royal decrees and other pertinent facts' (Wiseman 1970:45). Such records were of fundamental importance in enabling writers to draw out histories of particular sequences of events from the more general records, some of which accounts seem to have been used for composing the books of the Old Testament. Herodotus' remark of the Egyptians could be applied to other societies of the region: 'by their practice of keeping records of the past, [they] have made themselves much the best historians of any nation of which I have had experience' (II, 77). Archives are a prerequisite of history. And it was material drawn from these sources that the Hebrews, and possibly the Phoenicians before them (Grant 1970:10), began to put together into a more consecutive, albeit theocentric form, a development that seems likely to be connected with their use of the first alphabetic-type scripts.[6]

The keeping of chronicle type records is either event-dominated or else calendar-dominated. The event-dominated chronicle keeps track of 'important' occurrences whenever they take place: the death of a ruler, a natural disaster, the birth of a child. The alternative method provides a record of events on an annual basis and is therefore likely to be tied to the existence of a calendrical system that involves some kind of differentiation of the years. The first type of system is, in a sense, the written equivalent of the kind of oral recital of past events given by the spokesman (*okyeame*) of Ashanti chiefs, although in this case the ordering tends to be regnal, providing short summaries of the happenings in a certain reign. The second method was adopted by many priestly chroniclers whose recording was tied to a specific annual festival, such as the commencement of the year. This form was used by the Priestly Chroniclers of early Rome. The annalistic method of the Romans employed a year-by-year treatment based upon the annual list of consuls in the Fasti, which differed from the looser, episodic structure employed by the Greek historians (Grant 1973:36). The latter followed oral precedents and took a more narrative form. By means of these methods, the historical material could be extended (in a purely mechanical sense), developed (in terms of structural complexity) and reviewed (in the most literal as well as the most metaphoric sense). It was a combination of these methods that was used by Cato the elder: 'he scoffed at the trivialities of the Priestly Chronicles, and yet adopted their year-by-year chronology, while blending it with a Greek method of arrangement by subjects' (1973:38). Thus Rome provided another example of the utilisation of lists as a basis of chronicles, and of the chronicles in turn as a basis of history proper with its gradual differentiation from other ways of treating the past.

The lists which the Sumerians used as a basis for accounts of the past are described by Wiseman as '*the common basis of all Mesopotamian science and subsequent historiography*' (1970:41 – my italics). Such hyperbole requires some explanation. How are we to see the Mesopotamian achievements as being related to the mere compiling of lists? Throughout the region much of this activity was purely of an administrative kind, the kind we find in Ugarit, in Sumer and again in ancient Israel. The Hebrews, like their neighbours, did not lack census lists, lists of citizens by name, household, occupation or class; landowners, administrative boundaries, military rolls, records of booty, itineraries or geographical memoranda (cf. Num.; Gen. 5: 1–10; Neh. 11–12). But in Mesopotamia, these listings covered a yet wider field, for they included 'astronomical observations, the weather, prices of staple commodities and the height of the river on which the irrigation system and thus the economy depended' (p. 45). The records of human phenomena took the form of annals or chronicles, which were more elaborate (and hence less 'abstract' from one standpoint), even though the narrative element was limited. But the recording of 'natural' phenomena frequently took the form of lists of decontextualised observations that were later to form the bases of astrological and astronomical calculations.

What's in a list?

The questions that emerge from written data of this kind are illustrated in the earliest Babylonian astronomical texts, which include a tablet from the Hilprecht collection in Jena. This tablet begins with a list of numbers and names, which appear to indicate relations of distance between heavenly bodies, and after calculating the total of 120 'miles' poses the question, how much is one god (i.e. star) beyond the other god? And the text continues with a calculation, finishing with the customary formula, 'such is the procedure' and the name of the scribe who copied the text, together with the name of the one who verified it. Apparently arising from the recording of observational data, there is an attempt to translate those observations into precise numerical terms, and to pose the bizarre but eventually meaningful questions that lead to the growth of knowledge.

Other early documents give the names of planets etc. together with numbers in simple arithmetical progressions, and a third class of document presents the earlier records of actual observations. For example, for over a period of several years we have records of the appearances and disappearances of Venus, which were used to inform man (through the initiated) of divine prediction. Omen literature, which developed in the Babylonian period, also records specific features of the livers of sacrificial sheep; for this same purpose it uses representations of the liver in clay, a plastic model of the object upon which marks appear in a grid, a tabular formalisation of the space to be examined. The same omen literature records the appearance of celestial phenomena for similar reasons. Such observations, recorded in a large series of texts, provide examples of divinatory procedures that later took the form of judicial astrology and led to the horoscopic astrology of the Hellenistic age, associated with the invention of the zodiac.

Around 700 B.C.E., under the Assyrian empire, we find systematic observational reports of astronomers to the court, which were probably also associated with omens; Ptolemy notes that eclipse records were available to him from the reign of Nabonassar (747 B.C.E.) onwards. This phase led to the development of a systematic mathematical theory, centred above all on period relations, as well as to the invention of the zodiac (fourth century B.C.E.) which led the growth of knowledge in a different direction.

LEXICAL LISTS

The relation between record keeping and advances in empirical and even scientific knowledge is not difficult to perceive. But there is yet another way in which lists served not only to crystallise the state of knowledge, but to raise problems of classification and to push at the frontiers of a certain kind of understanding. I refer here to the kind of lists that are so well represented in the Sumerian lexicon and the Onomastica of Ancient Egypt, where we find not simply records of observations, past events, or the contents of a household or an estate, but lists of classes of object, such as trees, animals, parts of the body. Unlike previous examples we have discussed, abstract lists of this kind appear to have no immediate 'advantage' for those who compile them. Characteristically they appear to occur in school situations, where formal instruction is taking place. Indeed it is difficult to imagine them constructed in other situations. Some may have developed as a kind of exercise or 'game' (in the context of scribal training). There certainly seems to have been an element of this in the kind of alphabetic game that was being played in the Ugaritic example given above, where lists are made of names beginning with 'i' and of words beginning with 'y'. Such lists are much less activity-oriented than inventories of estates or lists of contributions to sacrifices; they represent an abstraction, a de-contextualisation, a game – and sometimes a conceptual prison. But at the same time they crystallise problems of classification and lead to in-crements of knowledge, to the organisation of experience. For what these lexical lists sometimes appear to explore is what 'structural seman-tics' seeks to do in a more elaborate way, namely, 'to discover certain relationships among the words in the vocabulary of a language' (Lehrer 1969:39, following Lyons 1963, 1968); in particular they are concerned with the organisation of items in a field on the basis of paradigmatic sets and occasionally of syntagmatic presuppositions.

The main source of lexical lists from earlier times is the enormous Sumerian series analysed by Landsberger and others, the study of which has given rise to a special technical term, *Listenwissenschaft*,[7] described as 'this essential part of ancient schooling and scholarship' (MSL IX:124). We find here lists which are basically similar to the great Egyptian Onomastica described by Gardiner but which are at once more comprehensive and less unified.

The nature and implications of these lexical lists were indicated some years ago by Chiera in his collection of texts from the temple school at Nippur. Firstly, there was the increased visibility of some existing principle of classification, or alternatively the introduction of new cri-teria, for 'the names are grouped in these lists according to some definite principle' (1929:I). For example, in Tablet No. 122, col. VII, 'the scribe had already written down all the names of gods preceded by the determinative. In this last column he lists the foreign gods without determinative'. In this way visual, non-oral signs are utilised to distinguish within the category of gods according to specific criteria, namely the origin of the gods concerned. Since over the long term gods were presumably entering and disappearing from the pantheon both from within and without the society, what we find is the use of a specific, and to some extent arbitrary feature (since foreign origin is a relative matter) to bisect the category on a semi-permanent basis. The chosen criterion over-rides all others in a manner that is not limited to a particular context; there is a process of over-determination, of over-generalisation with reference to a particular feature.

Chiera also calls attention to the desire to make these lists, and hence the categories, exhaustive. 'Every group of names, be it of stones, fields, or officials, is complete, perhaps too complete. In some instances the list comes to resemble some of the modern student exercises the chief aim of which is to compose as many sentences as possible with any given noun' (1929:2).

Not only were they exhaustive, they were also copied incessantly. Indeed they were in effect exercise lists, copied from 'an original document' (Chiera 1929:2) and found in all schools side by side with other texts. Later, about 2000 B.C.E. the standard glossary was being translated into Akkadian, as we see from the bilingual texts. In late Assyrian times, the scribes of Ashurbanipal made a round of the old temples in order to copy the lists for the royal library.

The copying of the lists was not a random affair; some were more frequently used than others. Chiera's study of the texts from the temple school at Nippur shows the following lists to have been duplicated:

subject	number
trees	84
stones	12
gods	9
officials	8
cattle	8
reeds	8
personal names	6
animals	5
leather objects	4
fields	3
garments	3
words compounded with *gar*	3
chairs	3
flocks	3
objects (*giš*)	3
birds	3

The following appear once: officers, copper objects, palm trees, trees and reeds, ships, stars and garments, cities, beds, doors, vessels, garments and reeds, phrases compounded with *ama*, boats, beverages, words compounded with *sol*.

The Sumerian lists analysed by Landsberger and others cover a very wide span of time and the nature of the changes over that period are indicative of their role in organising information. The earlier examples are often referred to as, for instance, Proto-Lú, contrasting with the canonical series Lú of a later date when the list had become standardised (MSL XII:87). This process of canonisation also meant a process of clarification, of formalisation. For example, while the canonical series Lú-ša (i.e. a vocabulary listing Sumerian words (as lú) on the left and Akkadian (as ša) on the right), were based upon Proto-Lú, 'the intrusion of the terms inapplicable to human beings, so frequent in the forerunner [i.e. the earlier version]...have been almost completely weeded out, on the other hand the series has been expanded by the inclusion of a large number of synonyms and figurative terms' (p. 87), for example, forty Sumerian words (words of a language now long unspoken) for king and queen. The Lú-ša series contains other lists of human activities including the 'standard Professions list, copies of which have been found in all the major archaeological sites; it occurs with the earliest remains of cuneiform script and continues to be faithfully copied until Old Babylonian times' (MSL XII:4).[8]

The Lú-ša series has a definite thematic unity, consisting of all lexical sources 'which list entries applicable to human beings: kinship terms, titles of a secular or religious nature, professional activities, social classes, states of the human body and mind, etc.' (MSL XII:xi). While there is thematic unity, 'no rigid hierarchy' is to be seen in the sequence, even though the text begins with administrative personnel. Other occupations tend to appear in related groups, e.g. artisans, musicians, temple personnel (MSL XII:16, referring to Early Dynastic list E).

Other lists do impose a hierarchy. The Emesal vocabulary begins, as does the Egyptian Onomasticon of Amenopě, with a list of the deities, and then descends to deal with the kin and servants of the gods[9]:

god
Ea
Damkina
Enlil
Enlil
his wife

Ninurta
Ninurta
his wife
sister of Ninurta
slave inspector of Ninurta

The Emesal vocabulary on Tablet no. II begins:

heavens
grave
man
lord
king
... continuing: 66. slave
                67. slave
                68. woman
... continuing with women until:
                87. female slave
                88. servants
                89. sheep

But while hierarchy and canonisation develop, there is still some room for movement over time, as is illustrated by certain changes from Proto-Lú in the Old Babylonian period. Some items seem to have entered the series 'by an attraction process which can be *thematic. . .;* [or] *graphic,* as when one sign is listed with all its meanings, regardless of whether they are pertinent or not to the main subject of the series. . .; or a combination of these processes that can be called grapho-thematic.'

The recourse to classification by graphic rather than thematic criteria seems to occur more frequently with the residual portions of the lexicon, as in Proto-Izi, rather than the central portions (i.e. Lú-*ša* and ḪAR-ra-*ḫubulla*). In the former this feature became more in evidence as time went on: 'soon, entries which shared the same initial sign were grouped together regardless of their meaning, and in some cases, even the morphology dictated the groupings. . .' (MSL XIII:3). The practice of arranging words according to their initial sign (sometimes an internal sign) utilises the acrographic or acrophonic principle, which becomes more and more prominent in this series until the canonical versions were characterised 'by an almost absolute dominance of the acrographic principle and by an attempt to make these lists *exhaustive*' (MSL XIII:4, my italics).

The process is described by Landsberger in the following words: 'When they attempted to make an inventory of Sumerian words, the native Mesopotamian scribes faced a problem familiar to any lexico-grapher in the first stages of planning a dictionary: should the entries be organized thematically, by subjects, or should they be arranged in a serial order based on graphic or phonological characteristics of the words? One can hardly speak of planning in the compilation of the Mesopotamian lexical lists as a whole, since they were the result of a slow process, which lasted for centuries and answered many different kinds of needs: scribal training, interpretation of traditional texts, com-position of new texts, and, undoubtedly, a certain amount of simple philological curiosity, spurred on by the desire of salvaging the words of an extinct language' (MSL XIII:3).

Thus writing emphasises a further classificatory principle inherent in language but that plays little explicit part in ordinary speech, namely, morphological similarity (including spelling), especial stress being laid upon the initial sign for the purposes of organising lexemes.[10]

One specific use of visual, morphological criteria, as we have seen, occurs when signs in Sumerian or determinatives in Egyptian are used to define a semantic field. Another criterion is 'uniqueness', i.e. the fact that the terms have not appeared elsewhere. The effect of apply-ing these two criteria, which tend to distinguish the semantic fields of speech from the written lists of the lexicographer, and sometimes of the linguist involved in componential analysis or field theory (Lyons 1968:472), is well brought out in the Sumerian list known as Proto-Izi:

'Section 1 (1–14). "Fire", including "flame", "ashes", "embers", "torches", "smoke", but excluding "cooking" and "hot" (also ex-pressed by (the sign) NE. In addition to this semantic limitation, the conditions for admitting a word to the group are: (1) the written word must have the sign NE (not necessarily in initial position), and (2) the word must not be found in previous lists' (MSL XIII:7).

Since these lists were used in school, they were given a specific in-structional form, a regular shape. Landsberger writes of one text (MAH 15850): 'In contrast to other school tablets, which never abandoned the fixed text-book sequence of lessons, it mixes material from the various stages of learning indiscriminately...' (MSL IX:141). These forms became more regular as we move from the Old Babylonian period onward, as we move from the 'forerunners' to the 'canonical' versions, the general character of which is again indicated by the comment Landsberger makes upon a negative case: 'we are still far from its systematization and its characteristic artificial (scholastic) distinctions' (MSL IX:147).

I have mentioned that proverbs were given more elaborate literary shapes by the scribes. So too the system of instruction, like most systems of written instruction, produced an 'inflation. . .of the vocabulary' (MSL IX:142). Landsberger speaks of a 'grotesque number of equations'.

The extent of this listing activity is associated by Landsberger with the nature of the Sumerian language; because of its transparent and unambiguous structure, it was suited to classifying the world. I would rather argue that it was the lists that helped to make Sumerian unambiguous, or rather less ambiguous, that the influence of writing on the use of language was more important than that of language on the use of writing.

THE EGYPTIAN ONOMASTICA

The dates of the Egyptian Onomastica are relatively late compared with the Mesopotamian lists, that is, from 1100 B.C.E.; they were used for teaching (*sebayet*) and were probably an adaptation of Assyrian lexicography, according to Wilson (Kraeling and Adams 1960:104). The kind of control these lists were thought to give to the scribes was associated with the internalisation in memory store of the items in their proper categories: 'they thought that just memorizing the writings of these things in categories had something to do with knowing and classifying phenomena'.

These particular educational forms, relying on the memorising of lexical lists, spread far outside the boundaries of Mesopotamia and were instrumental in expanding the influence of that culture into surrounding areas, to Iran, Armenia, Asia Minor, Syria, Palestine, and even Egypt in the New Kingdom; from all these countries we have 'a considerable body of school texts, especially lexical tablets and exercise texts' (Albright in Kraeling and Adams 1960:105). In Syria, for example, where the oldest known schools date from the eighteenth century B.C.E., 'native scribes taught Akkadian for century after century'. Gradually this foreign tongue was replaced by the vernacular, a form of Canaanite, but it required the introduction of a consonantal alphabet to break its hold over education. The parallel with Latin in the Middle Ages is a close one; its dominance was broken only with a further change in the mode of communication, namely, the introduction of print.

While they may have derived from Sumerian models, the Egyptian Onomastica related more directly to the world. Though sometimes referred to as glossaries, they are not alphabetically classified series of words, but 'catalogues of things arranged under their kinds' (Gardiner 1947:i, 5). Upon ostraca and elsewhere we have isolated words 'doubtless written for the sake of practice, and there is a whole class of

99

The domestication of the savage mind

Theban ostraca...that brought the stereotyped formulae of Middle Kingdom letters to the knowledge of youthful scribes' (Gardiner 1947:i, 3). Then there are the Late-Egyptian Miscellanies, often supposed to be wholly didactic in purpose, in which are incorporated 'long lists of natural products, vegetables, fishes, minerals and the like'; these were not merely spelling exercises, but designed 'to give instruction in the nature and sources of the things brought to the king by way of tribute' (p. 4). In other words, we have here another example of the way that lists of tribute, administrative lists, can be reanalysed and reformulated with the help of writing, in order to make lists of entities, classes of object in the natural world.

The Onomastica do not seem to have been manuals for teaching spelling, but rather developments of these lists in an academic, scholastic direction. They consist of 'a series of words or short combinations of words, each describing some entity or class of entities in the physical world' (Gardiner 1947:i, 35). So we are dealing here, as with the earliest Greek word-lists, with 'lists of entities rather than lists of words', with Onomastica rather than Lexica.

The two main Egyptian Onomastica are the Ramesseum, dating from the Middle Kingdom (Dynasty XIII–XIV), and the Amenopě, from the XX Dynasty. The former is a series of word-lists, with a separate line for every word and the determinatives (which appear to have been added afterwards) are 'divided by an interval from the preceding phonetic spelling, so that the species of things referred to can be rapidly and easily recognised by the reader, or rather would have been so recognised had the determinatives been less ambiguous than they usually are' (Gardiner 1947:i, 7). In two sections, short vertical lines give the classificatory headings, and every tenth line is numbered, the scribe providing a total of lines in the papyrus. The formality of the arrangement is further emphasised by the fact that the text was enclosed between parallel lines ruled lengthwise near top and bottom. The beginning is undecipherable, but appears to have included plant names and liquids. Nos. 122–33 deal with birds and these are followed (Nos. 134–52) by fishes. After fishes we have more birds and then quadrupeds. We shift to a list of southern fortresses, then twenty-nine towns, followed by loaves and cakes. From the bakery we pass to cereals and after a few obscure entries, forty-one parts of an ox, then condiments and fruit, ending with a series of twenty cattle names, such as 'A dirty red bull with white on its face'.

The Onomasticon of Amenopě is later and more elaborate. The scribe entitles his manuscript, in its most complete form (the Golénischeff version), 'Beginning of the teaching for clearing the mind, for instruc-

100

tion of the ignorant and for learning all things that exist: what Ptaḥ created, what Thoth copied down, heaven with its affairs, earth and what is in it, what the mountains belch forth, what is watered by the flood, all things upon which Rē῾ has shone, all that is grown on the back of the earth, excogitated by the scribe of the sacred books in the House of Life, Amenopĕ, son of Amenopĕ. HE SAID:'

There follows some 600 entries, though this was only part of the original (possibly 2000). In presenting this list, the author was not simply enumerating but also classifying, with rubrics often marking the beginning of a fresh category, though the cohesion of the categories is sometimes questionable. The whole composition is divided by Gardiner into the following sections:

 I Introductory heading.
 II Sky, water, earth (Nos. 1–62).
 III Persons, court, offices, occupations (Nos. 63–229).
 IV Classes, tribes, and types of human being (Nos. 230–312).
 V The towns of Egypt (Nos. 313–419).
 VI Buildings, their parts, and types of land (Nos. 420–73).
 VII Agricultural land, cereals and their products (Nos. 474–555).
 VIII Beverages (Nos. 556–78).
 IX Parts of an ox and kinds of meat (Nos. 579–610).

The degree of order in the Onomasticon of Amenopĕ can be exaggerated, but when Maspero edited this work, he gave it the title of *Un manuel de hiérarchie égyptienne,* thus recognising the fact that the scribe deliberately, intentionally, starts 'from the top with deities, demigods, and the king, and follows mankind through his various ranks and callings down to the humblest of free occupations, that of the herdsman' (Gardiner 1947:i, 38). Thus the author aimed at some sort of 'rational classification', an arrangement from the highest to lowest (II, III), and from general to particular (III, IV, V, IX)', while the list of Upper Egyptian towns follows an order from north to south. At a more detailed level, the Onomasticon exhibits sequences of words that have more or less close analogies elsewhere, e.g. in the administrative classification of land, the traditional order of the four inner organs identified with the four sons of Horus, the seven kinds of emmer and the six kinds of wine. We get not only traditional groupings of this kind, but also paired (binary) contrasts, for instance 'contrasted concepts like "darkness" and "light" (Nos. 13–14), "shade" and "sunlight" (Nos. 15–16), or persons paired in reference to sex like "male and female musician" (Nos. 214–15), though in Nos. 295–8 "woman" has had to be separated from "man" on account of the priority given to age-distinction in "man", "stripling", "old man"'. And Gardiner concludes in a sagacious manner that others would do well to heed: 'The state of affairs above outlined shows that no principle of contrast or kinship can be systematically employed as a means of eliciting the meanings; on the other hand, appeal to one or other of these principles may occasionally be useful as corroborative evidence of significations elicited on other grounds' (1947:i, 39) .

We can see here the dialectical effect of writing upon classification. On the one hand it sharpens the outlines of the categories; one has to make a decision as to whether rain or dew is of the heavens or of the earth; furthermore it encourages the hierarchisation of the classificatory system. At the same time, it leads to questions about the nature of the classes through the very fact of placing them together. How is the binary split into male and female related to the tripartite division between man, stripling and old man? In Gardiner's words 'Enough has been said to show that the relations between consecutive entries are by no means always on a dead level of equality, and that consequently we must always be on the look-out for some significant nexus of thought between neighbouring items' (1947:i, 39), though such a nexus may be completely absent in any particular case. In other words the same process is apparent here as that we found in looking at tables and at the Aristotelian discussion of opposites; the construction of simple tables, such as four square diagrams, two columns and two rows, can raise questions about the nature of opposites, contrasts, analogies and contradictions, that first bring out the greater complexities of speech acts, and then produce a schema that goes beyond 'common sense' and establishes a formal 'logic'. The fact that 'no principle of contrast or kinship' to use Gardiner's words, of 'polarity or analogy' to use the terms employed by Lloyd (1966) in his discussion of early Greece, is adequate, leads by a dialectical process to the formulation of more complex systems. The simplicities of so-called 'primitive classification' are, in part at least, the simplicities produced by the reduction of speech to lists and tables, devices that typically belong to early literacy rather than yet earlier orality .

As Glanville remarked, Amenopě had in mind a sort of catalogue of the universe, professing to enumerate the most important things in heaven, on earth, and in the waters, not for teaching children how to write but for instructing mankind about his world. 'Early thought', writes Gardiner (on what evidence it is difficult to see), 'was little interested in words. On the other hand it was intensely interested in things, and the classification and hierarchical arrangement of these may well have seemed a worthy ambition' (1947:i, 1). The first statement would be difficult to support; the Ancient Egyptians perhaps gave few indications of explicit grammatical or philological interest, as the author claims. However, one would not expect such an interest to flourish until writing appeared, when it would clearly be promoted by the adoption of an alphabetic script; and words can more easily be seen to be separate from things when they are seen to exist on their own, in written form. However, making explicit the hierarchies of classification implicit in linguistic usage and in man's perception of the world, and developing those systems into more elaborate, and sometimes more precise and 'accurate' classifications, is certainly an important activity in early literate societies, and one which could lead both to the type of scholastic preoccupation with the classification of food, prohibited and allowed, exemplified in Leviticus 11, as well as to the classifications that laid the basis for the development of zoology and botany (e.g. Kramer 1956:280). Not that either of these types of activity was absent from simpler societies, any more than were numerical systems. It is rather a question of the developments in these activities that writing encourages and permits.

As a simple example of the way in which organised arrangement in lists appears in 'scientific' texts and almost of itself enables the knowledge of the subject to advance, let us take the great Egyptian text, known as the Edwin Smith Surgical Papyrus, dating from the seventeenth century B.C.E., but possibly written down as early as 3000–2500 B.C.E. It consists of 377 lines in seventeen columns providing information on forty-eight cases. But these cases are subject to a very systematic arrangement. 'The discussion begins with the head and skull, proceeding downward by way of the nose, face and ears, to the neck, clavicle, humerus, thorax, shoulders and spinal column...' (Breasted 1930:33). Within each group of problems there was a specific principle of arrangement.

WRITING AND LISTING

The arrangement of words (or 'things') in a list is itself a mode of classifying, of defining a 'semantic field', since it includes some items and excludes others. Moreover it places those items in a hierarchy with the 'highest' items at the top of the column and the 'lowest' at the bottom. Logograms for numbers may then get attached to the ordered list, so that the items are numbered 1 to n, beginning at the head, ending at the tail.

But classification and hierarchisation can take more radical forms in writing, which may parallel, extend or even contradict the elementary

103

semantic classification of, say, animals or fruit. We have already seen
that the Onomasticon of Amenopě is rubricised. For example, on
the first page the word for 'dew' (No. 18) is picked out with a rubric;
it closes the series of celestial phenomena and ushers in a number of
terrestrial ones. Indeed it is an obvious 'mediator' between these two
classes.

Another way in which the class may be picked out in hieroglyphic
writing is indicated by the second of these groupings, which continues
until the rubricised word *dbw* commences a series of types of land. For
the category headed by 'dew' has a common determinative which
shows that all the items have some connection with water moisture. The
use of determinatives in this way is a form of classification which is
imposed by writing upon speech; it is a visual sign that characterises
the common features of series of objects or actions.

Just as words may be picked out in special colours or given distinctive written forms, so too the beginning and end of clusters can be indicated by spatial separation, by insetting, by diacritical marks and in
numerous other ways. And as the items within a list are set in an
implicit hierarchy by the order of listing (an order that may be indicated
by numbers), so too the first level clusters may be grouped in a similar
way, either by further levels of clustering (as in the kind of tree
diagram that forms the stock in trade of many scientists) or in a simple
linear hierarchy, which gives some overall order to the clusters and
their constituent items.

The systems of classification that are involved in these lists differ,
then, in certain respects from those that are 'implicit' in oral discourse.
Writing develops the process that Bruner regards as being specific to
human language, what he calls symbolic representation in contrast to
the representation by perceptual similarity that occurs with ikonic
representation (images). For language 'breaks up the natural unity of
the perceptual world – or at least imposes another structure on it',
since phonemes, morphemes and 'parts of speech' are all organised
discontinuously (1966:40–41). Writing draws out, crystallises and
extends this discontinuity by insisting upon a visual, spatial location
which then becomes subject to possible rearrangement. The explicit
formulation of category systems or semantic fields e.g. kinship termin-
ologies, zoological species and literary genres, is a function of the
reduction of classificatory terms to writing, and not simply writing in
a linear fashion but writing that takes words out of their speech context and places them, so abstracted, in a unilateral relationship with
words (concepts/morphemes, lexical units, possibly phrases) deemed
to be of a similar 'class', i.e. possessing certain common features which

may relate to the concrete world outside (i.e. animals, trees) or to some other ordering concern.

I do not wish to argue that the system itself is created by writing; classification is an obvious condition of language and of knowing. But it is clear that the oral situations, the conditions of utterance, in which individuals in most societies would formulate an exhaustive classification of terms for, say, trees or kin, are few, and certainly extra-ordinary. This is not to say that such wider systems of classing linguistic items do not exist at another level ('deeper', 'unconscious') and that these classes may not even take concrete linguistic forms in some cases (e.g. specific noun classes, modes of plural formation etc.). But they are rendered explicit by writing, and possibly only by writing.

The list is transformed by writing and in turn transforms the series and the class. I mean by 'transforming the series' simply that the perception of pattern is primarily (though not exclusively) a visual phenomenon. In certain areas, e.g. in respect of numbers, it would be extremely difficult to formulate a series (a patterned list) without first turning aural statements into visual ones, just because in the scanning of informational input the eye operates quite differently from the ear.

In saying that the list transforms (or at least embodies) the class, I mean that it establishes the necessity of a boundary, the necessity of a beginning and an end. In oral usage, there are few if any occasions when one is required to list vegetables or trees or fruit. One can visualise 'natural' situations in which one might list the clans, villages or tribes belonging to a wider collectivity: in these uses the idea of an exhaustive and exclusive list with binary choices (are they members of this class or not?) may be present. But the question, is a tomato a fruit or a vegetable? is the kind that would seem pointless in an oral context (and indeed trivial to most of us) but which may be essential to the advance of systematic knowledge about the classification and evolution of natural species. And it is the kind of question generated by written lists.

The process at work here could be called one of over-generalisation, and one can see quite clearly how it operates. In an oral discourse it is perfectly possible to treat 'dew' as a thing of the earth in one context and a thing of the sky in another. But when faced with its assignment to a specific sub-grouping in a list, or a particular column in a table, one has to make a binary choice; it has to be placed either up or down in rows, in the left column or in the right. The very fact that it is placed in a list which is abstracted from the context of ordinary speech gives the result of this choice a generality which it would not otherwise have had; the possibility of choice is now radically reduced because the item is placed in a prestigious list which may be 'authorised' by political and religious forces. Moreover, the list is then utilised as a teaching device as well as an instrument of learning, so that every schoolchild (though they were not all that numerous) learns where he should place 'dew' in relation to heaven and earth. Through a series of forced choices, binary choices, literacy established the victory of the overgeneralised schema. Of course this is not all loss or gain. On the latter side, questions are raised, and perhaps answered and preserved, in a way that one would not expect in oral discourse.

The emphasis I have given to the explicitness achieved by writing as a condition of the growth of knowledge may appear trivial, but is central to the theory I am advancing. Indeed what I have to say about categories and cognition is paralleled by work in the lexical field, especially by Hale among the Walbiri. Here he points out that while the Walbiri have a very simple colour terminology, they are able to perceive many more colour categories; and while they have a very simple numerical system, they can in fact count and can easily master the English system. Reviewing this work, Kay comments that it suggests a very general hypothesis about language evolution, namely that 'the progress of linguistic evolution may be traced in terms of lexical and syntactic devices that permit or require the *explicit expression* of certain universal semantic categories and relations that are present *implicitly* (at least) in all languages and all cultures' (1971:11–12, my italics). I would myself regard the reference to universals as unnecessary; but the process he describes seems to fit the one I connect with the introduction and development of graphic systems.

Something of this same process of the transformation of class, the transformation of structure (at least in the Piagettian sense of a bounded system capable of being isolated for analytical purposes), may lie behind certain problems that hedge the study of kinship terms. It seems hardly necessary to point out that without graphemes, you have no diagrams of the kind (see opposite page).

Yet is it not such diagrams that in fact tend to define the field of kinship as distinct from the field in which kinship terms are applied, i.e. to raise problems of primary and secondary fields, of core and extended meanings, of 'real' and 'metaphorical' usages? Is there likely to be any such perceptual boundary in native usage?

I do not wish to maintain that all usages of, say, the English term 'brother' form a Gestalt incapable of further subdivision. I mean only that the decision to include or exclude from a field or a class often has to be carried out in a binary manner when graphic representations are constructed (though the Venn diagram offers a partial alternative), and that this process, while possibly raising important problems for the growth of knowledge, may be quite divorced from the situation of the (oral) actor, whose field of perception is less differentiated, more homogeneous, than the one forced upon the (literate) reader.

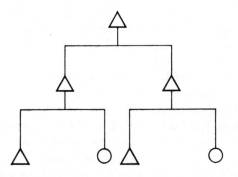

This situation has both advantages and disadvantages. Indeed, the sharper definition of classes is an earlier example of the increasing precision obtained by shifting from a loose verbal model to a precise formal one, of the kind involved in mathematical formulation or computer simulation. 'In verbal modes it is easy to overlook complications that result from the implications of statements that appear clear and unambiguous. Mathematical models allow no such leeway; the ambiguities must be resolved if the model is to work. This formalisation can be both bad and good' for precision is not helpful if the underlying assumptions are wrong or arbitrary, that is, chosen simply to keep the model going (Norman 1969:157).

The problem is not simply one of boundaries but one of ordering too. This limitation is brought out in Gardiner's own table that attempts to collate various lists of the towns of Upper Egypt. He insists that the use of this table demands intelligence, for in some respects it may be misleading, possible putting one town to the south of another where the real position is the reverse; 'if so', he writes, 'the wrong order in the table will have been due merely to the graphical necessity of showing one of the two places in front of the other' (1947:i, 41).[11] The table in question draws lists not only from the Onomastica, but from sources such as the taxation scenes from Theban tombs, one of which (No. 100) records the dues paid to the Vizier by local officials of various towns lying to the south and north of the Southern capital. 'To some extent the disposition of the scenes upon the walls imitates the actual geographical conditions, the southern entrance wall depicting the tribute-bearers from the South and the northern entrance-wall those from the

North (Gardiner 1947:i, 46). Moreover the towns on the south wall succeed one another in their true topographical position, providing an elementary kind of map.

Let me recapitulate the argument so far. Lists are seen to be characteristic of the early uses of writing, being promoted partly by the demands of complex economic and state organisation, partly by the nature of scribal training, and partly by a 'play' element, which attempts to explore the potentialities of this new medium. They represent an activity which is difficult in oral cultures and one which encourages the activities of historians and the observational sciences, as well as on a more general level, favouring the exploration and definition of classificatory schemas.

Little comment has been offered on the appearance of such lists, perhaps because their composition is viewed as a 'natural' activity, one that occurs in oral as frequently as in literate cultures. I have no representative sample of the linguistic acts of even one oral culture, but in my personal experience the occasions that would give rise to verbal lists are few and far between. The most obvious case is in the recital of genealogies, of ancestral names before a sacrifice. But genealogies are usually tied to existing social relationships, and in any case the pyramidal shape one finds in the diagrams of anthropological monographs have often been abstracted from a series of elicitations and enquiries built up from numerous people and over many occasions. The same is even more true of lists of animals or trees. Since these lists are not tied to social groups on the ground such as the division of a kingdom (though individual species may be linked to social groups, as in 'totemic systems'), the series are rarely if ever grouped together to form a genus or a 'kingdom' of their own. And even if they are so clustered, they would not represent a finite, exhaustive group of the kind we find in a written list because the items would have no definite spatial location, hence no precise beginning (middle) and end. And even if such a list is established orally, it has no permanent location (unless perhaps in the course of a narrative or fixed in some other standardised oral form). Hence it is unlikely to serve as a point of departure for an elaboration of the system, nor yet as an explicit model for other types of categorisation and classification.

LISTING AND COGNITION

Finally I want to suggest that the presence of writing, leading amongst other things to these developments in the activity of list making, alters not only the world out there but the psyche in here; at least a recognition of its role should modify our understanding of the processes involved.

I draw attention to the role of lists partly in order to explain the difficulties that members of other societies have in carrying out the kinds of activities devised by psychologists for testing 'cognitive growth'. Many of these experiments involve lists and listings of one kind and another. Remarking upon their importance for psychological discussions, Rohwer notes that, 'Since the turn of the century, tasks that require the learning of information from lists of individual items have been a mainstay of research on human learning and memory' (1975). An examination of a text book on memory (Norman 1969) or of readings on recent research (Postman and Keppel 1969) reveals the domination of tests based upon lists of decontextualised words, or pairs of words. The absence of extended comment upon the lists that occur in psychological tests and early writing systems would suggest that the psychologists and Orientalists concerned regarded this activity as 'natural'. On the contrary it seems to me an example of the kind of decontextualisation that writing promotes, and one that gives the mind a special kind of lever on 'reality'. I mean by this that it is not simply a matter of an added 'skill', as is assumed to be the case with mnemonics, but of a change in 'capacity'. I do not much like this particular dichotomy, which can be manipulated in various directions. My intended meaning seems similar to George Miller's when he writes, 'the kind of linguistic recoding that people do seems. . .to be the very life-blood of the thought processes' (1956:95). Writing, list making, involve linguistic recoding.

Let me take a particular example from a well known study on cognitive growth. In the first chapter of *Studies in Cognitive Growth*, Bruner writes that a second major theme of the book centres around 'the impact of culture in the nurturing and shaping of growth' (1966:1). 'We take the view', he continues, 'that cognitive growth in all its manifestations occurs as much from the outside in as from the inside out. Much of its consists in a human being's becoming linked with culturally transmitted "amplifiers" of motoric, sensory, and reflective capacities' (pp. 1–2). My concern is largely with the last of these and the role that writing has to play. I would argue that the graphic representation of speech (or of non-verbal behaviour, though this is of more limited significance) is a tool, an amplifier, a facilitating device, of extreme importance. It encourages reflection upon and the organisation of information, quite apart from its mnemotechnic functions. It not only permits the reclassification of information by those who can write, and legitimises such reformulations for those who can read, but it also changes the nature of the representations of the world (cognitive processes) for those who cannot do so, whether they are the non-reading element of societies with writing (a very large category over the five thousand years of written experience) or the population (usually children) that have not reached the point in time when they can read, either because they do not yet have the ability or because they do not yet have the opportunity.

Writing of the way inferences are drawn about people's 'representations' from the manner in which a person 'segments events, groups them, or organises, condenses, and transforms them' (p. 7), Bruner refers to the experiment where individuals are asked to name the fifty states of the Union. 'If he now "reads out" in this order, "Maine, New Hampshire, Vermont...", we can guess that the supporting representation for this recital is spatial. If the order is "Alabama, Alaska, Arizona ...", the support is inferred to be more list-like, ordered by an alphabetic rule'.

Bruner's use of the word 'list-like' is significant. So too is the presence of an 'alphabetic rule'. For clearly this method of organising information can only follow the invention and adoption of an alphabetic script. Not that the individual who responds in this way is necessarily literate; he might possibly have learnt the ordering orally, for it suffices that someone else at some stage has arranged the items in this way and then transmitted the results of the reorganisation by repetitive, that is, by rote learning.

Another form of reorganising, often adopted in lists (and particularly in shopping lists or itineraries, which are plans for sequential action) is the numbered list. The allocation of ordinals to names, words or transactions is characteristic of listings. But the value of alphabetic listings is that each word is automatically assigned a specific but logically arbitrary place in the system, a space that only that item can fill. It is thus of immense value in retrieval systems dealing with masses of disordered information, such as subscriptions for the telephone or students in a class. For the same reason it is useful for internal retrieval, where we often make use of mnemonics derived from the initial letters of words, a constituent it is virtually impossible to isolate orally.

The existence of the alphabet therefore changes the type of data an individual is dealing with, and it changes the repertoire of programmes he has available for treating this data. Whether or not it changes the hardware, the organisation of the central nervous system, and if so over what time span, is another matter, but on the analogy of language the possibility is there. In any case while avoiding dichotomous treatments of phylogenetic (and for that matter ontogenetic) development.

What's in a list?

and stressing the broad continuities of ability to respond to external inputs, I would argue that changes (differences) of the kind I have mentioned could be described as differences in modes of thought, or reflective capacities, or even cognitive growth (that is, if we want to assign meaning to phrases of this generality).

I would also suggest, and this point is developed in another context (Goody 1977), that writing not only affects the type of recall but the ability to recall; the alphabet makes possible a powerful form of classification in crystallising the possibilities of auditory ordering. So too the list, which increases the visibility and definiteness of classes, makes it easier for the individual to engage in chunking, and more particularly in the hierarchical ordering of information which is critical to much recall. If this is the case, we stand in danger of misunderstanding the import and the results of the tests we apply across the range of human cultures. Not that they are any less relevant for literate societies, many of whose activities depend upon such operations. But they may be quite irrelevant for members of oral cultures, who are less adapted to this form of activity and who participate neither in its gains nor in its costs.

6. *Following a formula*

1. Let them repeat four or fix verfes, (which you judge moft worthy to be committed to memory) by heart.

2. Let them conftrue the whole leffon *verbatim*, minding the proprietie of the words, and the elegancie of every phrafe.

3. Let them parfe every word Grammatically, as they have ufed to do in other Authours.

4. Let them give you the Tropes and Figures, the Derivations and Differences of fome words, and relate fuch Hiftories as the proper names will hint at, which they may perufe before hand in their Dictionarie. And let them not forget to fcan and prove every verfe, and to note more difficult quantities of fome fyllables.

    C.H. *The Masters Method or the Exercising of Scholars*, London, 1659

We have seen the limitations of the table for analysing the conceptual systems of oral societies, which arise from the fact that it is itself a product of the written culture it has helped to shape. The table is a fixed matrix consisting of vertical columns (or lists) and horizontal rows. These lateral placements are often taken as indicating either identity (analogy or equation) or else opposition (or polarity), though these possibilities only represent the extreme relationships of juxtaposed items. Once again, the formalisation of writing flouts the flexibility of speech, and it does so in a manner that is both distorting and generative.

    In this chapter I consider the special case of identity relations known as the 'formula' since this term has so often been applied to certain characteristics of standardised oral forms (such as the epic and the ballad).

    In everyday speech we are in no doubt about formulae. They are fixed statements of relationships in abstract form; indeed, they are largely unspoken, mainly unspeakable, graphic forms that bear a minimal resemblance to the speech of ordinary men, even bookish, literary men.

    Why then should the term have been used so widely in discussing oral forms, particularly standardised ones such as songs, epics and the like? Why has it been used for Yugoslav epic, for the works of Homer (Lord 1960), for the popular recitations of Ruanda (Smith 1975:25)?

Following a formula

Why has the term been used in an even wider way to describe non-literate cultures, as in the statement by a leading critic: 'Lengthy verbal performances in oral cultures are never analytic but formulaic. Until writing, most of the kind of thoughts we are used to thinking today simply could not be thought' (Ong 1971:2)?

The first question I want to answer has to do with the literary aspect of the formula, and the relationship between standardised oral forms and standardised written ones. But the problem is more widely related to the concerns called up by more evocative words and phrases such as the nature of myth, the sociology of knowledge and the characteristics of the 'savage mind'. And in trying to point up the differences and similarities between oral and literate modes, I shall use that repository of knowledge, that product of the 'savage mind' which I have collected and studied over a number of years among the LoDagaa of Northern Ghana and that I call *The Myth of the Bagre* (1972a). From the literary usage of formula, I will go on to discuss more widespread meanings listed by the dictionary, firstly in the scientific context and then the larger problem of 'formulation', and 'formalisation' and 'formalism', words with which, like 'form', it is etymologically connected.

The notion of formula in the writings of literary scholars was developed by Milman Parry in his well-known work on the Yugoslav epic and its structural affinities with Homer. The reason for treating this usage before the more common ones is because it was introduced specifically in an attempt to pin-point differences between oral and written forms of verse and prose, but specifically of metrical composition, a subdivision of what we have called standardised oral forms, whose standardisation takes the form of rhythmic utterances, often to the accompaniment of music.

I should add, in parentheses, that what I have called 'standardised oral forms' are clearly related to what Maurice Bloch writes of as 'formalised speech acts' (1975:13). The criterion of formalisation that he specifies in a contrast (though of a polar rather than a dichotomous nature) would certainly be relevant for considering the characteristics of standardised oral forms. But I envisage standardisation as operating over a wider range of utterance and as extending specifically to 'art' forms. Hence I cannot take the view that 'formalised language...is an impoverished language' (p. 13); on the contrary, it may be highly concentrated, full of ambiguity and resonance, poetry in fact. The difference of opinion stems, I think, from Bloch's concern with oratory; hence 'formalised language' is qualified as 'the language of traditional authority' and status is paramount; whereas my main interest is with the standardisation of 'art' forms which appear in societies both with and without hierarchy or centralisation. While certain types of utterance e.g. oratory and verse, are standardised or formalised as compared with ordinary conversation, I argue that writing permits a further stage of formalisation, the extreme version of which appears in the list and the table.

In his work on Balkan epic, Parry introduced the term 'formula' in order to get away from the restrictive connotations of words and phrases like 'repetitions', 'stock' or 'static epithets', 'epic clichés' and 'stereotyped phrases' that had been applied to Homer, to ballads and to other oral forms. Literary scholars had used these terms to refer to phrases like 'the blude-red wine' as well as to recurrent metaphors such as the comparison of the loved one and the rose which were recognised as standardised parts of the equipment of oral songsters, sometimes used for effect (to tie the poem together), sometimes as a fill-in. Parry defined the literary sense of formula as 'a group of words which is regularly employed under the same metrical conditions to express a given essential idea' (Lord 1960:30).

The difficulty about the use of the term 'formula' lies partly in the original metaphor, but more specifically in the extended connotations given by other authors. In his discussion of Tudor prose style in relation to the transition from script to print, Walter Ong deliberately applies the term to 'a sequence of elements in a passage of some length, to organisational formulas' (1971:39). This extension to 'over-all structural organisation' (p. 41) is in line with his thesis that Tudor prose style, often organised by means of the 'formulary structure' of rhetoric, of the oration, manifests a high degree of 'oral residue' which only disappeared with the Romantics and the rise of the novel.

But we can look at the problem in a rather different way. Reference to the Romantics (with their attachment to the speech of ordinary men) and to the novel (with its concern with dialogue and naturalism) reminds us that the relationship between utterance and text, between oral and written discourse, is a complex, dialectical process. If we assume that writing affects conceptual relations, patterns of thought, then its influence is not simply restricted to written communications. The rhetoric of the Greeks, Romans and the late medieval educators can hardly be taken to represent the customs, conventions or consensus of pre-literate speech, even formal speech, though it may share certain features in common. While rhetoric has to do with the organisation of oral forms, it displays a consciousness of those forms that seems to depend upon the deliberate analysis (*analytika* was Aristotle's term for logic) that writing makes possible, or at least does a great deal to promote. It displays the same relationship to public speaking as grammar (*technē grammatikē*, 'the art of letters of the alphabet', as Ong (1971:16) points out) does to utterance in a wider sense. It is a formalisation of oratory, brought about by the increased precision, the heightened consciousness of structural organisation, that writing can bring. In chapter 4 I suggested that the consciousness of polarity and analogy displayed by Greek writers, while based in a loose way upon 'primitive classification', was in fact a formalisation (in some ways, a distortion, in others a clarification) of categorical schema found in oral situations. The increased consciousness of words and their order results from the opportunity to subject them to external visual inspection, a process that increases awareness of the possible ways of dividing the flow of speech as well as directing greater attention to the 'meaning' of the words which can now be abstracted from that flow.

Again I do not mean to imply that oral speech is 'wordless', that morphemes cannot be and are not isolated for certain purposes, especially in the language-learning phase. But I know of no word for 'word' in either of the two West African languages with which I am reasonably familiar, namely, LoDagaa (or Dagari, a Gur language) and Gonja (or Gbanyito, Guang, a Kwa language). The LoDagaa have the word *yelbie*, child (possibly, seed) of speech, which I have heard teachers in modern schools use for 'word'. But on closer inspection it can refer, depending upon its context, to any segment of speech, to morpheme, phrase, line of a song, sentence, theme. It is a 'bit' of speech. In the beginning, then, was not the word but speech. When necessary its flow could be broken into parts by the use of a single term applied relatively. Writing changes this situation; at the cultural level, it enables people to analyse, break down, dissect, and build up speech into parts and wholes, into types and categories, which already existed but which, when brought into the area of consciousness, have a feedback effect on speech itself. People now speak words (though early writing systems did not insist on separation in the sentence, only in the list), are aware of ordering such as subject, verb, object (S.V.O.), of categories such as verb and adverb.

In seeing formal rhetoric as being connected with literate cultures rather than oral ones, I do not mean to imply that formalisation is absent from oral discourse. Apart from poetry, formal ways of address are often utilised in greeting, in prayer, in funeral speeches, while oratory can be found in the judicial and court activities of centralised states. Among the acephalous LoDagaa, I encountered no examples of formalised public speaking of quite the same kind as occurred in the great gatherings of the paramount chief of Gonja, where political manipulation was carried out by public speaking. But funeral speeches certainly displayed a special oratorical style. However, the consciousness of formal process that is displayed in 'rhetoric', and the conservation, the preservation, the congealing, the ossification of this process over time (so that what was once functional, or functioning, now becomes a rigid imposition) does seem to me to derive largely from the written mode. This very point is made by Ong when he writes: 'Rhetoric is thus the "art" developed by a literate culture to formalize the oral communication skills which had helped determine the structures of thought and society before literacy' (1971:49). The important word here is formalise; earlier he speaks of a fourth-century Greek writer on rhetoric, Aphthonius, as having 'codified in writing an oral institution', specifying that an eulogy should praise in succession a man's country, ancestors, education and 'actes', concluding with a favourable comparison (p. 39). The process is not simply one of 'writing down', of codifying what is already there. It is a question of formalising the oral forms and in so doing, changing them into something that is not simply an 'oral residue' but a literary (or proto-literary) creation.

The second difficulty about the use of the word 'formula' to describe oral compositions has to do with the view that it serves partly as a kind of mnemonic, partly as a kind of structural framework, a linking device. 'An oral culture can produce – that is, perform – lengthy oral epics, for these are made up of memorable thematic and formulary elements, but it has no way of putting together a linear analysis such as Aristotle's *Art of Rhetoric*' (Ong 1971:3–4). Both parts of his statement attract some support (though certain features of my first version of the Black Bagre should lead us to be careful of too firm assertions about the absence of 'linearity', unless we define that term somewhat more closely). But the reasons he gives for the possibility of producing or performing 'lengthy oral epics' seem to be less than adequate. We certainly find included in the Bagre some standardised designations of characters and, occasionally, standardised tales, not to mention phrases, themes or motifs that recur over time. But are memorisation and repetition critical to composition and performance? I would only see *memorable* themes and *repetitive* formulae as important conditions of performance if one understands an epic, legend, myth or other narrative genre to have a very high degree of continuity over time, as being the object of 'memory' and/or 'repetition'. If on the other hand one sees the performances of an epic as part of the process of continuous creation, of reconstituting and transferring elements, not in any mechanical sense (linguistic transformation provides too restricted a model), but in an imaginative way that allows a latitude, an autonomy,

116

a 'play' element, then they assume a secondary role. Why should it be *repeated* over time? Many participants think they are hearing or telling the same tale. But they have no text to effect such a comparison and my experience with the Bagre shows that their ability to compare and, what is more important, correct (since the reciters are senior men who 'know' by definition) is very limited. In any case, people enjoy a new twist and, in the absence of copy, may convince themselves that this change is in fact part of the true, the earlier version. Why should an oral poet not do what Shakespeare did with Kyd or Holinshed, and provide a re-creation of an old tale? In the context of written authorship we are unlikely to speak of a man's ability to transform as being linked to memorable themes and repetitive formulae, or to suggest that his failure to reproduce the *Spanish Tragedy* instead of writing *Hamlet* was due to a lapse of memory. Not only was exact reproduction far removed from his intention, we would not applaud this aim even had he espoused it. His aim was transformation, transformation of known plots and of accepted 'commonplaces'. As Ong remarks, 'From More to Shakespeare, adult Tudor authors turned to the collections (e.g. *Wit's Commonwealth*, 1597, or *A Treasury or Storehouse of Similes*) for ideas, phrases, illustrations, and even plots, just as they had done when they were schoolboys. The most resounding and most quoted passages of Shakespeare are generally his reworked versions of what anyone could find here. Like Alexander Pope a century later, Shakespeare was less an originator than a consummately expert retooler of thought and expression' (1971:80). In wishing to qualify this particular notion of originality, I would stress the importance of reworking the material of others, a process that (like rote learning) can be more extensively carried out in the literate than in the oral situation because one's repertoire is that much greater if one has the resources of Meeres or Cauldwell, of Plutarch or Boccaccio, at one's disposal, and because the reworking can be a more deliberate operation.

Despite the assumptions to which the use of the term 'formula' has led, the work of Parry and his student, Lord, gives concrete evidence of the role of memory and creativity in oral cultures. In his interesting discussion of how the singer learns his technique, Lord shows how a young man gets acquainted with the art of metrical singing, not by verbatim remembering but by constructing a song out of the phrases, themes and narratives that he has heard before. 'The singer cannot, and does not, remember enough to sing a song; he must, and does, learn to create phrases' (1960:43). So phrases get 'adjusted'; 'there is no rigidity in what he hears' (p. 33) and certainly none in what he does.

Under these conditions the formula becomes a flexible instrument in the singer's hands, a resource that he can call upon to fill the necessary length of line. Given this flexibility, a certain contradiction emerges. Assuming that we had the required sources, the search for repeated 'groups of words' in the work of either the Greek, Homer or the Yugoslav, Ugljanin, would seem to be less important than the search for creative modifications; yet it is towards the repetitive rather than the creative that the term 'formula' seems to push the analysis of oral forms.

I make this point about the implication of formula in the general sense because exact repetition, as both Parry and Lord were well aware, seems more characteristic of the written transmission of written literature than the reproduction of oral verse. Of course, metrical arrangements impose their own restrictions upon what can be said and how words can be used; its sentence structure is not that of ordinary speech and its 'memorableness' makes it liable to repetition. Equally the very speed of the performance makes for a reliance on certain set combinations; there is need for some marking of time. So that standardised oral forms of an extended kind contain a number of epithets, phrases, grammatical constructions that are repeated at different points in the performance; these can be described as 'formulae' in the restricted sense. We know too that whole chunks of descriptive verse may be transferred from one story to the next, as was the case with Yugoslav songs (Chadwick 1936:299ff; Lord 1967:68ff). In some cases, as perhaps in Homer (Page 1973) and in the Bagre, whole folktales may be incorporated into the longer work. But even the most standardised segments of oral sequences never become so standardised, so formulaic, as the products of written man. Reproduction is rarely if ever verbatim.[1]

I take my own example from communications between gods and men, which constitute an important sub-set of communications in all societies (even today the decline in earlier forms of communication with non-human powers is amply balanced by transcendental communications of a more general sort, including the range of what we may loosely call 'heightened states of consciousness'). In England, the typical example of such communication is the Lord's Prayer or Paternoster. We know that there is more than one English version, since it differs in the Authorised version (in itself an important concept for communicative acts) and in the various Revised versions. But we know what this range is and we can correct an individual who goes wrong, who does not fit the model in the mind.

The nearest equivalent among the LoDagaa is the Invocation to the Bagre. Like the Lord's Prayer, this is something everyone 'knows'. Just pronounce that opening, untranslatable, phrase, *Nmin ti*, and your hearer will immediately take up the refrain. If you continue, and make a mistake, he will at once correct you. Do we have here a fixed model, a model in the head as well as a model in the mind, the Lord's Prayer of the LoDagaa?[2] We have now collected a number of versions of the White Bagre, one in 1950, three in 1969–70, and several more in 1974–75. The last batch are partly from a different village, Lawra, and have not yet been fully examined. Those recorded in 1969 were all from Birifu; two were started by the same speaker. I have other partial renderings. The invocation only consists of a dozen or so lines, the beginning of a recital of some 10,000. In every single case there is some significant difference, some departure from the mode or model. Some of these departures might possibly be recognised by the speakers as 'mistakes'. However, in most cases, each individual will see his (current) version as 'right', and will correct others for getting it wrong, given the opportunity. The difference between this and the Lord's Prayer is that in the latter case people have all internalised verbatim the same model, which they can do because it continues to exist 'out there'; whereas in the first case, each individual possesses his own correct model, because there is no means of automatic correction, nor any definitive system of authoritative regulation. Any model we may erect is simply an averaging of the variations in the number of versions we happen to have collected; it is a statistical artefact, not the authorised version.

The idea that the standard oral forms of non-literate societies (the various genres) are the subject of generative transmission is one that I have pursued in another context (Goody 1977). Clearly, some forms are more generative, and hence more variable, than others. If we take that part of our tradition handed down by oral means (even though the fact that this transmission takes place within the context of a reading society makes a difference, in that inevitably folktales tend to get crystallised by the productions of Perrault, Grimm and the like, who in the guise of preserving a decaying art succeed in stifling possible changes), then we see differences between the different forms, depending upon the characteristics of the genre. Folktales, while they may preserve elements of earlier recitations, may change rather rapidly, as one can see from the various versions of 'The Three Bears', examined by E. A. Hammel (1972), or from the many versions of Cinderella (Cox 1893). On the other hand, shorter, metrical forms, such as the kind of children's song recorded by the Opies (1959), persist over relatively long periods. For young children, London bridge is still burning down, and the bombed churches of the City of London still peal out their chimes, even when these songs are not taught by means of the printed word. The child's drive towards repetition ensures their exact reproduction.

However given this range, we conclude that most of the standard oral forms of non-literate societies fall towards the variable rather than the repetitive ends of the continuum; that is, they may be standard both with regard to 'genre' and in contrast to the syntax of ordinary utterance, and standard too in certain aspects of their construction, but not necessarily with regard to their content.

I want to consider some general implications of this conclusion. In the first place, it implies a kind of rapprochement between the standardised oral forms of non-literate societies and the literature of literate ones, a rapprochement of the kind advocated by Ruth Finnegan (1970). Secondly it tends to dissolve the distinction adopted by many writers, between poetry and myth (Lévi-Strauss 1964) or between folklore and literature of the kind remarked upon by Todorov (1971:12, following Chklovski); the latter claims that whereas the literary work is completely organised, in folklore there is a greater independence of elements. Thirdly it tends to suggest that the analytical methods applied to these standardised oral forms should themselves be standardised, for we are not dealing with a different order of reality. I should add in parentheses that in so doing one must avoid the relativistic error of treating all literatures (like all societies) as identical. But if we reject this approach, we need to have some theory about the generation of difference which relies on something more than unspecified 'evolutionary' assumptions, or on the liberal recourse to metaphor and analogy (e.g. 'hot' and 'cold' societies). In Western cultures we appear to apply structural analysis to individuals rather than to cultures; the corpus is the works of Bernanos rather than the body of Bororo myth. Fourthly, it says something about the learning of literature and the composition of literature. And fifthly it emphasises the gradual differentiation in roles which has taken place with the development of written communication, especially with the advent of relatively simple alphabetic systems, between composers and reciters.

Let me expand upon this last point. In Ancient Greece the distinction takes the form of one between *aoidoi* (composers) and *rhapsodes* (reciters), and relates not only to the two roles themselves, but to the manner in which they obtain their knowledge (Kirk 1962:313). The professional reciters performed at public festivals and were subject to public regulations; it is said, for example, that Solon instructed them to follow the order of the Homeric poems, the second to start where the first left off, to avoid repetitions and omissions. From quotations in writers of the fifth century, it is clear that the text of the poem had by then become established and was familiar to the educated world; so that 'recitations must have conformed to this text, whether the reciters had written copies of it or not' (Chadwick 1932:i, 569).

120

Following a formula

In contrast to the rhapsodists are the minstrels, the composers. They are the producers as distinct from the reproducers of verse. Poetry and tale, song and epic, comes to them not from a text, nor even from an utterance, but from the Muses. In reading a text, or reciting an utterance, one is repeating a human communication. But the creative act, the recitation of an 'original' work, a 'new' song, often involves communication from the outside. The poet is *inspired* by the Muses (or by some experience) and his inspiration lies in the sphere of uncontrollable activity as distinct from the ordered action of the public reciters. Phemios, the minstrel in Ithaca, says to Odysseus (*Od* XXII. 347f.): 'I am self-taught; it was a deity that implanted poems of all kinds in my heart'. And Odysseus addresses the Phaeacian minstrel, Demodocos, in the following words: 'I praise thee far above all mortals, Verily thou hast been taught either by a Muse, a child of Zeus, or even by Apollo' (*Od*. VIII. 487ff.). In this way the distinction between the role of composer and reciter relates to the manner in which they acquire their knowledge, naturally or supernaturally, by copying or by inspiration, and hence to the cosmology itself; the body–soul dichotomy lies close to the heart of ideas of creativity.

Let me now turn from art to science and briefly discuss the more common use of the word formula. The first usage given in the O.E.D. has to do with 'a set form of words in which something is defined, stated, etc., or which is prescribed for use on ceremonial occasions etc.'. The emphasis is on the set form of words. The second usage has a similar theme. 'Recipe; (math.) rule or principle expressed in algebraic symbols'. In chemistry, it is the 'expression of constituents of a compound in symbols and figures'. And there is yet a further meaning that ties up with an earlier chapter just as 'recipe' pre-empts the title of our next: 'tabulation of facts etc. in symbols and figures'. Of course the classic case of a formula is the equation, which (again math.) is a 'formula affirming equivalence of two quantitative expressions, which are connected by the sign $=$', the sign that anthropologists have requisitioned for that supposedly equal partnership, marriage.

In this sense the formula is particularly dependent upon a certain kind of spatial arrangement. But the arrangement is also one that presumes equivalence of quantitative expressions. This is already a highly abstract i.e. non-speech-like concept, mainly because concepts of equality are difficult to handle in qualitative terms. Writing of Equality, Moral and Social, in *The Encyclopedia of Philosophy*, Benn remarks: 'The proposition "A and B are equal" may be descriptive or normative, but in either case it is incomplete without a statement of the respects in which the objects compared are deemed to be equal'.

Incomplete it may be, but it is the core of much mathematics, and is related to the kind of abstraction that dominates other forms of 'logical' operation. It is a concept generated by the abstractness of written formulae rather than by the exigencies of practical life. So too is the obverse of equality and identity, the assertion of opposition, of rigid contrast, achieved by setting 'black' against 'white'.

The formula, in this strict sense, is essentially a product of graphic reductionism. In the first place the flow of speech is arrested by words or symbols being given enduring visual forms and being withdrawn from the context of the sentence. In the second, the linear (or rather lateral) implications of writing develop into statements of equality, or of opposition, which are also formal statements of meaning. The lateral implications are not over-ridden by the hierarchical ones; though there may be a different emphasis in the directional movement of Chinese as against Arabic, writing itself involves lateral as well as vertical arrangements. As we have seen, these arrangements are formalised in the Table which asserts a relationship between items in rows as well as items in columns.

Typical of the formula in this strict sense is the equation involving horizontal equivalence signified by an equals sign. The formula of this type has normally dispensed with lexemes, using a more abstract and in most cases a more quantitative vocabulary consisting of letters (as in algebra), special signs, as well as logograms for numbers. These latter made them not only more abstract (since the numbers were not being used adjectivally to qualify particular objects) but also more general since they were not (as alphabets and number words are) tied to particular phonetic systems. '1 is 1 and always 1' in any language; in English, of course, it is 'one', in French something different.

Mathematics is international because its language is independent of phonetic systems; its concepts are inter-cultural because they are not phrased in a particular vernacular. And it is the existence of a notation far removed from speech that makes possible mathematical thinking and mathematical operations. Whatever relationship exists between the structure of mathematical systems and the structure of the human brain, the invention of a notation is clearly a prerequisite for the kind of highly abstract, decontextualised and arbitrary procedures that are typically represented by the formula.

One of the particular aspects of the formula that enables us to carry out computations is the ability to retain the balance or equality between the two sides by performing the same operations on each, subtracting $2x$ from each side or dividing by $n-1$. There is no non-visual way of doing this; the process depends upon spatial manipulation. Speech alone cannot do it; writing can. The visuo-spatial mode permits the development of a special kind of manipulation.

The formula also encourages the idea of a special kind of equality. In English speech, the verb 'to be' can be used to represent certain kinds of identity. God is love, wrote John the Evangelist. Turn this into a formula using the equals sign and we arrive at the statement God= love. But the meaning is different, for the second statement implies reversibility; the unidirectionality of speech gives way to the two-way traffic that graphic systems permit, though as far as reading rather than composing goes, prose flows in a single visuo-spatial direction.

This question of direction prompts me to make a short deviation. Writing, it has been suggested, introduces the directional factor into verbal communication. The brain is of course differentiated laterally with regard to speech, so too is the ear. But speech as output does not imply direction. Consequently early systems of writing displayed some ambiguity about direction until they settled down to a conventional system. We find evidence of this variability in the early alphabetic signs from Sinai in the second millennium and we find it again in a more recent invention, that of the Vai script in West Africa. Communication may go from left to right or from right to left; it may go from top to bottom or alternatively from side to side or up and down. More complex directional 'codes' may be used where there is a wish to keep the content hidden from the eyes of the world. But in the end, one direction dominates the others.

For most people, the allocation of dominant direction in the horizontal simplified the problem of reading, of decoding the graphemes. But it creates difficulties for the significant proportion of any community that are ambiguous about direction. To them it may not matter whether the phoneme 'th' is written 'ht'; or whether the syllable 'god' is written 'dog'. To the rest of the world, the order of letters is important; to those who have neither initial left hand nor right hand dominance, it may not be.

The problem of the dyslexic is totally different from that of the aphasic; it is partly a developmental problem, which could be mitigated if schools and the home placed less emphasis upon early reading; the head start for some may well be a dead loss for others. And it is a disability peculiar to scribal cultures, ones where the skills of writing and reading play a dominant part in the processes of communication. And it is related to the hemispheric differentiation of the brain whereby speech is associated with the left side and visuo-spatial activity (e.g. writing) with the right.

The linguistic aspects of the directional factor are also important. De

Saussure argued that the linguistic sign had two primordial characteristics. Principle I, so often repeated, affirms the arbitrary nature of
the sign. The second, less well known, asserts the linear nature of the
signifier. 'The signifier, being auditory, is unfolded solely in time from
which it gets its following characteristics: (a) it represents a span, and
(b) the span is measurable in a single dimension; it is a line' (1960:70).
Unlike nautical signifiers (e.g. flags) they can be presented only in succession; they form a chain.

The linear nature of spoken language can clearly be overstressed in
the sense that the 'line' of speech is certainly not a straight line, nor
does it have any necessary spatial direction, only a temporal one. In
this the spoken differs from the written word, where the line becomes
straight in either a sideways or downwards direction, never I think
upwards (unless downwards first). The consequences are radical, on
the nature of the output but more particularly on the nature of the
input, as well as on the receiver himself. Quite different organs are
brought into play and one can no longer say, with de Saussure, that
'the signifier, being auditory, is unfolded solely in time'; it is visual as
well as auditory, and while its linearity is increased, the fact that it
takes a visual form means that one can escape from the problem of the
succession of events in time, by backtracking, skipping, looking to see
who-done-it before we know what it is they did. Who, except the most
obsessive academic, reads a book as he hears speech? Who, except the
most avant-garde of modern dramatists, attempts to write as they
speak?

Clearly the understanding of language must be different under these
two situations, the oral and the written. The written language is not
simply a visual representation of the oral, as we have seen with lists.
Some individuals spend more time with the written language than they
do with the spoken. Apart from the effects on their own personalities
(such indulgence in intrapersonal communication must do something
to the psyche), what are the effects on language? How do written
languages differ from spoken ones? And how are some spoken
languages influenced by the fact that they also have a written register?

We are here in an area which touches upon those problems that have
become associated with working class as distinct from middle class
speech, with restricted as distinct from elaborated codes, with the
problems of schooling that involve taking people habituated to oral
converse and making them put down and read out a related but not
equivalent language in written symbols.[3] In some cultures and at some
times, of course, the written language has diverged to such an extent
that it is not simply a matter of dialect shading but of an outright

difference in language. I refer here to the situations, and they are many, and a virtually (but not entirely) pure artefact of writing, where the language of 'scholarship' (i.e. the school) is totally distinct from the language spoken by the teachers or the pupils, that is, from the vernacular. Such a situation already existed in Mesopotamia; Assyrian scribes had to learn Sumerian before they could learn to read. A similar course of events took place in Phoenicia (Ugarit) with Assyrian itself and it happened with Aramaic, Hebrew, Greek, Latin (throughout Western Europe), with Sanskrit and Pali in Asia, while written Chinese has been described as a totally different language from *any* of the spoken versions (Rosemont 1974). This extreme case, which is common enough, did not simply entail a mechanical job of learning another language. The 'categories of the understanding' were also influenced by the preservation of the unspoken language, as for centuries the categories for analysing the English language were based upon those appropriate, or more appropriate, to a foreign tongue, namely, Latin, the only evidence for which was literary. The relationship between written versions of the 'same' language, e.g. German, French or English, is more subtle, but none the less worthy of examination. Yet very little investigation has appeared in this field.

Returning to the main line of the argument, I come to the third aspect of my present interest in the formula, namely the relationship to formalisation in a more general sense. Let us look briefly at some of the ways in which writing may influence standardised oral forms. It is obvious, I think, how heavily the novel and the play depend upon writing. Drama, narrative, sermons, all exist in oral cultures; but their forms are radically different. Take drama. Although today no longer constrained by Aristotelian rules, it is still subject to a number of specific organisational regulations that mark it off from the dramatic activity of oral cultures embodied in ritual or in play. In the first place one requires a text in order to orchestrate a complex production, and certainly to repeat one. Just as one requires a score to compose, and certainly to play, a symphony.

The existence of a text or score implies the existence of rules of procedure, which tend to get more elaborate not only because of the reduction of speech to writing, but because writing draws attention to itself and makes explicit what was formerly implicit. I want to take my examples here from two areas, one proverbial, the other grammatical.

The influence of writing manifests itself even upon such thoroughly 'folk' material as proverbs, those encapsulations of popular wisdom. One of the favourite subjects for scholars wishing to write down a language for the first time is folk literature, proverbs especially. The effects, particularly upon utterance-embedded forms, is interesting. For by taking the proverb out of the context of speech, by listing it along with a lot of other similar pithy sentences, one changes the character of the oral form. For example, it then becomes possible to set one proverb against another in order to see if the meaning of one contradicts the meaning of another; they are now tested for a universal truth value, whereas their applicability had been essentially contextual (though phrased in a universal manner).

In the Sumerian case, there is even a question as to how many of these proverbs had a popular as distinct from a 'literary' origin. For there is a special group of proverbs dealing with scribes, while others display an abundance of rhetorical figures and numerous complex forms of parallelism, which suggest their composition by the literati (Gordon 1959). In any case it was the scribes who selected and arranged the proverbs in the more or less standard order in which they are found in collections and who used these for the purposes of instruction. At the elementary stages of his education, a pupil may have used a tablet on which was written a single proverb 'to copy and perhaps to memorise' (Gordon 1959:20). Some texts of this kind were not only prepared for memory but from memory as well.

This use of writing to build up an organised collection of previously distinct units, distinct in the sense that they occurred only in context, is an example of a process that is visible in the treatment of the king-lists as well as the epics to which I have earlier referred. The epics, it has been suggested, consisted of separate tales brought together by the process of writing. In the case of the king-list we seem to be dealing with originally separate lists which have been put together 'as if they were consecutive' (Jakobson 1939:161), but which were in reality contemporaneous; separate lists from separate towns were listed serially rather than in parallel, a transformation that no doubt occurred because of the character of the written process in its initial stages.

The way in which the collection of proverbs was put together in standard form is itself interesting. With few exceptions they fell into groupings which have in common either the initial signs of each individual proverb or the subject matter of the proverbs in the group (Gordon 1959:26).

The same kind of listing, with its consequent formalisation, also occurred with certain grammatical texts, which are at once more speech-like than the pure lists, but at the same time provide a high degree of formalisation of speech. Of Emesal tablet III the editor notes that it is more 'grammatical', listing numerals and adverbs, but still abstracted from the context of discourse. However we also find, as in

126

the Old Babylonian Grammatical texts, formal sentence structures that sound like the exercises of modern linguists.

> it is this one,
> it is these
> more than this one
> he is greater than this one (p. 49).

And again:

> it is we
> it is you
> it is they
> it is not we
> it is not you
> it is not they   (p. 51).

Leading to the more than grammatical questions:

> what are we?
> what are you?
> what are they?

It would be extravagant to argue that statements of the order, I am what I am, Cogito ergo sum, and similar phrases that have resounded down the centuries of written culture were generated as responses to the existential questions posed in a formal manner by academic grammarians instructing their pupils. But the decontextualised form of the question appears to raise issues of greater generality than would occur in most oral contexts where the phrase 'what are we?' has a more concrete significance, implying perhaps an incompleted sentence, expressing desperation. What are we going to do? What *are* we? Or to take a more likely example, 'Who am I (to query a superior?).'

I began this chapter by considering the relationship of 'formula' (in the way it has been used by literary critics) to the development of verbal forms. While the exigencies of oral composition meant the use of a certain number of set phrases, it seemed wrong to think that the content was necessarily fixed and transmitted by verbatim memory. Rather, it was early writing systems that emphasised copying and repetition, that separated the roles of composer and performer. In the scientific use of the term, formulae were more clearly the product of graphic reductionism. Finally in the more general sense we saw writing as creating a greater consciousness of form and formalisation. But such formalisation, always conserving, was not always conservative, for it was an essential prerequisite of the rapid growth of knowledge in the last five thousand years, lying at the basis of central developments in the arts but more especially in the sciences. Writing is critical not simply because it preserves speech over time and space, but because it transforms speech, by abstracting its components, by assisting backward scanning, so that communication by eye creates a different cognitive potentiality for human beings than communication by word of mouth.[4]

7. The recipe, the prescription and the experiment

3 *Witch.* Scale of dragon, tooth of wolf;
Witches' mummy; maw, and gulf,
Of the ravin'd salt-sea shark;
Root of hemlock, digg'd i' th' dark;
Liver of blaspheming Jew;
Gall of goat, and slips of yew,
Sliver'd in the moon's eclipse;
Nose of Turk, and Tartar's lips;
Finger of birth-strangled babe,
Ditch-deliver'd by a drab,
Make the gruel thick and slab:
Add thereto a tiger's chaudron,
For th' ingredience of our cauldron.

Note. 'Egyptian mummy, or what passed for it, was formerly a regular part of the *Materia Medica*'; 'Turks and Tartars were not only regarded as types of cruelty. . .but. . .they were *unchristened*, and hence valued by the witches.'

Macbeth, Act IV, Scene I

The organisation of the kind of non-familial household required by a king's court, a standing army or an educational college tends to generate lists and tables of a variety of kinds, both of the food to be purchased, prepared and consumed (the rations), and of the individuals who are entitled to these benefits (the personnel). These lists not only 'reflect' certain aspects of the social organisation; they also determine other aspects, in that they have certain implicit features (such as hierarchy and lateral placement) that influence behaviour, as well as other explicit features that prescribe it. Moreover through these formulations they make possible what would present enormous difficulties in an oral society, both in the field of social organisation as well as in the growth of knowledge. The development of major branches of medicine, slow as it has been, depends upon the ability to examine critically a list

129

of ingredients, their mode of employment, and reports of the results, then to share and diffuse this knowledge for the use of practitioners and their patients.

There are three kinds of nominal list which it is convenient to distinguish at this point. Firstly there is the nominal roll, which lists the members of a group (e.g. a school class or army platoon) who are or should be present, or who are entitled to certain privileges (e.g. the list of the members of a guild or the Fellows of a college). In this type falls the ration list of an army, since entrance on the roll and participation in the activities of the organisation are two sides of the same coin. Where they are not, we get a selective list, sometimes self-inscribed, which indicates those members who have put their names down or who have been chosen for a certain activity, such as dining in Hall or going out on patrol. Thirdly the retrospective, as distinct from the prospective, list gives the names of those individuals who were in fact present, who did attend, a type of list which may obviously be used outside the kinds of 'corporate' situations mentioned before.

When the Fellows of St John's College, Cambridge, dine together each evening, two pieces of paper lie upon the table, the menu and the dining-list.

The list of diners is an example of the second type of nominal list mentioned; it is self-inscribed and indicates, both to the kitchens and to other Fellows, who has decided to dine that evening. It is worth examining since it displays a number of the characteristics of lists in general. Firstly it insists upon an explicit hierarchy; the list has to be arranged so that the items, names of persons in this case, are one above another, from top to bottom. It is true that horizontal 'strings' of names, found in the plurality of authors of some academic papers, place one item *before* another, thus implying priority, or seniority, running from left to right. But left to right is a more 'conventional' movement than that from top to bottom. Indeed, systems of writing that begin at the right and move in the opposite direction, such as Arabic and Hebrew, clearly have a different order of priority. No-one, I think, has employed a system of writing that starts at the foot of the page and moves to the top, then jumps to the bottom again. The vertical hierarchy is more compelling, more insistent, than horizontal differentiation; it is the difference between head and foot in one context and right and left on the other.

Indeed, so compelling is the idea of hierarchy in a written list that extraordinary steps have to be taken to avoid the implications of higher and lower, first and last, with their associations of differential power or responsibility. To get over the problem, the signatories of a letter

ROUND ROBIN, *addressed to* SAMUEL JOHNSON, L.L.D. *with* FAC SIMILES *of the Signatures.*

We the Circumscribers,
having read with great pleasure, an
intended Epitaph for the Monument of D.
Goldsmith, which considered abstractedly, appears to
be, for elegant Composition and Masterly Stile, in
every respect worthy of the pen of its learned Author,
are yet of opinion, that the Character of the Deceased as
a Writer, particularly as a Poet, is, perhaps, not delineated
with all the exactness which D. Johnson is Capable of
giving it. We therefore, with deference to his Superior Judgement, humbly request, that he would at least take the trouble
of revising it; & of making such additions and alterations
as he shall think proper, upon a further perusal: But
if We might venture to express our Wishes, they would
lead us to request, that he would write the Epitaph
in English, rather than in Latin: As We think that the
Memory of so eminent an English Writer ought to be
perpetuated in the language, to which his Works are
likely to be so lasting an Ornament, Which we
also know to have been the opinion of
The late Doctor
himself.

London. Published as the Act directs, 10 April 1791, by Charles Dilly.

131

have to place their names in a circle, producing a Round Robin of the kind sent to Dr Johnson by his friends when they wanted to make some slight protest about the use of Latin for his obituary of the dramatist, Oliver Goldsmith (page 131), to which the Doctor replied that he would 'never consent to disgrace the walls of Westminster Abbey, with an English inscription'. In this way the Round Robin has similar functions to the Round Table, namely, to avoid the linear hierarchy implicit in the list as part of a figurative table and the seating plan as part of a physical one.

The hierarchy of the dining-list is distinct, with the Master at the top followed by the President (known by their titles, rather than their names), then other Fellows appearing in strict order of seniority. Because it is written down in the form of a list and placed upon the table at which the meal is eaten, the hierarchy is always visibly present in front of every diner. Indeed during the meal, Fellows can be seen consulting this list, not merely to ascertain the names of guests or younger Fellows, but to confirm their own position in the daily ranking. The hierarchy is therefore more linear than in most oral societies. It imposes itself in an immediate way, making the ordering more 'meaningful' to the actors than it has any right to be, seniority for this purpose depending simply upon date of election. But the list in the form of a single column also gives a peculiar shape to the hierarchy; unlike the positions in a table of organisation, no one can be equal to any one else. There is no horizontal placement; every item must be vertically ordered, even if this means forcing hierarchy on what is in practice a looser form of social organisation.

I do not want to imply that unilineal ranking is only to be found in written cultures. Clearly many forms of spatial and temporal ordering may place individuals in distinctive ranked positions of this kind e.g. the file of Gonja chiefs that greet the paramount at the annual Damba celebration, or the recipients of the kava cup at a Tongan festival; a central phase of mass ceremonies is often devoted to such ordering. My point is that the list provides an ordering whether you want it or not.

The list of those dining has particular as well as general characteristics. Towards the lower end, individuals begin to be given initials as well as titles and surnames. In earlier days, lists of county cricket teams, and even international ones, used to indicate who was paid as a professional and who played as an amateur by giving the names of the latter with their initials, and the former without; so that an entry read H. D. G. Leveson Gower in one case, and Hobbs on the other. Each year, an important fixture in the cricketing calendar was the match of Gentlemen against Players, those with initials against those without. In the case of the list of diners, it is the Fellows who have no initials, and those 'with dining rights' who are defined in a more specific manner. It would perhaps be a waste of time to seek out the reasons for this distinction, the use or non-use of initials being simply an arbitrary 'diacritical' feature to set apart the two categories. But it might be suggested that the Fellows, who are known to each other, require minimal marking, the others maximum, for both in cricket and in Hall, Smiths (and others with similar names) are excluded from the rule when there is more than one of them present: in case of ambiguity initials are provided.

One further discriminating feature in the dining-list is the lateral displacement of certain names, that of guests. They appear partly in a different column and partly under the name of their host, indicating their protected but interstitial status.

Finally, the most distinctive feature of the usual list is its exclusively male character. Some lists contain the names of women. These would appear not as Fellows but (and only recently) as guests and very occasionally in the category of those having dining rights. Otherwise women in the College, as the list indicates by implication, occupy the non-academic roles, serving at table, making beds, typing letters. The differentiation, indeed discrimination, between the roles of the sexes is radical, and is clearly illustrated in the dining-list.

The second piece of paper lying on the table is the menu, the list of rations as distinct from the list of those entitled to them. Conventional in form, it presents the shape of the meal to come. The shape is a regular one; variation falls within a restricted range, although deliberate changes do occur over the longer run. The first course consists of the soup, or an equivalent preparatory dish such as antipasto or *hors d'oeuvres*; it is followed by the main course, a hot dish of meat and vegetables, occasionally fish (especially on Fridays); cold meat, vegetarian dishes and alternatives to pork are available on request. For the third course three alternatives are announced, namely, a fruit pie, cheese and a sweet. In addition, the menu specifies the wine to be served, but not the beer which may be taken instead. This omission indicates two aspects of the menu. Firstly, there is no need to specify constants; the menu deals, and enables the individuals concerned to deal, with variables. Secondly, though the first reason probably covers the omission of beer, the inclusion of the foreign at the expense of the local is typical of the language of this and most high-status English menus, with their frequent recourse to restaurant French.

The role of the written menu in a restaurant is somewhat different

133

since it specifies not the variations offered diachronically (from day to day) to a fixed Fellowship, but the alternatives offered synchronically (on one day) to a variable clientele. In the first place it acts as an advertisement, when placed in the window to attract custom. Secondly, it helps the proprietor to offer and the client to choose among a wider range of dishes. Some years ago there used to be a small Italian restaurant in Frith Street, Soho, where there was no menu; the waiter came up to the table and asked:

'Whadyawan?'

To which the standard answer was,

'Whadyagot?'

He then reeled off the lists of *plats du jour* and shouted your answer down the stairwell to the kitchen below. Such a procedure is possible in small 'family' restaurants where the range of dishes is limited. But the offer of a wider choice *necessitates* a recourse to writing, because even if the waiter could recall a much longer (and frequently-changing) list, his client would be unable to make up his mind among these dishes because he cannot scan the choices available to him. Alternatively, he would be likely to plump for the first or the last dish named, or possibly to seize upon a name that he had heard before. An arbitrary or conservative choice would be made because of the difficulties of scanning.

The use of the written menu for the sale of meals in restaurants and (to a lesser extent) in hotels is easy to understand. But its adoption for high-status dinners is equally interesting because it implies not only the complete separation between consumers and preparers, between table and kitchen, but also a marked separation between the servers (standing, mobile) and the consumers (sitting, immobile), since information about the content of the meal is mediated impersonally by a piece of paper. Of course, matters of prestige enter directly into the whole situation. Written communication is valued above oral; the menu in itself has a high status, the symbol of luxury and of choice, of the great rather than the little cuisine. The menu is appropriate to the special occasion, the non-domestic meal, the repast prepared by men rather than women.

The two pieces of paper placed on the High Table of St John's College represent only the surface structure; behind it lie two other schedules of differing kinds that serve to organise and frame the meal. The first is the board that carries the graces said before and after dinner. However well he knows the grace, the designated speaker holds this board in front of him, and half reads, half recites the prayer. The rendering itself provides a continual subject for comment at the

134

dining tables, a conversational opener used almost as frequently as the weather or the passage of the term. Any alteration is seen either as an unconscious mistake or else as a deliberate attempt to alter a highly ritualised pattern of speech.

The grace itself is a variant of one recited in many Cambridge Colleges. The existence of these variations shows that some 'creative' innovation has taken place in the past. However, what is presently required is strict conformity to a written original, which together with the comments of the listeners (whose model is the identical printed sheet), serves to correct any deviation.

The consecration not only asks for the blessings of the universal God upon this particular meal; it. also intercedes on behalf of those bene-factors of the College who have provided for the repast. In this way the communal meal is marked off from ordinary life and the consumption of food and wine made into something more than either hunger or gluttony demands; it provides a 'sacred frame'.

The fourth schedule that organizes the meal, in a secular rather than a sacred way, is the recipe, one of a number of lists that adorn the kitchens, including the nominal roll of available staff (the 'strength' rather than the 'establishment'), and the duty roster that allocates them particular times of work. Behind the recipe lies the shopping list, that is, the list of objects required to implement the recipe, which at once precedes and succeeds the in-gathering of the unprepared (not neces-sarily raw) food. Since the immediate source of food may be neither the market nor the field, but rather the storehouse where it has found its way as the result of either primary production or the collection of tribute, lists of tribute and stores are in themselves closely connected with the shopping list, though they consist of statements of what has been done rather than prescriptions (the suffix 'pre' combined with the verb 'write' indicating its nature) for what should be done. The shopping list is a way of constructing the future schedule of an indi-vidual or group, a schedule of movements in space and in time, relative to the requirements of the household economy; it is not simply a state-ment of what one wants, for writing permits a person to re-order the items in relation to the source of supply; articles to be bought at the greengrocer's can be grouped together, and this set put next to that to be bought at the baker's, the shop next door; thus the shopping list can be made to represent future movements of a fairly precise kind.

Basically, we have three types of list concerned with the meal itself, one connected with the 'production' of the food for the kitchen, i.e. the shopping list, one connected with the preparation of the food, i.e. the recipe, and one with the consumption of food, i.e. the menu. Each of these is a PLAN in the sense given to that word by Miller, Gallanter and Pibram (1960) and they are plans in which the externalisation of the organising mechanism makes it more determinative, more enduring, more inclusive and more formal. The first and the third I have briefly considered. Let me now turn to the recipe, which has implications over a wider field than the meal, since it lists not only what ingredients are required but what actions have to be carried out in order to produce the menu. Etymologically the word derives from the Latin verb, to take (as does the cognate, receipt), and was originally used by physicians in the abbreviated form of R or ℞, 'to head prescriptions, and hence applied to these and similar formulae'. But the medical meaning was soon supplemented by the culinary usage, and by 1500 we find 'recipe brede gratyd, and eggis' (*Babees Book*, Harl. MS. 5401) which, in the eighteenth century became generalised to 'a statement of the ingredients and procedure necessary for the making or compounding of some preparation, esp. a dish in cookery; a receipt'. Indeed the word 'receipt' is essentially an early version of the same, being used in its medical sense in Chaucerian times, and defined by the Oxford English Dictionary in virtually identical terms, the context once again being medical as well as culinary. A usage of 1703 refers to 'Medicinal and Cookery receipts collected from the best authors'.

The point about a recipe or a receipt that emerges from these dictionary definitions and literary usages is their essentially written character. The recipes are collected in one place, classified, then serve as a reference book for the doctor or the cook, for the sick or the hungry, as in Dryden's line, 'The Patients, who have open before them a Book of admirable Receipts for their Diseases' (Dryden, *Juvenal* Ded., 1697). For recipes, once collected, have then to be tried: 'There is not a receipt in the whole extent of chemistry which I have not tried' (Malkin, *Gil Blas* XII. iv para 5, 1809). And once recipes are set down and tried in this manner, then some turn out better, or more approved, than others: Steele writes of 'The most approved Receipt now extant for the Fever of the Spirits' (*Spectator* No. 52 para 3). In these effective remedies, common elements can easily be identified and their effects assessed: 'In all good receites and medicynes Amomium is ofte ido' (Trevisa, *Barth.* De P. R. XVII, viii. Bodl. M.S.). Experiment, assessment, the isolation of common elements, all are encouraged by the written recipes, whose very existence changes the course and nature of teaching: 'A Booke...teachinge the waye of making diverse good and excellent Receiptez' (Sloane M.S. 2491 If. 73, c. 1500). For the recipe now exists independently of the teacher; it has become depersonalised and acquired a more general, universal quality.

The written character of the recipe is brought out in the second, and nowadays more usual, meaning of receipt. As early as 1442 we find the Rolls of Parliament referring to the 'bookes of receyte', containing the '*written* acknowledgement of money or goods received into possession or custody'. The goods of course might be tribute, taxes, gifts or alms, but the common characteristic is that their acceptance should be confirmed by means of a written document (or at the very least a signature at the foot of a printed one), which can then serve as evidence that the transaction has taken place, either to the employer of an intermediary or to a court of law, both situations assuming a certain degree of social or physical distance between the transacting parties, a distance that writing itself promotes. For this purpose a receipt-book may be used and in the seventeenth century, significantly, this same term was used for a book of medical or cooking recipes.

The recipe or receipt, then, is a written formula for mixing ingredients for culinary, medical or magical purposes; it lists the items required for making preparations destined for human consumption. Clearly oral cultures also follow relatively standard procedures for such purposes. What then is gained or lost by committing such instructions to writing?

Let us look at some of the very earliest examples. Towards the end of the third millennium B.C.E., a Sumerian physician decided to collect and record his most prized medical prescriptions. Kramer describes this tablet as the first pharmacopoeia. In one way the claim is nonsense; earlier man certainly had his *materia medica* related to the classifications of plants, animals and minerals. What we have here is the first *written* pharmacopoeia, the importance of which was that it provided the starting point for a series of incremental developments associated with the storage, categorisation and development of medical information.

The text presented by Kramer indicates not only the materials employed but also the mode of employment, e.g. salves applied externally (often mixed with wine), filtrates also applied externally (often prepared by decoction), liquids to be taken internally (often mixed with beer); indeed, some of the chemical operations were similar to those used for producing alkali ash and fat. Here we shift from the simple list to the recipe itself, which consists of two parts, the list plus the instructions, the ingredients plus the action. The instructions are of two kinds, one for its preparation and one for its consumption, corresponding to the recipe and the mode of employment, the former characteristic of cooking, the latter of medicine. Indeed, in the latter case (and occasionally in the former), the mode of preparation may be deliberately hidden from the outside world, either by a form of secret writing or by sketchy instructions whose meaning will be understood only by members of the craft. In the present case, the recipes lack proper indications of quantities, an omission which may have been a deliberate way of concealing the secrets of the trade. For these recipes were often connected with crafts that required special preparations for their particular tasks. The dyer's craft, for example, probably developed in the Neolithic but became much more complex in the urban civilisations of the Near East. Early Egyptian pictures show coats of varied hue, including striped cloths of many colours. In the temple workshops of Mesopotamia, the sacred vestments of the gods and priests had to be given the correct colours and patterns. Egyptian dyers had books of recipes (though we know them only from the third century A.D.). 'They contain the notes of an alchemist from ancient recipe books describing the dyeing of cloth with alkanet, safflower, saffron, kermes, madder, and woad' (Forbes 1954:249), the specification of which would clearly encourage the elaboration of colour terminology. We also find recipes for the manufacture of chemicals such as alum needed in dyeing. But while it was useful to write down such recipes so that a more elaborate technology could be developed and communicated, the aim was also to restrict communication to the in-group, the initiated. Indeed it was to prevent identification by the uninitiated that in Akkadian the substance was deliberately referred to by a pseudonym, 'lichen from the tamarisk' (Forbes 1954:263). The secrecy of such recipes was doubtless associated with an early structure of guilds in which trade secrets were passed down only between members. The written recipe-book is more open to the world, so that deliberate steps have to be taken to preserve its secrets.

In so far as they constituted lists, these books of prescriptions led to the kind of explicit arranging and rearranging of data that we earlier observed with proverbs and more generally and more generatively with concepts and classes, rules and procedures. But being also prescriptions for taking action, they formulated a programme as well, leading to an extension of the repertoires of specialist and layman alike, as well as to 'trying out' recipes (i.e. 'testing', 'experimenting') and to a comparative assessment of the results.

The first approximation to recipes in the culinary sense comes from the northern Semitic city of Mari, on the upper Euphrates. In the documents found in Room 5 of the royal palace, dating from the earlier part of the second millennium, there were 300 tablets representing lists of produce (cereals, oil, sesame, honey, wine, dates); of livestock, clothing and precious metals, as well as lists of personnel and inventories (Birot

The recipe, the prescription and the experiment

1960:245). In type the texts are similar to those found in Room 100 except that the number dealing with comestibles is much higher, amounting to about two-thirds (Bottéro 1956). For Room 5 was in the part of the palace, given the name of *quartier de l'intendance*, which held the archives relating to food for the royal table (Bottéro 1958).

The texts from Room 5 consisted largely of lists of comestibles issued for the king's table, *le repas du roi*, provided for his family, his domestic staff and many of the palace officials, who were also officials of the realm. This meal consisted of solid food (*akalum*) and fermented drink (*šikarum*). In addition, other lists made provision for the *kipsum*, or meal for the dead kings; food for the living and the dead was recorded in a similar manner. Some of the lists end with the phrase 'for the table of the king', and others 'pour les esprits infernaux'. An example of a short list of the former kind is the following:

1 *kur*   4 *qa* of bread KUM;
1 *kur* 10 *qa* of leavened bread(?);
70 *qa* of cake;
28 *qa* of *šipku*;
2 *qa* of *arsânu*;
7 *qa* of oil
2 *qa* of honey;
8 *qa* of sesame (Birot 1964:35)

But in addition to these lists of food issued, we also find some dealing with the elaboration of the different constituents which initiate us into the activities of the kitchens themselves (Birot 1964:1), though in a very summary way.[1] These proto-recipes, indicating actions as well as objects, verbs (or adverbs) as well as nouns (or pronouns), took a very simple form:

1 pot of honey
for the cake (Birot 1964:97)

followed by a date and a seal. In other words they have shifted from a mere list of comestibles to specifying what the constituents are to be used for, i.e. to prescribing a set of actions. So the two facets of a culinary recipe take the same kind of shape as the medical prescription; the list of constituents is followed by a summary description of the processes to which they are to be subjected (often using shorthand technical terms relevant only to this specific *written* context). While writing down recipes does not have quite the same relevance for the growth of knowledge as recording the preparation of other concoctions (with which it is at first closely associated), nevertheless the recipe has important implications for the extension and differentiation of the repertoires of cooking that accompanied the differentiation of culture and society associated with the technological developments of the Bronze Age, when cooking took on a specific 'class' aspect.[2] Equally, the elaborateness of the modern cuisine depends essentially upon the literacy of its practitioners. There the recipe (as in purchase, the receipt) reigns supreme, essentially a literate product. The production of collections of recipes (i.e. cookbooks) is a significant part of the book trade, forming a steady sale for any publisher so engaged. In the daily and weekly press, individual recipes form a standard ingredient of the 'women's page'. Even the rural areas of our own culture are often dominated by the book, though this might take the form of an exercise book filled with recipes gathered from home, neighbours and news-papers; I recently found half a dozen volumes of this kind of recipe-book when going through the belongings of a maternal aunt in north-east Scotland. Nevertheless there were and are certain urban–rural differ-ences in Europe which, while not absolute in any sense, embody the reliance on the shop and market as distinct from the garden and the farm and learning by word of book rather than by word of mouth.

Country cuisine of course often depends upon an implicit recipe in the sense that each meal requires the assemblage of the ingredients followed by a phase of preparation based upon 'tradition' rather than cookbook. The methods learnt in the context of family living are acquired by direct rather than indirect means, by observation rather than by reading, by watching rather than by the kind of testing that might have constituted a possible model for the genesis of the experi-mental method; indeed the dissemination of recipes and books of household management among the English middle classes was a fact not unconnected with the dissemination of knowledge by the Royal Society. Knowledge of cooking acquired by participation rather than by instruction is necessarily conservative (in one sense of the word) and tied to the ingredients readily available, placing less emphasis on the fulfilment of a set of written 'orders' and more upon the utilisation of the contents of the cupboard in an improvisation upon certain *recettes de base* (base recipes). It is the constraints and freedom of the *bricoleur* as opposed to those of the scientist, where exact measurement may be a prelude to discovery and invention.

The attraction of regional cooking is precisely that it is tied to what grandmother did ('*les gaufres de mémé*') and to the 'natural' ingredi-ents she used rather than to the recipes that are diffused by writing (or rather, by print, since the standardisation of typography also spelt out the standardisation of food) and whose wide range of ingredients was made possible first by the size of the steamship and later by the speed of the aeroplane, which in turn transformed the esoteric into the quotidian.

Until the advent of printing, the European literature on cooking was essentially a literature for the Court or for noble households. As such, it was eclectic in a regional sense, taking recipes from here and there and elaborating them into dishes 'fit for a king', to use the words of an English nursery rhyme, though the same idea is found in early Arab literature (see Rodinson 1949, Roden 1968). For the upper classes, literature (as for example, the Roman treatise entitled the *Deipnoso-phists*) helped to bring together the recipes (or more usually the out-lines of recipes) gathered from different places and hence requiring the import of any exotic ingredients native to those localities. At this level the existence of a specific written recipe for, say, mullet in hummus, exercises a constraining influence on the actors involved in the preparation of this plate, because it suggests the trying out of a new dish, following a recipe and accumulating the ingredients needed. Of course, verbal norms are also constraining, but the written recipe exercises rather a different kind of normative pull, both at the level of court recipes (which are seen as the noble, even the right and proper, thing to do) and at the level of the *bourgeois gentilhomme* learning about such behaviour from a cookbook. In this respect, peasant cook-ing is different. Firstly, it relies less on precise quantities, which tend to be specified exactly in the written recipe. Secondly, it tends to be less tied to specific ingredients; one can substitute more easily if one does not think one is preparing *tripe à la mode de Caen*, but simply cooking a dish of tripe for supper. Thirdly, there is more flexibility with regard to procedures.

Perhaps I can interpolate a personal example. When we first came across that Cantal dish, *l'aligot*, we found a recipe printed on the back of a picture postcard (though it is equally available in *La Cuisine occitane*). We took some trouble to accumulate the specified cheese (Tome de Cantal) which was not available in any of the local shops but occasionally at markets, and to follow the instructions given there. Later, upon enquiring about the dish in a restricted area around where we lived, we found several households giving us recipes that differed considerably from one another. There was little 'cultural' standardisa-tion of the mode of preparation, even though the ingredients remained relatively constant.

While literate cooking is constraining (if one follows the book), it is so partly because, as in the case above, it often provides instruction ('programmed learning') for individuals who do not themselves know how to prepare the dishes. In the town, where children spend a large part of their time at school and are not required to make a great contribution to the house or garden, individuals often learn cooking indirectly from books rather than directly from the familial setting. Such a process necessitates 'following a (written) recipe', rather than learning by participation i.e. by oral means. But in situations such as the initial elaboration and later transmission of a courtly cooking, writing appears to have played an important role, firstly, in the accumulation and learning of a wider repertoire of recipes, and secondly, in the retention and organisation of that repertoire.

In completely oral societies, at least as far as the ordinary household in Africa is concerned, opportunities for learning and transmission are quite limited. Cooking is usually carried out in the open, and hence generally in the more communal rather than the more private space. Therefore the pressures towards conformity and homogeneity will be greater than in a peasant society in Europe where households are smaller, meals more private. But in any oral culture new recipes have to be learnt by one individual from another in a face-to-face situation. The concrete context would stress the relation of teacher to pupil, e.g. of mother to daughter. For oral learning tends to reduplicate the 'initial situation', the process of socialisation. With the cooks of courts, once again, to learn is often to place oneself in a subordinate position towards another. But all this is avoided if one can use a written source, which is 'objective', 'neutral', 'impersonal', as far as human relations themselves are concerned.[3] One can learn in privacy as an adult even better than as a child; one can learn to change one's cooking, change one's ways of behaving, without seeking the direct advice of others. Hence the widespread circulation of *printed* works on cooking, etiquette and household management (*manuscript* works tend to be confined to the few who don't need them to the same extent) at a period when the changing socio-economic structure made mobility, social and geographical, a characteristic feature of the life of Western Europe. Indeed one might say that on the domestic level, the publication of manuals of 'correct' behaviour made possible the rapid assimilation of social climbers. It also contributed, in a wider sense, to the weakening of sub-cultures in the society, since the 'secrets' of one group were being made public to all others, although it took the political change of universal suffrage, the economic change of mechanised industrialisation and the communications change of radio and, above all, television, to produce the present pressure towards national, even international, uniformity that characterises the global village.

The second point concerns the development of a wider repertoire of recipes. In oral cultures, procedures for preparing food can be complex, not so much in terms of what is placed on the table, but in the preparation itself. In West Africa the time taken in preparing millet grains for the porridge, or in making shea-butter, or rendering manioc fit for consumption, all complex processes, is very considerable. But the number of recipes that can be held in oral memory is limited, while those that can be held in written form are unlimited. If one had information upon the different recipes in actual use by a particular woman in a West African society, the total number would be relatively small. Indeed the same is no doubt also true of most peasant and urban households in Europe, especially where the wife is working outside the home as well as within. However, an individual can always consult his own recipe-books, published cookbooks or the columns of the newspaper, in order to extend the number of dishes that he can prepare. Thus the written recipe serves in part to fill the gap created by the absence of Granny, Nanna or Mémé (who has been left behind in the village, or in the town before last), by the feeble communication of culture between mother and daughter (often because of the alternative activities of either or both), and by the possibility of the easy and inexpensive resort to prepared meals, such as fish and chips, delicatessen, T.V. dinners or convenience foods of all kinds. In fulfilling this function the cookbook is also instrumental in extending the range of a society's cuisine as well as that of a particular individual.

While the use of written recipes may emphasise and enshrine differentiation of a hierarchical kind, as well as permitting the accumulation of modes of preparation from many localities, it has limited implications for the growth of knowledge. Such is not the case with the medical recipe mentioned earlier. I have already noted the kind of power over the systematic arrangement of material that writing gave to the study of surgery in the shape of the Edwin Smith Papyrus. Wounds, fractures and dislocations are covered in a relatively systematic way that was to become the accepted one, namely *a capite ad calcem*, from head to toe (Sigerist 1951:305). Other medical works do not display such an overarching system although the Papyrus Ebers has a definite beginning and end. This papyrus is a compendium devoted to a number of subjects of interest to the physician, usually introduced by an Incipit, such as 'The beginning of the physician's secret: knowledge of the heart's movements...'; it mostly consists of 'collections of recipes with prescriptions for the treatment of internal diseases, of diseases of the eyes, of the skin, of women, and other ailments' (Sigerist 1951:313). The relation with incantations is close (indeed the boundary is always blurred) and the medical recipe may well be seen as emerging from the spell, just as the prescription in its turn was close both to the provision of cosmetics and to the dietetic or culinary recipe; one required the external application of *materia medica* and related substances, the other the internal consumption of powders, solids and fluids of various kinds.[4]

But the fact that these remedies were set down in the papyrus meant that they could also be made the subject of comment and addition. Whatever had been put down in writing received immense authority, and it is significant that Thoth, the god of writing, was also the patron of physicians. In the introduction to the Papyrus Ebers, Re, the sun god, says: 'I will save him from his enemies, and Thoth shall be his guide, he who lets writing speak and has composed the books; he gives to the skillful, to the physicians who accompany him, skill to cure. The one whom the god loves, him he shall keep alive' (Sigerist 1951:287). While the god had given all knowledge, this knowledge could nevertheless be augmented, by marginal notes and colophons, so that the learning contained in the manuscripts surpassed that of any one individual. Indeed the practice of medicine split into a number of specialisms, and roles proliferated; as Herodotus noted of Egypt, 'every physician is for one disease...and the whole country is full of physicians' (Herodotus II, 84).

The incorporation of medicine in a written text may well have led to the same split that the arts displayed between composers and reciters, at least in Greek medicine which owed so much to Egypt. For a Greek alchemical treatise defines the difference between the physician on the one hand and the magician on the other; the former acts 'mechanically and by books', while the other is a priest, acting 'through his own religious feelings' (Gardiner 1947:268; Sigerist 1951:364). Here the doctor as 'scientist' is being contrasted with the healer as priest; the former has to act by the book, the latter is more free to let his spirit roam, to seek for new remedies, to fill the interstices of the written word with inspired messages from the gods. The cost of book learning was a restriction on spontaneity.

In Mesopotamia, medicine developed along similar lines. Their medical texts were somewhat more carefully arranged, being 'collections of cases arranged systematically under a certain heading', the principle of classification being etiological, symptomatic or clinical (Sigerist 1951:417). These works were not only copied but edited as well; indeed they may have been the least static books in the scribal libraries. Many tablets consisted entirely of recipes, while others listed symptoms and prognoses, but they were added to and changed over time. This gradual process of accumulating, writing down, assessing and augmenting a set of acts designed to relieve the ills of mankind is

144

clearly continuous with the diagnosis and curing of disease in oral cultures. But the systematisation of knowledge, combined with the incremental activity involved in the training of literate physicians, meant that a large step had been taken on the road to 'modern science', to 'rational medicine', to 'logico-empirical activity', whatever phrase one deems appropriate. It is the kind of step in the 'domestication of the savage mind' that is so ill-described by means of our current binarisms, which smack of the body–soul dichotomy that has for so long been a central feature of human thought. I prefer instead to link these changes with those in the technology of the intellect, the means as well as the modes of communication that enabled man to make these advances in human knowledge.

8. The Grand Dichotomy reconsidered

> 'He composed a book also, which he entitled... Of the Division of Nature, extremely useful in solving the perplexity of certain indispensable inquiries, if he be pardoned for some things in which he deviated from the opinion of the Latins, through too close attention to the Greeks. In after time, allured by the munificence of Alfred, he came into England, and at our monastery, as report says, was pierced with the iron styles of the boys whom he was instructing, and was even looked upon as a martyr...'
>
> William of Malmesbury on Johannes Scotus
> (transl. by J. A. Giles 1847:119).

At the beginning of this book, doubts were expressed about the dichotomous approach to the study of cognitive developments in human culture, to the characterisation of modes of thought, to the growth of knowledge, that runs through so much discussion in the field of comparative sociology and philosophy, largely because the we/they division penetrates so deeply our everyday speech.

The pervasive dichotomy between primitive and advanced societies, provides for some the frontier between anthropology and sociology, for others the divide between them and us, between the bricoleur and the scientist, between the non-logical, the non-rational, as against the logical and the rational, while some even see the one as the field for symbolic interpretations of social action, the other as calling for the application of a utilitarian calculus, the calculus of practical reason as against 'culture'.[1]

Let us consider how far the effects of changes in the mode and means of communication can be held to account for the dichotomous distinctions between what various writers have called by terms in the following list:

| primitive | advanced |
| savage | domesticated |

146

The Grand Dichotomy reconsidered

traditional	modern
'cold'	'hot'
(closed)	(open)
(developing)	(developed)
pre-logical	logical
mythopoeic	logico-empirical

I have suggested that this dichotomous treatment is inadequate to deal with the complexity of human development. Moreover, we have seen that it proposes no reasons for the difference and no mechanisms for change. On the contrary, it accepts a typology that phrases what might possibly be acceptable as a polarised field in terms of a binary division.

The problem can be partly resolved, the Grand Dichotomy refined, by examining the suggested differences in cultural style or achievement as the possible outcome of changes in the means of communication, an outcome that will always depend for its realisation on a set of socio-cultural factors. In Chapter 3, I discussed Horton's characterisation of the difference between the 'open' and 'closed' situations and tried to show how some of the features he isolates might be better explained in terms of the potentialities of literacy.[2] The same I believe can be done for some of the central features that mark Lévi-Strauss' division between hot and cold societies and that were discussed in the opening chapter. These characteristics were summarised as follows:

Domesticated	Wild	References (1952)
'hot'	'cold'	309
modern	neolithic	24
science of the abstract	science of the concrete	3
scientific thought	mythical thought	33, 44
scientific knowledge	magical thought	33
engineer(ing)	bricoleur(-age)	30
abstract thought	intuition/imagination/perception	24
using concepts	using signs	28
history	atemporality;	348, 47,
	myths and rites	321

I don't regard this list as either an exhaustive or a satisfactory statement of the difference between the simpler and the more complex societies (to use Bouglé's happier distinction), but it provides a focus for contemporary discussion and hence requires further comment in the light of the present argument. The first two items have little content, unless the hot and cold are taken to refer to the speed of change, and more specifically cumulative changes at a societal level. From whatever vantage point we view this change, the shifts to writing and then to print must be considered of critical importance in both formalising and increasing the flow of information that has been a precondition of many of the features that differentiate the prehistoric societies of the Neolithic and Palaeolithic from the 'modern' civilisations that followed.

What does the rest of the contrast amount to? In the simplest terms, it is a contrast between the domination of abstract science together with history, as against the more concrete forms of knowledge (e.g. of the 'bricoleur' or handyman), combined with the mythical and magical thought and practices of 'primitive' peoples. I take it that the contrast between using concepts and signs corresponds to the abstract/concrete dichotomy.

The notion of a shift of emphasis from magic and myth to science and history has been the commonplace of anthropological discourse since its very beginning. Moreover, there has always been a tendency to interpret these terms as descriptions or indices of modes of thought and action that one could dichotomise by words like primitive and advanced. However, another current of opinion has concentrated upon analysing the technical achievements of simpler societies and calling attention to the mythical or magical elements of our own, though the former tended to be regarded as precursors and the latter as survivals.

The very existence of these two trends, both expressed in the work of Lévi-Strauss, points to the inadequacy of the notion of two different modes of thought, approaches to knowledge, or forms of science, since both are present not only in the same societies but in the same individuals. Moreover the very terms of the analysis, especially magic and myth, are slippery to handle, relics of some earlier folk contrast with religion on the one hand (as in sixteenth-century England) and history on the other (as in fifth-century Athens).

The emergence of what we call history was linked very closely with the advent of writing, as the implicit distinction with prehistory suggests. It was not the presence of documents in themselves, though preservation and storage were essential prerequisites. Lévi-Strauss claims that 'there is no history without dates' (1966:258), but it would be truer to say there is none without archives. However, dates are also dependent upon a graphic system, as he himself intimates, but does not explicate, in his comment on Sartre's view of history and historical continuity. The general code of history consists, he suggests, in 'classes of dates each furnishing an autonomous system of reference. . .It operates by means of a rectangular matrix:

148

where each line represents classes of dates, which may be called hourly, daily, annual, secular, millennial for the purpose of schematisation, and which together make up a continuous set' (1966:260–1). The whole process he describes is a fine example of the kind of formalisation that is encouraged by visuo-spatial communication, and particularly by the setting down of language in written form.

It is not only the existence of archives or the formalisation of information that makes history possible, but the kind of critical attention that one can devote to the original documents and to the comments of others, particularly when one can examine different versions side by side. And finally, there is the combination of recording and reformulating that is involved in written composition itself.

These points are not obscure. But they are often obscured by the formulations of those, historians, philosophers and others, who tend to think of the establishment of discontinuity (by means of folk dichotomies or historical periods) as in themselves a form of explanation. In the end we may do no better than establish such a dichotomy or attribute the differences to the spirit of nation, the culture or the times. In the present case, I think we can. It is not accidental that the sequence of operations that are intrinsic to history, recording, formalising, scanning and reformulating, were also intrinsic to the science of antiquity that developed on the basis of the logographic scripts of the Fertile Crescent.

Why should magic disappear with this development of science? Let us set aside for a moment the very real definitional problems and assume we are dealing with a question of substance. To the extent that magic is to be understood as a set of procedures for changing the world, 'symbolically' or not, to this extent they have to give way to a rival set. To the extent that spells and other attempts to control the course of events are dependent upon the magic of the word, to this

149

extent they tend to give way to the worship of the book. But I would reject the argument that these are 'systems of thought' competing on an equal footing. The magic of the spell is dependent, at least in part, upon the virtual identity of the speaker and spoken. How can one separate a man and his words? How can I imagine myself as destined to speak another language or in another way? Writing puts a distance between a man and his verbal acts. He can now examine what he says in a more objective manner. He can stand aside, comment upon, even correct his own creation – his style as well as his syntax. Hence the attitude to writing differs from that towards oral performance. But it is not so much the immediate change as the long-term one that reduces the sphere of magic. Skorupski concludes his examination of Horton's ideas with the remark: 'Science no doubt contains "traditional" elements of legitimation. . .nevertheless. . .it is a "rational" rather than a "traditional" mode of thought' (1976:204). I argue that it is a 'rational' mode of thought (and again, I set aside the problems connected with Weberian and with folk terminology) because of the availability of certain procedures. Those associated with the use of writing rank first and foremost, since this technique permits a different kind of scrutiny of current knowledge, a more deliberate sorting of *logos* from *doxa*, a more thorough probing into the 'truth'; and it is the same procedures that open the way to the systematic recording and analysis of data that marked the astronomical tables of Babylon and the geometrical theorems of Euclid, as well as to the formalisation of classificatory schemes and to the repetitive exploration of the effects of one action upon another.

When people speak of the development of abstract thought out of the science of the concrete, the shift from signs to concepts, the abandonment of intuition, imagination, perception, these are little more than crude ways of assessing in general terms the kinds of processes involved in the cumulative growth of systematic knowledge, a growth that involves elaborate learning procedures (in addition to imaginative leaps) and which is critically dependent upon the presence of the book.

That the development of science and of systematic knowledge led to a diminution in the cosmocentric aspects of religion and magic (Skorupski 1976) is as clear as in the case of history and myth. It contributes to what can be characterised in more general terms as the process of secularisation, a process that has had many discontinuities but which cannot be reasonably described either in dichotomous terms or in relativistic ones. The shift from the science of the concrete to that of the abstract, in other words the development of concepts and formulations of an increasingly abstract kind (side by side with the

150

more concrete), cannot be understood except in terms of basic changes in the nature of human communication.

In this way we can avoid not only the Grand Dichotomy but also the diffuse relativism that refuses to recognise long-term differences and regards each 'culture' as a thing on its own, a law unto itself. So, on one level, it is. But that is not all there is to say about any set of relations, however clearly defined the boundaries may be. The set exists in the context of a specific constellation of productive relations and of a particular level of technological achievement. The technology, which creates possibilities for, and places limits upon, a wide range of social interaction, changes in the same general direction throughout human history. By 'general', I mean to allow for some backward movement (the decay of the 'useful arts' that W. H. R. Rivers observed in certain areas of Melanesia), as well as for the development of a plurality of differing traditions. Nevertheless, there is direction, especially in the areas of what has been called 'control over nature' and 'the growth of knowledge', and this movement is related to developments in the technology of the intellect, to changes in the means of communication and, specifically, to the introduction of writing.

I am aware that throughout this discussion I too have tended to drop into a dichotomous treatment of utterance versus text, the oral against the written. But, as has been emphasised, the changes are numerous, so too are the relationships centring upon these changes. In many early writing systems, the means of communication are vested in the priests; in others, the secular component is stronger. But one common feature of societies where literacy is confined to a particular group (that is to say, virtually all communities before recent times), is that the content of certain literate texts is communicated by literates to non-literates, though this material is of course transmitted only between the literates themselves. The teacher expounds, the audience responds or memorises, but is not necessarily literate. Indeed, most schooling takes precisely this form, for this is the way one is supposed to teach. So, too, did drama which uses a written play to communicate with what in Elizabethan England was an audience that did not and could not have access to the script, the book of words. Equally, the sermon expounds a written text to a congregation who may themselves be unable to read the Holy Book. In each case we are dealing with a performance by literates before an audience which may be unable to read. And this position is one which some priestly, mandarin or scribal groups may wish to retain, even when developments in the means of communication make such restrictions technically unnecessary and socially unprofitable. Nevertheless, the scribal culture continues;

The domestication of the savage mind

the *literati* hold onto their monopoly; the mandarinate maintains control.

In other cases, specialist literacy may lead to a turning inwards which confines literate communication to the select few and which therefore raises problems about the cultural status of its products, and the relation between the 'two cultures', the oral and the literate. For example the epilogue of the Law Code of Hammurabi (Old Babylonian I) states that it was 'destined to be read to any wronged man so that he could discover his rights'. But the judges were not in fact literate so the code was relegated to the schools (Landsberger, in Kraeling and Adams 1960:98). More surprisingly, it is claimed that the famous Mesopotamian myths, the Creation Epic and Gilgamesh, were 'edited only in schools' (p. 98). Not only did epic material of this kind form a very small part of the total product of writing, but it appeared relatively late on the scene, not as a national epic but apparently formalised in the schoolroom. Indeed Kramer argues that the audience for most literary activity of this period consisted of other scribes rather than the world at large (Kraeling and Adams 1960:110).[3] Parker makes a similar point about some segments of the written material of Egyptian origin, such as hymns; many of the school texts 'inculcated. . .moral principles' while the pupil was learning to write (Kraeling and Adams 1960: 113).

This situation of specialised literacy not only produces its own particular written forms but its oral ones as well. I mean by this that the oral component in societies with writing may be influenced in a whole variety of ways by the presence of this additional register. In developing this point, it is helpful to think of three major types of linguistic situation:

1 where language takes a purely oral form;
2 where language takes both written and oral forms (for all or for a proportion of people);
3 where language takes a written form only, either because the oral one has died out or because it never existed.

These three types roughly correspond to Swadesh's distinction between:

1 local languages;
2 world languages;
3 classical languages.

It is situations of this second kind with which I am mainly concerned, for until the end of the nineteenth century literacy was almost universally confined to the few rather than the many, sometimes for technical, sometimes for religious, and sometimes for class reasons. Under

152

specialist literacy of this kind, the majority pursue their daily life in the oral register, so that a literate and an oral tradition exists side by side. Indeed, in many early societies the use of writing was not simply specialised (i.e. confined to scribes) but was also restricted (i.e. in its range of application).

Perhaps the extreme case of restricted literacy comes from the history of Minoan–Mycenaean writing, which appears to have been used exclusively for administrative purposes; 'of written literature, indeed, not one scrap survives' (Dow 1973:582). The oral transmission and composition of 'literature' must have continued side by side with this early bureaucratic use of writing. But can we assume (as Parry and Lord tend to do) that the contents of oral communication (e.g. the structure of standardised oral forms) did not change as a result? Clearly, much depends upon the extent of literacy, both in terms of the numbers and status of the literate, and the range and extent of their activity. Both were so small in Crete that literacy died out with the sacking of the palaces in about 1200–1100 B.C.E. But the fact that some interaction inevitably takes place between literate and non-literate members of the community, and that the former are often in the socially and culturally dominant positions, suggests the possibility that the oral tradition may itself undergo significant changes even in this half-way stage. I refer not only to the specific content of communication, where it is obvious that the beliefs of the non-literate can be influenced by the advent of religions of the Book or by the performance of a play by Shakespeare. But the classificatory schemes and styles of communication that prevailed under the oral tradition may themselves be affected in important ways. As an example, not to demonstrate certainty but to suggest possibilities, I take a Table, pictured in a painting from Steiermark, Austria, dating from the early eighteenth century and described as 'Beschreibung und Konterfei der Europäischen Nationen' (Table 6). Ten nations are presented in the columns; the rows classify them according to seventeen criteria, behaviour, illness, likes etc. The attribution of specific characteristics to neighbouring peoples is probably universal among human societies. But here this tendency becomes formalised in such a way that each nation *must* be classified according to each of the seventeen features, even though the procedure places an enormous strain on the system and upon its credibility. For each space in the Table *has* to be filled; the scheme allows of no empty boxes; the matrix abhors a vacuum. Indeed, as the looser classification of everyday speech becomes formalised in this way, the Table shifts from being a record of a classificatory system to being a kind of reference book, a ready reckoner of national character,

Table 6   The European Nations

Brief description of types to be found in Europe and their different characteristics	Spanish	French	Belgian	German	English	Swiss	Pole	Hungarian	Muscovite	Turk or Greek
Names	Spanish	French	Belgian	German	English	Swiss	Pole	Hungarian	Muscovite	Turk or Greek
Manners	Haughty	Frivolous	Sly	Open-hearted	Well-mannered	Strong	Peasant	Disloyal	Malicious	Fickle as April weather
Personality	Credulous	Patient and garrulous	Jealous	Passable	Warm-hearted	Cruel	Timid	Inhuman	Quite unlike the Slavs	A young devil
Intellect	Clever and wise	Cautious	Sagacious	Witty	Resistant	Ruthless	Disdainful	Still less	No skill whatsoever	Superficially clever
Physical features	Masculine	Childlike	Reluctant	Superior	Effeminate	Ordinary	Medium build	Sanguine	Infinitely rough	Tender, sensitive look
Skills	In writing	Military affairs	Canon Law	Secular law	Worldly-wise	The free arts	Different languages	Latin	In speaking Greek	Political affairs

Names	Spanish	French	Belgian	German	English	Swiss	Pole	Hungarian	Muscovite	Turk or Greek
Costume	Respectable	Variable	Respectable	Slaves to fashion	Frenchified	Fustian	Long-skirted	Very colourful	Chains	Like women
Faults	Haughty	Deceitful	Randy	Extravagant	Restless	Credulity	Braggart	Treacherous	Windbags	Even greater windbags
Likes	Flattery and praise	Warfare	Gold	Drink	Voluptuous	Expensive food	The aristocracy	Causing a disturbance	Little figs	Self-love
Diseases	Constipation	Peculiar to themselves	The plague	Bodagra	Consumption	Colic	Rupture	Influenza	Asthma	Anaemia
Their country	Fertile	Well-cultivated	Pleasant	Good	Fertile	Mountainous	Wooded	Fertile and rich in minerals	Full of ice	Pleasant
War virtues	Courageous	Machiavellian	Cautious	Invincible	Heroes at sea	Passionate commitment	Uncertain	Like pirates	Well-organised	Lazy
Worship	The best of everything	Goodness	A little better	Still more pious	Fickle as the moon	Busy beehives	Believe all manner of things	Activity	Apostate	The same
Their master	A monarch	A king	A patriarch	A kaiser	Now one, now the other	Freehold	Somebody elected	The unlovable	Volunteer	A tyrant
Excesses of	Fruits	Merchandise	Wine	Grain	Self-effacement	Ore pits	Defence-works	In all things	Cinnamon	Soft and gentle things
Pastimes	Games	Intrigue	Chatting	Drinking	Work	Eating	Brawling	Laziness	Sleeping	Being ill
Animal-comparison	An elephant	A fox	A lynx	A lion	A horse	An ox	A bear	A wolf	A donkey	A cat
Life ends	In a boat	In battle	In a monastery	In wine	In water	On the ground	In a manger	By a sword	In the snow	In fraud

a producer rather than just a product, comparable to the sorts of tables used by astrologers and other specialists to inform the 'man in the street' about the nature of the universe in which he finds himself. But, as the reference to 'reckoners' suggests, the influence of the book is not confined to literate contexts alone. For example, the format of a table may itself be internalised as part of visual memory, which is in many ways more 'literal', more precise, than oral memory, being dominated by the reconstitution of a total image rather than a set of less articulated sounds; a tabular layout may structure verbal memory, influence classification and recall, as well as encourage certain cognitive procedures, such as the abhorrence of the empty box, that are in some respects foreign to the purely oral situation. Once such essentially graphic devices as the alphabet or the mathematical table have been learned, they can be used to organise information of a wide variety and great quantity without the use of pen and paper.

The influence of writing on form and content is yet more clear-cut in the field of literature. The ways in which this use of language is dominated by the idea and reality of visual inspection would hardly require comment, were it not so often neglected. Recall T. S. Eliot's description of 'the intolerable wrestle with words and meanings' in *The Four Quartets.*

> So here I am, in the middle way, having had twenty years –
> Twenty years largely wasted, the years of *l'entre deux guerres* –
> Trying to learn to use words, and every attempt
> Is a wholly new start, and a different kind of failure
> Because one has only learnt to get the better of words
> For the thing one no longer has to say, or the way in which
> One is no longer disposed to say it. And so each venture
> Is a new beginning, a raid on the inarticulate
> With shabby equipment always deteriorating
> In the general mess of imprecision of feeling,
> Undisciplined squads of emotion. And what there is to conquer
> By strength and submission, has already been discovered
> Once or twice, or several times, by men whom one cannot hope
> To emulate – but there is no competition –
> There is only the fight to recover what has been lost
> And found and lost again and again: and now, under conditions
> That seem unpropitious. But perhaps neither gain nor loss.
> For us, there is only the trying. The rest is not our business.

If I characterise the kind of struggle in which Eliot was engaged as specific to the written register, I stand in danger of being misunderstood, to be thought to maintain that oral verse is by contrast automatic, collective, 'traditional'. This is not at all what I mean. But the intolerable wrestle takes on a different hue when words are laid out clinically on the page before me, capable of being struck out, re-ordered, substituted, pored over, reflected upon. And as has been suggested once the reflection has taken place, in the context of writing, it obtains a hold over oral composition itself. Look at the formalisation of metre, the complexities of rhyme and the development of strophic form that mark written poetry. It can be readily understood that the sonnet form is the product of writing; but, once produced, it can then be composed orally, without the intervention of eye or hand.

The increased formalisation of literary genres is typical of the written mode, partly because of the addition of a visuo-spatial element and partly because of the new capacity to reorganise verbal material in different ways. An extreme case of the influence of the visuo-spatial element is Herbert's poem on *Easter-wings* where the typography mirrors the iconography of a wing:

Easter-wings.

Lord, who createdst man in wealth and store,
Though foolishly he lost the same,
Decaying more and more,
Till he became
Most poore:
With thee
O let me rise
As larks, harmoniously,
And sing this day thy victories:
Then shall the fall further the flight in me.

My tender age in sorrow did beginne:
And still with sicknesses and shame
Thou didst so punish sinne
That I became
Most thinne.
With thee
Let me combine
And feel this day thy victorie:
For, if I imp my wing on thine,
Affliction shall advance the flight in me.

But in a different way it is reflected in the whole tradition of Islamic calligraphy, where the scribe can take no liberties with the verbal content of the Koran but is encouraged to elaborate complex patterns for the eye.

But it is not simply a question of typographic tricks or styles of calligraphy, but of the manipulation of the visuo-spatial context as a whole. An obvious case is the kind of anagrammatic reference favoured by the metaphysical poets; Herbert's anagram on the Virgin ('How well her name an *Army* doth present'), like Richard Crashawe's playing with his own name ('Was Car then Crashawe; or Was Crashawe Car, Since both within one name combined are?'), are (unlike the pun) impossible in speech. Neither of these specific examples has much to recommend it. But the kind of scrutiny they represent is intrinsic to the scholarly activity as a whole, to all it has had to offer both to the growth of knowledge and to tabulated nonsense.

Once again the scrutiny may give rise to changes in 'standardised oral forms', in the structure and diction of songs or epics. Utterances differ in their degrees of formalisation, and we do not doubt that features such as the 'formula' (Lord 1960) or semantic parallelism (Fox 1971) are features of orally composed verse.[4]

> Hear, O ye kings;
> give ear, O ye princes;
> I, even I, will sing unto the Lord;
> I will sing praise to the Lord God of Israel.
> Lord, when thou wentest out of Seir,
> when thou marchedst out of the field of Edom,
> the earth trembled, and the heavens dropped,
> the clouds also dropped water.
>
> (Judges 5:3–4)

The effect comes of course not from repeating a formula so much as from ringing the changes, the balance between repetition and innovation. But features such as these are not necessarily abandoned with the introduction of writing;[5] formality may be yet further formalised, and it would be a mistake to consider the verse which we find in early written cultures as necessarily displaying an oral residue rather than a literary elaboration. Following a formula is not confined to the oral register; the lists that appear in Homer are not necessarily evidence of oral composition any more than Pythagorean or Aristotelian tables. Deductions about the nature of the oral tradition that derive from written sources require the closest scrutiny. Most transcription transforms, often in complex ways; one can never be quite sure what utterance the 'text' represents.

The Grand Dichotomy reconsidered

Of course there are considerable differences between short, rhythmic songs and longer works, but it could be argued that the highly formal qualities of some verse found in the early written record derive not so much from the oral tradition per se but represent a heightening, an extension, of certain features under the pressure of a writing system that encourages the development of forms of patterning that possess a visuo-spatial component. The most favourable situation for this development would appear to be one where a literate speaker was communicating to a non-literate audience, but the very existence of metrical and semantic components developed by literates may influence the oral composer as well. To take a parallel example, oratory may get formalised into rhetoric by the intervention of writing.

The particular issues of the formula and of semantic parallelism are the marginal cases and are not intrinsic to my discussion. More central is the position of the table and the list. The latter is connected in a direct and intimate way with cognitive processes. For the making of the kind of lists, actual or figurative, that I have called shopping lists is part of the more general process of planning human action. Indeed in their book on *Plans and the Structure of Behavior* Miller, Gallanter and Pibram note that 'planning can be thought of as constructing a list of tests to perform' (1960:38), where the test is part of the pre- and post-operational phase of activity and the list is a way of representing the 'hierarchical organization of behavior' (1960:15). It is not so much the making of plans, the use of symbolic thought, as the externalising and communication of those plans, transactions in symbolism, that are the marks of man. And it is precisely this kind of activity that is promoted, encouraged, transformed and transfigured by writing, as a moment's observation of the list-making activities of one's close kin or associates will confirm. It represents one aspect of the process of decontextualisation (or better 'recontextualisation') that is intrinsic to writing, not merely as an external activity but as an internal one as well. To put the matter in another way, writing enables you to talk freely about your thoughts. Of course all speech is programmed by the brain and therefore subject to monitoring by the inner ear; most of what we call thought is silent speech. But only a small proportion of what we reflect upon actually turns up as an interpersonal communicative act, i.e. A to B re X, even though the intrapersonal communications (reflections) may be of great potential importance.

There are several reasons why these reflections do not make it into the aural arena. Perhaps there was no auditor at the particular moment, and the fleeting thought is difficult to store for a future occasion. Or

159

they were censored, in the manner postulated by Freud, by some internal device; or the auditor may be in a position of authority, or hostile, bored, or simply interested, as most of us are, in our own concerns and therefore willing to engage in a give-and-take on common ground, but resistant to the idea of listening to a monologue, to the unrelenting exposition of another's thoughts, except under certain social conditions, the court case, the funeral speech, the marriage address, the prayer to God.

But writing gives us the opportunity for just such a monologue that oral intercourse so often prevents. It enables an individual to 'express' his thoughts at length, without interruption, with corrections and deletions, and according to some appropriate formula. Of course what is required for this purpose is not simply a mode of writing, but a cursive script and the kind of instruments that permit rapid recording. For the purpose of recording internal or external discourse, thoughts or speech, pen and paper are clearly better than stylus and clay, just as shorthand is more efficient than longhand, the electric than the manual typewriter. But once the initial recording has taken place, then revision relies upon visual inspection and subsequent reformulation.

To conclude this conclusion, it does not require much reflection upon the contents of a book to realise the transformation in communication that writing has made, not simply in a mechanical sense, but in a cognitive one, what we can do with our minds and what our minds can do with us. I have tried to look at some of the ways various writers have talked about 'other cultures' in contrast to our own to see whether it is possible to give more precision, more meaningfulness, to the supposed differences by attempting to assess the contribution of changes in the means of communication. By discussing mechanisms as well as differences, I have tried to map out an approach to the problem of cognitive processes, the 'nature of human thought', *l'esprit humain* (to use the formulae of Chomsky and Lévi-Strauss respectively), which attempts to take account of the effects of differences in the mode of communication between and within human beings. I want particularly to stress the relevance of this internal aspect since the role of the inner ear and the contribution of writing in clarifying one's own thoughts are rarely given much recognition by those who see the elements in communication as a matter of the external relations between human beings (or social persons); the outstanding case, not always the limiting one, is the audience of one, myself, for even at this level the 'social setting' is all-important, an essential prerequisite of the kind of cognitive process we are familiar with. As Durkheim pointed out, the social factor is internalised. But internalisation is not a matter of imprinting on a *tabula rasa*, a wax impression; it is part of an internal dialogue, of which 'the nature of the human mind' (the initial structure in Chomsky's Descartian usage, the programmed, developmental structure in the Piagettian sense) and the continued reaction with what is outside (the environment in the sense of books as well as deserts), all play their part.

Some may find this too eclectic a way of approaching the development of human thought, one that gives some comfort to the rationalist as well as the empiricist, to *intro*spection as well as to *in*spection. However, the polemic that is generated by treating theory as a matter of binary opposition does not always provide the best atmosphere for intellectual advance; unsatisfactory solutions are often provoked by unsatisfactory formulations, and Chomsky's reversion to a seventeenth-century dichotomy is hardly adequate except as a weapon to attack the more extreme statements of behaviourist views (and to show that radicalism is not the sole preserve of the latter). Moreover, this approach tends to define the 'nature of human thought' at the species level, at the level of the universal elements of language, especially universal grammar, grammatical structure, since the deep structure of meaning is related to the surface structure of the sound by grammatical transfiguration (1968:25).[6]

I am not suggesting that one can ignore this level. But problems of human thought cannot be treated in terms of universals alone. Not only anthropologists have called attention to differences in cognitive styles in various cultures; the specification of difference is a commonplace and common-sense reaction to the clash of cultures. Some linguists have tended to explain cognitive differences at the level of differences between specific languages and one recalls the exciting attempt of Benjamin Lee Whorf to specify the implications of different languages for cognitive patterns and social systems. In Western industrialised societies, Standard Average European was accredited with the presence of formalised texts, with record keeping, with lists and with formulae. This interesting argument does try to face up to the problem of difference. But it fails, in a strikingly obvious way, to recognise the influence of external social factors upon language. All these features are connected with European languages only because they are *written*. The desire to relate these characteristics to linguistic variables, narrowly defined, is an example of the frequent domination of intellectual effort by the formal boundaries of academic territories. Nevertheless it is curious that so few men of learning should have paid any attention to the conditions of the reproduction of their own forms of knowledge and its influence on human thought. Vygotsky spoke of the historical conditions for the determination of man's consciousness and intellect. While we may wish to modify the notion of determination, the role of changes in the means and mode of communication (of which language is just one element, though the most important) have to be investigated over time, in developmental terms that are historical as well as sociological and psycho-biological, that take account of written text as well as of oral utterance. For writing is no mere phonograph recording of speech, as Bloomfield (and others) have assumed; depending on social as well as technological conditions, it encourages special forms of linguistic activity associated with developments in particular kinds of problem-raising and problem-solving, in which the list, the formula and the table played a seminal part. If we wish to speak of the 'savage mind', these were some of the instruments of its domestication.

6 szér, ... Frankness.
6 smunda, ... Dreams.
Ox Eye, ... Patience,
Palm, ... Victory.
Pansy, ... Thoughts.
Parsley, ... Festivity.
Pasque Flower, ... You have no claims.
Patience Dock, ... Patience.
Passion Flower, ... Religious superstition.

(There is a language, 'little known',
Lovers claim it as their own.
Its symbols smile upon the land,
Wrought by Nature's wondrous hand.
    The Language of Flowers)

Notes to the text

1. EVOLUTION AND COMMUNICATION, pp. 1–18

1 When Talcott Parsons undertook a comparison of social systems, he was directly confronted with the problem of dealing with 'social evolution' (1966:v).

2 'It is universally the case that...the child's *use* of language is caegorical' (Bruner 1966:32).

3 By language here I mean a specific constellation of attributes of aural systems of communication (see Hockett 1960).

4 The kind of visual estimating of items of six and below has been called 'subitizing' and has been related to the structural limits of the human brain (Kaufman *et al* 1949; see also Miller 1956).

2. INTELLECTUALS IN PRE-LITERATE SOCIETIES?, pp. 19–35

1 I am indebted to Thomas Hodgkin for drawing my attention to this book. His article 'Scholars and the revolutionary tradition: Vietnam and West Africa' (*Oxford Review of Education*, 1976 (2): 111–128) is a valuable contribution to the discussion.

2 M. Granet, *La Pensée Chinoise*, Paris (1934).

3 See Merton (1957 [1941]:490) for some further references to the influence of Durkheim. To this list one should add Doutté's useful work on North Africa (1909).

4 See for example D. Tait's account of the market cycle of the Konkomba of Northern Ghana (1961).

5 The problem of infinite variants is recognised by Lévi-Strauss (1970:7), but is set aside by means of the analogy with language. As a linguist works with a selection of total speech, so too mythologists can derive the structure (= syntax) from any myth, or set of myths. Clearly, if we are interested in the cognitive content of myths, we are looking at semantics rather than syntax, which involves very different considerations. But in any case, the linguistic analogy falls down, since language is the instrument of the poetic or narrative communication we loosely refer to as myth, not the end result. Clearly it does matter to Lévi-Strauss which particular version of a myth he uses as a point of departure for his analysis, as he shows in his discussion of the 'key-myth' (a concept which in itself indicates the limitations of the linguistic analogy).

3. LITERACY, CRITICISM AND THE GROWTH OF KNOWLEDGE, pp. 36–51

1 See, specifically, J. Goody and I. P. Watt, 'The consequences of literacy', *Comparative Studies in Society and History* (1963:304–345).

2 I am indebted to E. A. Havelock, *Preface to Plato*, Cambridge, Mass., 1963, and to David Olsen, 'The bias of language in speech and writing', in H. Fisher and R. Diez-Gurerro (eds.), *Language and Logic in Personality and Society*, New York, 1976.

3 I am much indebted to discussions with D. Gjertsen, Department of Philosophy, University of Ghana.

4 Joseph Needham's view of primitive thought owes much to Lévy-Bruhl, a fact that influences his interpretation of the Chinese achievement: 'The selection of "causes" at random from this undifferentiated magma of phenomena was called by Lévy-Bruhl the "law of participation" in that the whole of the environment experienced by the primitive mind is laid under contribution, i.e. participates, in its explanations, without regard either for true causal connection or for the principle of contradiction' (J. Needham 1956:284).

5 I do not myself see how the suggestions that Watt and I put forward concerning the consequences of literacy can be considered a 'great-divide theory', since we treat 'literacy' as a variable. Moreover, it is clearly only one of many changes in the *mode of* communication which might influence the *content* of communication. Since I am referring to Ruth Finnegan's article in the volume on *Modes of Thought* (1973) that she edited with Robin Horton, I should add that Horton's article takes a somewhat different position than the one I have commented upon here.

6 See my 'Religion, social change and the sociology of conversion' in *Changing Social Structure in Ghana* (London, 1975).

7 For a more recent discussion see S. J. Tambiah (1968) and T. Todorov (1973).

4. LITERACY AND CLASSIFICATION: ON TURNING THE TABLES, pp. 52–73

1 In some societies, such as those of aboriginal Australia, such schema may be much closer to the actor's conceptualisation. Usually a more limited schema and a more flexible format for portraying the relationships between the social group and its environment are more appropriate (e.g. Field, 1948). We are dealing with variables not with constants, and the critical question is the problem of evidence.

2 Author's translation.

3 On the influence of the printing press, see Eisenstein (1968).

4 On the restricted significance of binary classification, see Cherry (1966: 36).

5 The article by Beattie makes a number of the points I have discussed here, though not in the specific context of the distinction between oral and written modes of communication. For a reply to a reply, see Needham (1973), and for yet further discussions, see Beattie (1976) and Needham (1976).

6 Lloyd notes that 'several commentators have suggested that in certain ancient Near Eastern societies. . .not only was Nature understood in terms of Society, but there was simply no conscious distinction drawn between the realm of Nature on the one hand and the realm of Society on the other' (1966:211). On the manifest level at least, such statements call into question the interpretation of, for example, Greimas and Rastier: 'It is accepted, in accordance with the description of Claude Lévi-Strauss, that human societies divide their semantic universes into two dimensions, Culture and Nature, the first defined by the contents they assume and with which they invest themselves, the second by those

which they reject', e.g. culture (permissible sexual relations) versus nature (unacceptable relations) (1968:93).

7 Lloyd makes much the same points in considering the prevalence of theories based upon opposites among early Greek writers (1966:80).

8 See William Empson, *Seven Types of Ambiguity* (1930) and much else besides.

9 Of the Bambara, Griaule writes:

'There too Water and the Word were the foundations of spiritual and religious life. There too coherent myths provided a key to institutions and customs; and there were many indications that, beneath the various ritual forms and patterns of behaviour characteristic of the African peoples of these regions, lay hidden the main features of one religion and one conception of the organisation of the world and the nature of man' (1965:217–218).

5. WHAT'S IN A LIST?, pp. 74–111

1 See also Speiser and Albright in *City Invincible* (eds. Kraeling and Adams), 1960.

2 This is a point I would like to follow up in a different context. But a reading of Dewdney, *The Sacred Scrolls of the Southern Ojibway* (Toronto, 1975) suggests to me that some of the characteristics of the mythology and classificatory schema of the Americas may be related to the more elaborate iconography found there; my implicit contrast is with Africa.

3 '(Writing) exists for the sole purpose of representing (language). . .the spoken forms alone constitute the object' (de Saussure 1960:23–24).

4 Writing not of Ugarit but of the Phoenicians, the Jewish historian Josephus noted in the first century A.D. that they 'made the largest use of writing, both for the ordinary affairs of life and for the commemoration of public events' (*Against Apion*, II, 6). For a recent survey of the precursors of the Greek and Roman historians, see M. Grant, *The Ancient Historians*, London, 1970, to whom I owe this reference, and *The Idea of History in the Ancient Near East*, ed. R. C. Dentan, New Haven, Conn., 1966.

5 For schedules from Nimrud in the eighth century B.C.E., see J. V. Kinnier Wilson, *The Nimrud Wine Lists*, British School of Archaeology in Iraq, 1972.

6 This was the consonantal alphabet. I qualify the term 'alphabetic' because of the absence of vowel signs, an absence that leads Gelb to insist upon their syllabic character. Whatever word is used, the system was simpler than earlier scripts.

7 W. von Soden (1936), but according to Landsberger (MLS IX:124) only 'elaborated by W. von Soden'.

8 See also A. Falkenstein, *Archäische Texte aus Uruk*, 1936, where he recognises the importance of lists and the fact that they were among 'the earliest remains of writing'.

9 B. Landsberger (ed.) (MSL III:1955).

10 'The structure of Proto-Izi constantly vacillates between the thematic repertoire of words and a list organized according to the initial signs. The compilation of Proto-Izi, with the various associations of words formed by semantic links, similarities in spelling, and even morphological shape, but without a detectable organization plan, constitutes a most interesting tendency (even if doomed to failure) in the history of lexicography' (MSL XIII:7).

11 Here the problem arises from the reduction of two-dimensional space to linear lists; other representations do not have altogether the same limitations.

6. FOLLOWING A FORMULA, pp. 112–128

1 For a discussion of the oral-formulaic theory in relation to Old English verse, see Shippey, 1972. He too points out that formulaic repetitions are used in many examples of early written verse (1972:96) and therefore accepts the idea of a 'transitional text'.

2 The phrase *Nmin ti* stands for the whole invocation in the same way that Our Father (Paternoster) stands for the whole prayer, and the Jewish 'Shima' (Hear) is understood straight away as 'Hear O Israel, the Lord our God is one God, etc.' One important liturgical form consists of a leader uttering the first word (e.g. 'Credo') and the congregation repeating the word and continuing with the rest in unison. I owe this observation to Michael Black.

3 See Vacheck 1973; Greenfield 1972.

4 This chapter would have gained from a reading of Ruth Finnegan's *Oral Poetry* (Cambridge, 1977) and Geoffrey Kirk's *Homer and the Oral Tradition* (Cambridge, 1976) which were not available at the time of writing.

7. THE RECIPE, THE PRESCRIPTION AND THE EXPERIMENT, pp. 129–145

1 'Parfois, cependant, une rédaction plus précise indique l'élaboration que celles-ci doivent subir, ou bien le produit résultant de cette élaboration, ou encore, peut-être, l'article auquel elles doivent être associées ou mélangées pour obtenir un mets déterminé' (Birot 1964:2).

2 See my forthcoming piece on 'The Sociology of Cooking'.

3 See Esther Goody's Malinowski Lecture for 1975 (1977).

4 These substances which, as *materia medica*, are internalised for curing, may be forbidden as foods, e.g. the flesh of the pig in Ancient Egypt.

8. THE GRAND DICHOTOMY RECONSIDERED, pp. 146–162

1 In his book, *Culture and Practical Reason*, Marshall Sahlins accepts the argument for two societies, two theories, only to dismiss it at a later stage. However, he retains for analytic purpose the gross distinction, the 'crude' comparison between 'bourgeois' and 'tribal' societies that characterises so many studies of a structural kind, and his analysis is certainly committed to a binary stance.

2 The philosophical ground has recently been surveyed by Skorupski (1976), whose contribution is particularly useful on some of the issues raised by Horton (with whom he worked). My third chapter would certainly gain from a consideration of a number of his points. Critical of the implications of Horton's dichotomous treatment, he nevertheless cannot pursue the analysis outside the boundaries provided by his analytic procedures and by the limited range of the ethnographic evidence used in these encounters (especially Evans-Pritchard's study of the Azande of the Sudan). He does not therefore consider the mechanisms of change or differentiation but only problems of a definitional and 'logical' order.

3 This statement does not command universal acceptance; Speiser thinks of Gilgamesh as a national epic, Landsberger as a school text. While the two points

of view are not altogether exclusive, the second view would certainly modify the status of Gilgamesh as myth.

4 LoDagaa funeral chants are full of semantic parallelism which is very much part of the rhythmic structure and has little or nothing to do with other forms of binarism.

5 'Les textes poétiques se caractérisent par l'établissement, codifié ou non, de rapports d'équivalence entre différents points de la séquence du discours, rapports qui sont définis aux niveaux de représentation "superficiels" de la séquence' (Ruwet 1975:316).

6 While this is one interpretation to be assigned to Chomsky's general statement, it is only one.

References

Albright, W. F. (1968), *Yahweh and the Gods of Canaan*. London.
Anderson, P. (1974), *Passages from Antiquity to Feudalism*. London.
Beattie, J. H. M. (1968), 'Aspects of Nyoro symbolism', *Africa*, 38:413–442.
  (1970), 'On understanding ritual', in B. R. Wilson, ed., *Rationality*. Oxford.
  (1976), 'Right, left and the Banyoro', *Africa*, 46:217–235.
Beidelman, T. O. (1961), 'Hyena and rabbit: a Kaguru representation of matri-lineal relations', *Africa*, 31:61–74.
Bendix, R. (1960), *Max Weber: An Intellectual Portrait*. New York.
Benn, S. I. (1967), 'Equality, moral and social', *The Encyclopedia of Philosophy*. New York.
Berlin, B., and Kay, P. (1969), *Basic Color Terms: their Universality and Evolution*. Berkeley, California.
Birot, M. (1960), *Textes administratifs de la salle 5 du palais* (Archives royales de Mari IX). Paris.
  (1964), *Textes administratifs de la salle 5 du palais* (2e partie) (Archives royales de Mari XII). Paris.
Bloch, M. ed. (1975), *Political Language and Oratory in Traditional Society*, London.
Bloomfield, L. (1933), *Language*. New York.
Bottéro, J. (1956), *Textes administratifs de la salle 110* (Archives royales de Mari VII). Paris.
  (1958), 'Lettres de la salle 110 du palais de Mari', *Revue d'assyriologie et d'archéologie orientale*, 52:163–176.
Braimah, J. A. and Goody, J. (1967), *Salaga: the Struggle for Power*. London.
Breasted, J. H. (1930), *The Edwin Smith Surgical Papyrus*, 2 vols. Chicago.
Bruner, J. S. *et al.* (1966), *Studies in Cognitive Growth*. New York.
Bunzel, R. (1932), 'Zuñi Origin Myths', *Forty-seventh Annual Report of the Bureau of American Ethnology*. Washington.
Cassirer, E. (1944), *An Essay on Man*. New Haven, Conn.
Chadwick, H. M. and N. K. (1932), *The Growth of Literature*. Vol. I. Cambridge.
  (1936), *The Growth of Literature*. Vol. II. Cambridge.
Cherry, C. (1966), *On Human Communication*. 2nd edn. Cambridge, Mass.
Chiera, E. (1929), *Sumerian Lexical Texts from the Temple School of Nippur*. Chicago.
Chomsky, N. (1968), *Language and Mind*. New York.
Cole, M. and Scribner, S. (1974), *Culture and Thought*. New York.
Cooley, E. H. (1909), *Social Organisation*. New York.
Cox, M. R. (1893), *Cinderella, 345 Variants* (Folklore Society Monograph No. 31). London.

References

Culpeper, N. (n.d.), *The British Herbal and Family Physician* (1st edn. 1649 London).

Dentan, R. C. ed., (1966), *The Idea of History in the Ancient Near East*. New Haven, Conn.

de Saussure, F. (1960), *Course in General Linguistics*. London (1st French edn. 1916).

Dewdney, S. (1975), *The Sacred Scrolls of the Southern Ojibway*. Toronto.

Dieterlen, G. (1952), 'Classification des végétaux chez les Dogon, *Journal de la Société des Africanistes*, 22:115–158.

Douglas, M. (1966), *Purity and Danger*. London.

Doutté, E. (1909), *Magie et religion dans l'Afrique du Nord*. Algiers.

Dow, S. (1973), 'The linear scripts and the tablets as historical documents (a) Literacy in Minoan and Mycenaean lands', in I. E. S. Edwards, C. J. Gadd, N. G. L. Hammond and E. Sollberger, eds., *The Cambridge Ancient History*, Vol. 2, Part I, *History of the Middle East and the Aegean Region c. 1800–1380 B.C.* Cambridge.

Durkheim, E. (1915), *The Elementary Forms of the Religious Life*. Glencoe, Illinois (1st French edn. 1912).

(1933), *The Division of Labour in Society*. New York (1st French edn. 1893).

Durkheim, E. and Mauss, M. (1903), *Primitive Classification*. Transl. and ed. by R. Needham, London, 1963.

Eisenstein, E. L. (1968), 'Some conjectures about the impact of printing on Western society and thought: a preliminary report', *Journal of Modern History*, 40:9–56.

Empson, W. (1930), *Seven Types of Ambiguity*. London.

Evans-Pritchard, E. E. (1934), 'Lévy-Bruhl's theory of primitive mentality', *Bulletin of the Faculty of Arts* (Cairo), 2:1–36.

(1937), *Witchcraft, Oracles and Magic among the Azande*. Oxford.

(1940), *The Nuer*. Oxford.

Falkenstein, A. (1936), *Archäische Texte aus Uruk*. Leipzig.

Field, M. J. (1948), *Akim-Kotoku: an Oman of the Gold Coast*. London.

Finnegan, R. (1970), *Oral Literature in Africa*. Oxford.

Forbes, R. J. (1954), 'Chemical, culinary and cosmetic arts', in C. Singer *et al.*, eds., *A History of Technology*, Vol. I, *From Early Times to Fall of Ancient Empires*. Oxford.

Fox, J. J. (1971), 'Semantic parallelism in Rotinese ritual language', *Bijdragen tot de taal-, land- en volkenkunde*, 127:215–251.

Frazer, J. (1890), *The Golden Bough*. London.

Gardiner, A. H. (1947), *Ancient Egyptian Onomastica*. London.

Gay, J. and Cole, M. (1967), *New Mathematics in an Old Culture*. New York.

Gelb, I. J. (1963), *A Study of Writing*. 2nd edn. Chicago.

Goody, E. N. (1977), 'Towards a theory of questions' (Malinowski lecture, 1975), in E. N. Goody, ed. *Questions and Politeness: Strategies in Social Interaction*. Cambridge.

Goody, J. (1959), 'Ethnohistory and the Akan of Ghana', *Africa*, 29:67–81.

(1962), *Death, Property and the Ancestors*. Stanford.

(1968a), ed., *Literacy in Traditional Societies*. Cambridge.

(1968b), 'The myth of a state', *J. Mod. African Studies*, 6:461–473.

(1968c), 'Time: social organisation', in *International Encycl. Soc. Sciences*, 16:30–42. New York.

(1969), *Comparative Studies in Kinship*. London.

169

The domestication of the savage mind

(1972a), *The Myth of the Bagre*. Oxford.

(1972b), 'Literacy and the non-literate', *Times Literary Supplement*, 12 May 1972. (Reprinted in R. Disch, ed., *The Future of Literacy*. Englewood Cliffs, New Jersey, 1973).

(1975), 'Religion, social change and the sociology of conversion', in J. Goody, ed., *Changing Social Structure in Ghana*. London.

(1976a), 'Civilisation de l'écriture et classification, ou l'art de jouer sur les tableaux', *Actes de la Recherche en Sciences Sociales*, 87–101.

(1976b), 'Literacy and classification: on turning the tables', in R. K. Jain, ed., *Text and Context*. Philadelphia.

(1977), 'Mémoire et apprentissage dans les sociétés avec et sans écriture: la transmission du Bagre', *L'Homme*, 17:forthcoming.

Goody, J., Cole, M. and Scribner, S. (1977), 'Writing and formal operations: a case study among the Vai', *Africa*, forthcoming.

Goody, J. and Watt, I. P. (1963), 'The consequences of literacy', *Comparative Studies in History and Society*, 5:304–345.

Goody, J. and Wilks, I. (1968), 'Writing in Gonja', in J. Goody, ed., *Literacy in Traditional Societies*. Cambridge.

Gordon, C. H. (1965), *Ugaritic Textbook* (Analecta Orientalia, 38). Rome.

Gordon, E. I. (1959), *Sumerian Proverbs: Glimpses of Everyday Life in Ancient Mesopotamia*. Philadelphia.

Granet, M. (1934), *La Pensée chinoise*. Paris.

Grant, M. (1970), *The Ancient Historians*. London.

(1973), *Roman Myths*. London.

Greenfield, P. M. (1972), 'Oral or written language: the consequences for cognitive development in Africa, the United States and England', *Language and Speech*, 15:169–177.

Greimas, J. and Rastier, E. (1968), 'The interaction of semiotic constraints', *Game, Play, Literature*. Yale French Studies, No. 41.

Griaule, M. (1948), *Conversations with Ogotemmêli*. English transl., London, 1965.

Hammel, E. A. (1972), *The Myth of Structural Analysis: Lévi-Strauss and the Three Bears* (Addison-Wesley modules in Anthropology, No. 2). Reading, Mass.

Havelock, E. A. (1963), *Preface to Plato*. Cambridge, Mass.

(1973), *Prologue to Greek Literacy*. Cincinnati.

Hirst, P. Q. (1975), 'The uniqueness of the West', *Economy and Society*, 4:446–475.

Hockett, C. (1960), 'The Origin of Speech', *Scientific American*, 203:88–96.

Hodgkin, T. (1976), 'Scholars and the revolutionary tradition: Vietnam and West Africa', *Oxford Review of Education*, 2:111–128.

Horton, R. (1967), 'African traditional thought and Western science', *Africa*, 37:50–71, 155–187.

Horton, R. and Finnegan, R. eds., (1973), *Modes of Thought*. London.

Hussey, M. (1967), *Chaucer's World: A Pictorial Companion*. Cambridge.

Jakobson, T. (1939), *The Sumerian King-List*. Chicago.

Kaufman, E. L., Lord, M. W., Reese, T. W., and Volkmann, J. (1949), 'The discriminations of visual number', *Am. J. Psych*, 62:498–525.

Kay, P. (1971), 'Language, evolution and speech style'. Draft paper.

Kinnier Wilson, J. V. (1972), *The Nimrud Wine Lists*. British School of Archaeology in Iraq.

Kirk, G. S. (1962), *The Songs of Homer*. Cambridge.

(1970), *Myth: its meaning and functions in ancient and other cultures*. Cambridge.

170

References

Kraeling, C. H. and Adams, R. M. eds., (1960), *City Invincible*. Chicago.

Kramer, S. N. (1956), *From the Tablets of Sumer*. Indian Hills, Colorado.

Kuhn, T. (1962), *The Structure of Scientific Revolutions*. Chicago.

    (1970), 'Logic of discovery or psychology of research?', in I. Lakatos and A. Musgrave, eds., *Criticism and the Growth of Knowledge*. Cambridge.

Lakatos, I. and Musgrave, A. eds., (1970), *Criticism and the Growth of Knowledge*. Cambridge.

Landsberger, B., ed., (1955), (MSL III) *Materialen zum Sumerischen Lexicon* III. Rome.

    (1967), (MSL IX) *Materialen zum Sumerischen Lexicon* IX. Rome.

    (1969), (MLS XII) *Materials for the Sumerian Lexicon* XII. Rome.

    (1971), (MSL XIII) *Materials for the Sumerian Lexicon* XIII. Rome.

Lehrer, A. (1969), 'Semantic cuisine'. *Journal of Linguistics*, 5:39–55.

Lévi-Strauss, C. (1956), 'Les organisations dualistes, existent-elles?', *Bijdragen*, 112:99–128.

    (1960), 'On manipulated sociological models', *Bijdragen*, 116:45–54.

    (1962), *La Pensée sauvage*. Paris. (Engl. transl. London, 1966.)

    (1968), 'The concept of primitiveness', in R. B. Lee and I. De Vore, eds., *Man the Hunter*. Chicago.

    (1970), *The Raw and the Cooked. Introduction to a Science of Mythology*, London. (1st French edn. 1964.)

    (1973), *From Honey to Ashes*. London. (1st French edn. 1966.)

Lévy-Bruhl, L. (1910), *Les Fonctions mentales dans les sociétés inférieures*. Paris. (Engl. transl. by L. A. Clare, *How Natives Think*. London, 1926.)

Lloyd, G. E. R. (1966), *Polarity and Analogy*. Cambridge.

Lord, A. B. (1960), *The Singer of Tales*. Cambridge, Mass.

    (1967), 'The influence of a fixed text', in *To Honor Roman Jakobson*, vol. II, *Janua Linguarum*, series major 32. Paris and The Hague.

Lyons, J. (1963), *Structural Semantics* (Publications of the Philosophical Society, 20). Oxford.

    (1968), *Introduction to Theoretical Linguistics*. Cambridge.

Maranda, P. and E. K. (1971), *Structural Models in Folklore and Transformational Essays*. The Hague.

Maranda, P. and E. K. eds. (1971), *Structural Analysis of Oral Tradition*. Philadelphia.

Maspero, G. (1888), *Un Manuel de hiérarchie égyptienne*. Paris.

Masterman, M. (1970), 'The nature of a paradigm', in I. Lakatos and A. Musgrave, eds., *Criticism and the Growth of Knowledge*. Cambridge.

Maybury-Lewis, D. (1960), 'The analysis of dual organizations', *Bijdragen*, 116:17–44.

Merton, R. K. (1941), 'Karl Mannheim and the sociology of knowledge', *J. Liberal Religion* 2. (Reprinted in *Social Theory and Social Structure*, revised edn. 1957. Glencoe, Illinois.)

    (1945), 'The Sociology of Knowledge', in G. Gurvitch and W. E. Moore, eds., *Twentieth Century Sociology*. (Reprinted Merton, 1957) New York.

Miller, G. A. (1956), 'The magical number seven, plus or minus two: some limits on our capacity for processing information', *Psychol. Rev.*, 63:81–97.

Miller, G., Gallanter, E. and Pibram, K. (1960), *Plans and the Structure of Behavior*. New York .

Mounin, G. (1970), *Introduction à la sémiologie*. Paris.

171

Murdock, G. P. (1941), *Ethnographic Bibliography of North America*. New Haven, Conn.

Nadel, S. F., (1942), *A Black Byzantium*. London.

Needham, J. (1956), *Science and Civilisation in China*, Vol. 2, *History of Scientific Thought*. Cambridge.

Needham, R. (1956), Introduction to English translation of E. Durkheim and M. Mauss, *Primitive Classification*. London.

(1967), 'Right and left in Nyoro symbolic classification', *Africa*, 37:425–452.

(1976), 'Nyoro symbolism: the ethnographic record', *Africa*, 46:236–246.

Needham, R. ed. (1973), *Right and Left: Essays on Dual Symbolic Classification*. Chicago.

Nesbit, W. M. (1914), *Sumerian Records from Drehem*. New York.

Norman, D. A. (1969), *Memory and Attention*. New York.

Nougayrol, J. (1962), 'L'influence babylonienne à Ugarit, d'aprés les textes en cunéiformes classiques', *Syria*, 39:28–35.

Ong, W. J. (1971), *Rhetoric, Romance and Technology*. Ithaca, New York.

(1974), *Ramus, Method and the Decay of the Dialogue*. New York.

Opie, I. and P. (1959), *The Lore and Language of Schoolchildren*. Oxford.

Oppenheim, A. L. (1964), *Ancient Mesopotamia*. Chicago.

Page, D. (1973), *Folktales in Homer's Odyssey*. Cambridge, Mass.

Parsons, T. (1937), *The Structure of Social Action*. New York.

(1966), *Societies: Evolutionary and Comparative Perspectives*. Englewood Cliffs, New Jersey.

Popper, K. (1963), *Conjectures and Refutations*. London.

(1970), 'Normal science and its dangers', in I. Lakatos and A. Musgrave, eds., *Criticism and the Growth of Knowledge*. Cambridge.

Postman, L. and Keppel, G. eds. (1969), *Verbal Learning and Memory*. London.

Pulgram, E. (1951), 'Phoneme and grapheme: a parallel', *Word*, 7:15–20.

(1965), 'Graphic and phonic systems: figurae and signs', *Word*, 21:208–24.

Radcliffe-Brown, A. R. (1922), *The Andaman Islanders*. Cambridge.

Rattray, R. S. (1913), *Hausa Folklore*. Oxford.

Roden, C. (1968), *A Book of Middle Eastern Food*. London.

Rodinson, M. (1949), 'Recherches sur les documents Arabes relatifs à la cuisine', *Revue des études islamiques*, 17–18.

Rohwer, W. D. Jr. (1975), 'An introduction to research on individual and developmental differences in learning', in W. K. Estes, ed., *Handbook of Learning and Cognitive Processes*, vol. 3: *Approaches to Human Learning and Motivation*. Hillsdale, New Jersey.

Rosemont, H. Jr. (1974), 'On representing abstractions in archaic Chinese', *Philosophy East and West*, 24:71–88.

Ruwet, N. (1975), 'Parallélismes et deviations en poésie', in *Langue, discours, société: pour E. Beneviste*. Paris.

Sahlins, M. (1976), *Culture and Practical Reason*. Chicago.

Scribner, S. and Cole, M. (1973), 'Cognitive consequences of formal and informal education', *Science*, 182:553–559.

Shils, E. (1968), 'Intellectuals', in *Encyclopedia of the Social Sciences*, New York.

Shippey, T. A. (1972), *Old English Verse*. London.

Sigerist, H. E. (1951), *A History of Medicine*, I: *Primitive and Archaic Medicine*. London.

References

Skorupski, J. (1976), *Symbol and Theory: a philosophical study of the theories of religion in social anthropology*. Cambridge.

Smith, M. G. (1957), 'The social functions and meaning of Hausa praise-singing', *Africa*, 27:26–45.

Smith, P. (1975), *Le Récit populaire au Ruanda* (Classiques africains). Paris.

Soyinka, W. (1976), *Myth, Literature and the African World*. Cambridge.

Tait, D. (1961), *The Konkomba of Northern Ghana*. London.

Tambiah, S. J. (1968), 'The magical power of words', *Man*, 3:175–208.

Todorov, T. (1971), *Poétique de la prose*. Paris.

(1973), 'Le discours de la magie', *L'Homme* 13:38–65.

Turner, V. W. (1967), *The Forest of Symbols*. Ithaca, New York.

Vachek, J. (1939), 'Zum Problem der geschriebenen Sprache', *Travaux du Cercle linguistique de Prague*, 8:94–104.

(1959), 'Two chapters on written English', *Brno Studies in English*, I:7–34.

(1973), *Written Language* (Janua Linguarum. Ser. critica, No. 14). The Hague.

von Soden, W. (1936), 'Leistung und Grenze sumerischer und babylonischer Wissenschaft', *Die Welt als Geschichte*, 2:411–464, 509–577.

Wartofsky, M. W. (1967), 'Metaphysics as a heuristic for science', in R. S. Cohen and M. W. Wartofsky, eds., *Boston Studies in the Philosophy of Science* III, New York.

Weber, M. (1947), *The Theory of Social and Economic Organization*. (Engl. transl.). London.

Whorf, B. L. (1956), *Language, Thought and Reality: Selected Writings of Benjamin Lee Whorf*. New York.

Wilson, B. R. ed. (1970), *Rationality*. Oxford.

Wiseman, D. J. (1962), *The Expansion of Assyrian Studies*. Inaugural Lecture, School of Oriental and African Studies, University of London.

(1970), 'Books in the Ancient Near East and in the Old Testament', in P. R. Ackroyd and C. F. Evans, eds., *The Cambridge History of the Bible* Vol. 1, *From the Beginnings to Jerome*. Cambridge.

Woolley, L. (1963), 'The beginnings of civilization', *History of Mankind: Cultural and Scientific Development*, Vol. 1, part 2. London.

Worsley, P. M. (1955), 'Totemism in a changing society', *Am. Anthrop.*, 57:851–861.

Wu Ching-Tzu (1957), *The Scholars* (transl. by Yang Hsien-Yi and Gladys Yang). Peking.

Yates, F. (1966), *The Art of Memory*. London.

Abreviations

A.H.	anno Hegirae, dating from the flight of Mahomed in A.D. 622
B.C.E.	before the Common era
IASAR	Institute of African Studies (Legon, Ghana), Arabic collection
L.D.	LoDagaa
MAH	Musée d'Art et d'Histoire, Geneva
MSL	Materials for the Sumerian Lexicon
VAT	Vorderasiatische Tontafelsammlung des Berliner Museums

Index

Index

cuisine: 143; country, 140; the great, 134
Culpeper, N., 60, 61
cult, mobility of, 43
cultural code, 61
culture, 64, 164; practical reason as against, 146
cuneiform, 76; tablets, 79
cursive script, 160
Cushing, F., 57–58

de Saussure, F., 77, 124
'dead' languages, 79, 125
decontextualisation, 78, 94, 109, 122, 127, 159; of knowledge, 13
deep/surface structure, 161
depersonalised, 44, 77, 136
developing/developed, 2, 147
Dieterlen, G., 59
differentiation, 143
dining list, 130, 133
direction (in writing), 123
distribution of rations, 82
diviner, 30, 62, 67
division: mathematical, 12; Platonic method of, 70
Dogon, the, 59
domesticated/wild, 147
double-entry book-keeping, 89
Douglas, M., 42, 45
Durkheim, E., 11, 14, 20ff, 54, 62, 160, 163
duty roster, 135
dyslexia, 123

education, classroom, 13
empty boxes, 153, 156
epic, 112, 116, 126, 152, 158, 166
epistemology, 41
equation, 121
etiquette, 142
Evans-Pritchard, E. E., 23
event lists, 90
evil, the problem of, 28
exercise-lists, 95
experiment, 136, 138
explicit/implicit, 105–106

folktales, 119
'forerunners' (to the 'canonical' versions), 98
formal instruction, 94
formalisation, 107, 127, 157–158; of classificatory schemes, 150; of information, 149, 153; of speech acts 113

formula, 17, 53, 75, 86, 112ff, 158
Frazer, J., 20, 23
funeral, 87; LoDagaa, 84–85, 167; speeches, 115, 160

gemeinschaft/gessellschaft, 25
Gelb, I. J., 82–83, 165
genealogies, 81, 91; recital of, 108
genres, 104, 119, 120, 157
geometrical theorems (of Euclid), 150
glossaries, 99
Gonja, 132; eastern, 90; kingdom of, 31; language, 115
grammar, 115; universal, 161
grammatical texts, 126
Grand Dichotomy, the, 146ff
graphic reductionism, 122, 127
Great Divide, the, 3, 151, 164
greeting, 115
Griaule, M., 54, 58–59, 67, 165
growth of knowledge, 90, 146, 151
guilds, 138

Havelock, E. A., 75, 164
Hebrews, the, 92
Hertz, R., 62
hierarchy, 97, 101ff, 111, 129, 130, 132
history, 2, 14, 150; archives as prerequisite for, 91, 92, 148; role of lists in development of, 90
Hodgkin, T., 163
homeostasis, cultural, 14
Homer, 26, 112, 114
horoscopic astrology, 93
Horton, R., 2, 17, 38, 41–46, 150, 166
hot/cold, 2, 147
household management, 142

ikonic representation, 104
incantations, relation with recipes, 143
incest, 45
individualism, 14
innovation, repetition and, 158
intellect, technology of the, 10, 81
intellectuals, 24
internalisation, 160
inventory, 80, 86, 88, 94
Islam, 18, 31, 42; calligraphy, 158
itinerary, 80, 92

judicial astrology, 93

Kalabari, the, 42
'key-myth', 163
king-list, 80, 90, 91, 126
knotted ropes, recording by means of, 83

176

Index

knowledge: growth of, 90, 127, 146, 151; sacred, 60; systematisation of, 145
Koran, the, 158
Kramer, S. N., 79, 83, 137, 152
Kuhn, T. S., 33, 42, 44, 47–50

labour, division of, 14
langue and *parole*, 76
Landsberger, B., 94, 96–99, 152, 165
lateral: direction, 86; placement, 129
ledgers, 82
left hand, 62; and diviner, 67
left to right, 130
Lévi-Strauss, C., 2, 4–8, 23, 147–149, 163, 164
Leviticus, 103
Lévy-Bruhl, L., 2, 4, 11–13, 164
linear nature of spoken language, 124
linguistic re-coding, 109
list, 17, 53, 75, 80ff; administrative, 85, 92, 100; census, 92; dining, 130, 133; event, 90; exercise, 95; king, 80, 90, 91, 126; lexical, 80, 93, 94; of classes, 94; of entities, 100; prospective, 87; ration, 130, 133; retrospective, 80, 130; selective, 130; shopping, 80, 135; sign, 83, 84; text, 83
Listenwissenschaft, 80, 94
literacy: alphabetic, 14; restricted, 31, 151–153; specialised, 152
literati, 31, 32, 76, 152
literature, 153
locational sorting device, 84
LoDagaa, 12–13, 17, 28–31, 38, 63, 66–67, 84–85, 115, 118, 167; language, 115
logic, 37, 71, 114; binary, 71; establishment of a formal, 102; 'our', 11; rules, 41
logical/non-logical, 146
logical operations, 122
'logical' order, 166
logical/pre-logical, 2, 12
logicality, 47
logico-empirical activity, 145
logico-empirical/mythopoeic, 2, 147
logograms, 75, 122
logographic scripts, 149; systems, 83
long-term memory, 87
Lord, A. B., 26, 112, 114, 117–118
Lord's Prayer, the, 118–119
Luria, A. R., 11, 37

magic (folk contrast with religion), 148
magic/science, 3, 149

magicians (contrasted with physicians), 144
Malinowski, B., 5–6, 24–25, 38
mandarin or scribal group, 151, 152
Marx, K., 11, 46
materia medica, 129, 137, 144, 166
matrix, 53, 75, 112, 153
Mauss, M., 54
meaning: in parallel, 86; surface, 35
medical works, 143–144
memorisation, 116
'memory', 85, 117, 126, 151; 'artificial', 71; oral, 143; verbal, 156
menu, 130, 133
mnemonic, 109–110, 116
mobility, social and geographical, 142
'modern science', 145
modes of thought, 1, 19, 81, 111, 146, 148
monologue, 160
morphological criteria, 98
multiplication, 12; tables, 54
myth, 2, 24, 113, 150, 163, 165, 167; key-, 163; of the framework, 33; Zuñi origin, 54, 57
myth/history, 3, 14, 90, 148

nature, 64, 164
Ndembu, the, 66
Needham, J., 40, 68, 163
Needham, R., 54, 62–65, 164
needs, 5
nominal roll, 130, 135
nomothetic thinking, 68
non-logical, 146
non-rational, 146
numbers, 122
Nyoro, the, 62–65, 67

omen literature, 93
Ong, W., 71, 78, 114ff
Onomastica (of Ancient Egypt), 94, 96, 98–102, 104
open/closed, 147
opposites, among early Greek writers, 165; Aristotelian discussion of, 70, 102
opposition: assertion of, 122; or polarity, 112
oral forms, standardised, 113
oral: situations, 78; 'tradition', 27
oratory, 114, 115
originality, 117
orthodoxy (of the book), 37
over-generalisation, 95, 105

Index

paradigm: change in, 48; different uses of the word, 49; in 'normal' science, 33
Parry, M., 26, 113–114
Parsons, T., 3, 163
payments, to officials, 82
performer, 127
pharmacopoeia, 137
philosophers, 71
philosophy, 47; emergence of 44
Phoenician, 84–85, 91; –Hebrew alphabet, 85
physicians, 144
pictograms, 75
'pictographic' writing, 79
plans, 80, 87, 136, 159
polarity, 112, 114; and analogy, 102, 115
Popper, K., 2, 33, 41, 47
practical reason, 146
prayer, the, 160
pre-capitalist/capitalist, 2
prescription, 135, 137ff, 143
priest, 151; the healer as, 144
primitive/advanced, 3, 146, 148
print, printing, 14, 34, 46, 77, 99, 114, 140, 141 164
procreation, 39
'programmed learning', 141
property marks, 82
proverbs, 98, 125

Radcliffe-Brown, A. R., 66
Ramus, P., 71
'rational classification', 101
rational/irrational, 2
'rational medicine', 145
rational mode of thought, science as a, 150
rational/non-rational, 146
rationality, 37, 47, 48
rations, 87, 129; list, 130, 133
recall, 111, 156
receipt, 136, 137
recipe, 17, 121, 135ff; proto-, 139
reciters, 120, 144
'reckoners', 156
record keeping, 93
'redistributive' economies, 82
reductionism, graphic, 53
repetition, 116, 158
restricted/elaborated codes, 124
restricted literacy, 31, 151–153
rhetoric, 114–116; curriculum of, 71; 'formulary structure of', 114
ritual/rationality, 3

Rohwer, W. D., 109
rote learning, 117
Round Robin, 131–132
Round Table, 132
Ruanda, popular recitations of, 112

scepticism, 28, 37, 42, 43, 45, 47
school, 94, 95, 98, 125; texts, 83, 152, 166
science, 148–150; emergence of, 1; 'modern', 145; of the concrete, 150
scientist, 140, 146; the doctor as, 144
scribes, 98–101, 152; groups, 151; training, 94, 98
script: cursive, 160; Vai, 123
'secondary elaboration' (of theories), 42
secret, 142, 143; writing, 138
'semantic field', 103, 104
semantic parallelism, 158–159, 167
sermon, the, 151
shrines, turnover of, 30
signature, 137
simple/complex, 2, 147
Skorupski, J., 150, 166
specialised literacy, 152
specialist's elaboration, 61
spoken and the written, the, 77
standardised oral forms, 113, 118–119, 153, 158
status/contract, 3
structural semantics, 94
'subitizing' 163
subtraction, 12
Sumerian lexicon, 94
syllabic alphabets, 75, 84; systems, 83
syllogism, 11, 44

table, 12, 13, 17, 53ff, 75, 102, 112, 122; mathematical, 156, multiplication, 54; Round, 132
'taboo', 42, 45
technology of the intellect, 151
text, 19, 37, 75, 114, 125, 158; analytical study of, 71; -books, 83; -lists, 83
thought, modes of, 1, 19, 81
time, concepts of, 45
Tongan festival, 132
traditional/modern, 2
tribute, 100, 137; receipts of, 82, 87
Turner, V., 66
Tylor, E. B., 23

Ugarit, 76, 85, 88–89, 92, 94; lists, 88; tablets, 87

178

Index

universal, 136; grammar, 161; truth
   value, 126
universals, linguistic, 77, 161
utility, 13
utterance, 19, 37, 75, 86, 105, 114, 115,
   151, 158

Vachek, J., 77
Vai, the, 18; script, 123
verbatim, 118
votive inscriptions, 79
Vygotsky, L., 9, 161

Wartofsky, M., 48

we/they, 1, 146
Weber, M., 11
Whorf, B. L., 9, 161
wild/domesticated, 2, 7, 24
Wiseman, D., 79–80, 91–92
word, 115; divider, 85; signs, 82

Yin/Yang, 40
Yugoslav epic, 112

zodiac, 68, 69, 93
Zuñi: clans, 55–58; origin myths, 54, 57,
   60